Jewish Days

50

FARRAR
STRAUS
GIROUX

Also by Francine Klagsbrun

Words of Women (editor)

The First Ms. Reader (editor)

Free to Be . . . You and Me (editor)

Too Young to Die:
Youth and Suicide

Voices of Wisdom:
Jewish Ideals and Ethics for Everyday Living

Married People:
Staying Together in the Age of Divorce

Mixed Feelings:
Love, Hate, Rivalry, and Reconciliation
Among Brothers and Sisters

BOOKS FOR YOUNG READERS

Sigmund Freud: A Biography

The Story of Moses

The First Book of Spices

Psychiatry: What It Is, What It Does

Freedom Now!
The Story of the Abolitionists

Also Illustrated by Mark Podwal

Voices of Wisdom:
Jewish Ideals and Ethics for Everyday Living

The Golem (by Elie Wiesel)

The Six Days of Destruction (by Elie Wiesel)

A Passover Haggadah (by Elie Wiesel)

Dybbuk: A Story Made in Heaven (by Francine Prose)

BOOKS BY MARK PODWAL

Let My People Go: A Haggadah

A Book of Hebrew Letters

A Jewish Bestiary

The Book of Tens

Golem: A Giant Made of Mud

JEWISH DAYS

A Book of Jewish Life and Culture

DAYS

Around the Year

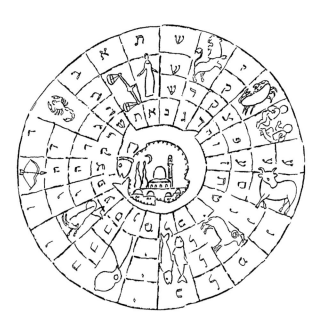

FRANCINE KLAGSBRUN

Illustrated by

MARK PODWAL

FARRAR STRAUS GIROUX ✦ NEW YORK

We thank our editor, Elisheva Urbas, for her enthusiasm for this project,
her learned suggestions, and her perceptive insights into both text and drawings.

Grateful acknowledgment is made for permission to reprint biblical passages
from the *TANAKH: A New Translation of the Holy Scriptures*
According to the Traditional Hebrew Text. Copyright © 1985 by The Jewish Publication Society.

Library of Congress Cataloging-in-Publication Data

Klagsbrun, Francine.
Jewish Days : a book of Jewish life and culture around the year/
Francine Klagsbrun ; illustrated by Mark Podwal.
p. cm.
Includes bibliographical references and index.
1. Fasts and Feasts—Judaism. 2. Religious calendars—Judaism.
3. Jews—Anniversaries, etc. I. Podwal, Mark H. II. Title.
BM690.K57 1996 296.4'3—dc20 96-15392 CIP

With loving memories of my parents
Anna and Benjamin Lifton
F K

For Michael and Ariel
M P

CONTENTS

Jewish Days

PREFACE
The Times of Our Lives

JEWS AS A PEOPLE HAVE BEEN MORE OFTEN CONNECTED TO TIME THAN TO PLACES OR THINGS. The Bible, the Talmud, and other Jewish texts tend to pay greater attention to the nature of events than to the places where they occurred. Twice in Jewish history there has been a great Temple in Jerusalem where people came to worship and priests performed majestic ceremonies. But when each of those Temples was destroyed, worship and ceremony continued in homes and synagogues wherever Jews lived. The Temples were less important than the time hallowed within them.

The philosopher Abraham Joshua Heschel spoke of "holiness in time" as a basic characteristic of Jewish religious practice. Prayer in the morning, afternoon, and evening punctuates time in every day. Each week the Sabbath sanctifies time in an evening and day set apart from all others. Jews greet every new month as sacred time, celebrated through prayer and ceremony. And throughout the year a continuous cycle of holidays and festivals gives a sense of spiritual renewal to the passing time.

But even when not sacred, time has special meaning in the four-thousand-year-old history of the Jewish people. The biblical commandment to remember events and peoples in that history forms the core of Jewish identity. So time and memory become intensely intertwined in Jewish thought, and historical occurrences make up the underpinnings of the Jewish calendar. Feast days, for example, that may have begun as seasonal celebrations at planting or harvest times acquired other, more significant, historical meanings over the years. Thus Passover, originally a spring harvest holiday, became a great festival of freedom, honoring the deliverance from slavery in Egypt.

Other historical experiences may not be observed as regular feasts or fast days but are deeply embedded in Jewish consciousness as decisive moments never to be forgotten. The expulsion of the Jews from Spain in 1492, for instance, continued to be noted on Jewish calendars more than a hundred years after it happened. Five hundred years later, Jews in many lands still saw fit to memorialize it for an entire year with lectures, concerts, books, and exhibitions.

And then there is a kind of time in Jewish life that does not fit into the cycle of holidays, is rarely commemorated with public ceremonies, and cannot even be pinpointed in history. Who can say precisely when the wicked cities of Sodom and Gomorrah were destroyed, or Miriam the Prophetess died, or Aaron fashioned the golden calf? Yet tradition has assigned dates on the Jewish calendar to such biblical episodes because of their lasting imprint on Jewish imagination.

This is a book about time—the sacred and historical days in the Jewish experience and the biblical days marked on the calendar by tradition. It is a book about the Jewish holidays but also about historical events that have shaped Jewish life, and persons whose lives have made an impact on Jewish history. Neither an encyclopedia nor a standard book of days, it does not attempt to cover every key date in Jewish existence or present capsule information about every day on the Jewish calendar. Its aim instead is to analyze, interpret, and illustrate a variety of subjects that together present a diverse tapestry of Jewish culture, a weave of holiday practices, historical remembrances, biblical narrative, and rabbinic explanation—with a thread of mystical thought woven through.

❖

The book is arranged around the months and days of the Jewish calendar, and that calls for some explanation. First, the Jewish calendar reckons the years according to a traditional date established for the creation of the world: some 5,757 years ago, or 3,760 years before the beginning of the Common Era. The year 2000 on the general, Gregorian, calendar, for example, is 5760–61 on the Jewish one. That method of dating came into general use during the period of the *geonim*, men who headed great academies of learning in Babylonia between the eighth and eleventh centuries.

Second, unlike the general calendar, which is based on the sun, the Jewish calendar is based primarily on the moon. A Jewish month begins with the appearance of the new moon, a tiny slice of light in the sky. It ends after the moon has completed an entire cycle, waxing until it becomes full and then waning until it can no longer be seen.

A lunar year is approximately 354 days long, 11 short of the solar year. With that time difference, from year to year Jewish dates fall on different days of the solar calendar—Passover may be

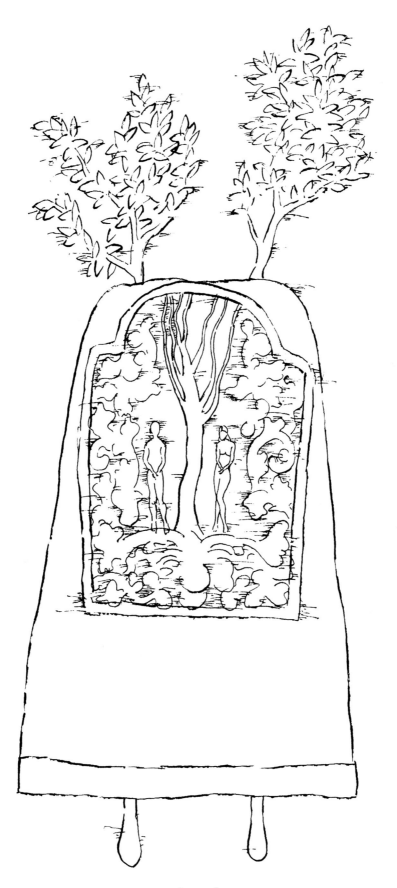

at the end of March one year and the middle of April the next. But the dates always fall during the same season—Passover is always celebrated in the springtime. This is because the Hebrew Bible itself dictates that Passover should come in the spring, other holidays in the fall. To keep the holidays in their specified seasons, centuries ago scholars intercalated the lunar calendar to the solar by adding an extra month seven times in every nineteen years. This "leap" month, Adar II, is inserted between the months of Adar and Nisan and occurs about once every three years.

A lunar month lasts about twenty-nine and a half days, which has been translated into Jewish months of either twenty-nine or thirty days. Jews celebrate the beginning of each new month as a minor holiday called *Rosh Hodesh*, literally, the "head of the month."

In ancient times, before astronomical calculations were perfected, the *Sanhedrin*, the supreme court in Jerusalem, would fix the calendar on a monthly basis. Witnesses would testify that they had sighted the new moon, and basing its judgment on that testimony, the court would proclaim the new month. The court's proclamation was essential for dating the month's festivals correctly, and word of it would be sent throughout the land of Israel and to Jews living in the Babylonian Diaspora. At first the rabbis used beacon fires to broadcast the news; later, messengers carried it.

But while awaiting word, and unsure of when the new month started, Diaspora Jews began to observe two days as the new moon. That led them to add an extra sacred day at the beginning and end of major festivals, known in Hebrew as *Yom Tov Sheni Shel Galuyot*, the "Second Festival Day of the Diasporas." After the calendar was set, the custom of adding those extra days continued, perhaps as a way of differentiating between Diaspora Jews and those in Israel. It continues still today among Orthodox and Conservative Jews outside Israel. Reform Jews have dropped it.

The holidays that have extra days in the Diaspora are the biblical festivals of Passover, Sukkot, and Shavuot but not the later, national ones of Hanukkah and Purim. This book includes second festival days as holidays.

❖

So much for years and months. Jewish days themselves are counted from evening to evening, starting at sunset one day and ending at nightfall the next. The practice follows the biblical description of Creation: "And there was evening and there was morning, a first day" (Genesis 1:5). The Hebrew word for evening is *erev*, as in *erev Pesah*, Passover eve. But the term *erev* may also refer to the entire day on whose evening the holiday begins, because so much preparation for the next day takes place then. That is how it is used here: the holiday eve carries the date of the day before the holiday although technically the eve and next day are part of the same twenty-four-hour period. Passover is on the fifteenth of Nisan, but Passover eve is dated on the fourteenth.

Exceptions to the evening-to-evening count are minor fast days. The Day of Atonement and the fast of the Ninth of Av are the only two fast days that extend from one evening to the next. All others last only from morning to evening. In earlier times, extremely pious people also fasted on Mondays and Thursdays as a form of repentance, the days (along with the

Sabbath) when the Torah scroll is read in synagogue. A small number still keep the practice today.

Various days of the week have their own lore. Medieval Jews regarded Mondays and Wednesdays as unlucky times for starting a new enterprise, because the stars were not propitious then. It was risky even to leave one's home on Wednesday evening, when the demon Agrat came out to torment folk. On the other hand, Tuesday, the third day of the Jewish week, still has a reputation for being lucky. That is because in the biblical account of Creation, the statement "And God saw that this was good" appears twice in connection with the third day (Genesis 1:10, 12). In Israel, this has made Tuesday the most popular day for weddings.

❖

When Mark Podwal and I first conceived of this book, a model we had in mind was the traditional *Minhagim* book. Developed during the Middle Ages, these books were detailed compilations of customs and practices written by Jews in different lands. The most popular had extensive illustrations and followed the order of the Jewish year. As *Jewish Days* took form, we kept the concept of a highly illustrated and interpretive book built around the calendar. We decided, however, to omit life-cycle events such as circumcisions and weddings that were often part of the customs books so we could add historical and legendary material along with the holiday essays.

One fundamental guideline we used for selecting a subject was that a Jewish date related to it be known and recognized. For individuals, that frequently meant the *yahrzeit,* or anniversary of the person's death, because Jews ritually commemorate death dates more often than birth dates. In Jewish thought, only after a person has lived a lifetime can we truly pay tribute to him or her.

Aside from the festivals and fast days, the topics chosen represent the most decisive occurrences and most influential personalities in Jewish history. Because traditionally women rarely held public roles in Jewish life, they tend to be underrepresented in the biographical essays. However, women's viewpoints are emphasized throughout—a reflection of my own commitment to Jewish feminism.

Both the text and illustrations draw on classic Jewish sources. Most prominent are the Hebrew Bible and the Talmud, the great compilation of Jewish law and lore codified between 200 and 500 C.E. The Talmud is made up of the Mishnah, the code of Jewish law redacted by Judah HaNasi (Judah the Prince) around 200 C.E., and the Gemara, discussions and elaborations on the Mishnah. Often cited here also is the *midrash,* which refers both to interpretations, homilies, and maxims of the talmudic sages and to collections of those materials.

Our hope for *Jewish Days* is that people with little knowledge of Judaism will find it a compelling pathway to Jewish ideas and beliefs, and that those with more extensive backgrounds will discover new insights and new challenges here. It is a book that can be read and enjoyed from cover to cover, but doesn't have to be. Because it is a book about time and events in Jewish life, it can be entered in any season, and reentered time and again.

FRANCINE KLAGSBRUN
NEW YORK CITY

SHABBAT

The Sabbath Rest

EFORE I FULLY UNDERSTOOD THE HOLINESS OF THE DAY, BEFORE I TRULY APPRECIATED ITS BEAUTY, AND BEFORE I COULD INTERPRET ITS RITUALS, I KNEW THE SABBATH WAS A "MIRACLE." That was how my father always spoke of it, from the time I was a child and well into his hundredth year of life. In Hebrew it is called *Shabbat,* but he used the Yiddish *Shabbos,* still preferred by numbers of Jews.

"When I was a young man, an immigrant from Russia," he would say, "the United States had no labor laws regulating working conditions. People worked long hours, seven days a week, without rest. But imagine, more than three thousand years ago the Bible commanded that all work stop for an entire day every single week, and not only for the ancient Israelites but for all who lived among them, including slaves. And not only for people, but for animals as well. What a revolutionary practice that was. What a miracle!"

A miracle indeed. No such day existed in the universe until it appeared full-blown in the Hebrew Bible. Other ancient peoples had certain "evil days" during the month when the king had to restrict his activities to avoid trouble. Some also had unlucky days that coincided with the full moon in the middle of the month. But none had a fixed day in every week of every month of every year in which all work stopped and all creatures rested—yes, even the animals.

The command to keep this day of rest is the fourth of the Ten Commandments, and as such appears in two places in the Hebrew Bible. Each makes clear that the rule extends, as my father so lovingly reiterated, to husband and wife, and everyone in their household— "you, your son or daughter, your male or female slave . . . your cattle," and "the stranger who is within your settlements" (Exodus 20:10). But the rationale differs in each place.

The Book of Exodus connects the Sabbath to Creation and God's rest after forming the world. "For in six days the Lord made heaven and earth and sea," we read, " . . . and He rested on the seventh day; therefore the Lord blessed the sabbath day and hallowed it" (20:11). The Book of Deuteronomy emphasizes the day's humanitarian purpose and grounds it in the liberation from slavery in Egypt. The Sabbath is given to every person in the household "so that your male and female slave may rest as you do," Scripture says. It continues: "Remember that you were a slave in the land of Egypt . . ."(5:14–15).

The two versions of the commandment also begin with different words: in Exodus, "Remember the sabbath day and keep it holy"; in Deuteronomy, "Observe the sabbath day and keep it holy" (5:12). Tradition holds that God uttered both words, "Observe" and "Remember," simultaneously, so intertwined are they. In observing Shabbat, Jews imitate God, who ceased from all activity on the seventh day. In remembering their own history of being enslaved, they recognize the need of even their lowliest servant to be freed on the Sabbath from the burdens of daily labor. Together, the observing and remembering keep the Sabbath day holy and blessed.

Legend tells us that God actually created the Sabbath on the seventh day. Scripture says, "on the seventh day God finished the work which He had been doing" (Genesis 2:2), and the ancient rabbis wondered what that meant. After all, they reasoned, the world had already been created in six days. What did it lack that required finishing on the seventh? Rest, they answered, and tranquillity, and peace, and quiet—Shabbat.

The laws for keeping the Sabbath are abundant and detailed. The Mishnah, codified around 200 C.E., describes them as "mountains hanging by a hair," for "there is little Scripture and many rules." In truth, the Bible gives few instructions about how to observe this day other than to refrain from work. With this general rule, the rabbis of the Talmud developed meticulous regulations, arriving at them, paradoxically, almost poetically. They noted that injunctions about the Sabbath accompany each biblical passage that instructs the Israelites on how to build the Tabernacle, their sanctuary in the wilderness. From that they deduced that the rules for constructing the sanctuary contain the secrets of the Sabbath laws.

Accordingly, they outlined thirty-nine categories of work forbidden on the Sabbath, all of them forms of labor used in constructing the Tabernacle. "They sowed, therefore you must not sow," the rabbis said. "They reaped, therefore you must not reap . . ." These major groups the sages called *avot*, or fathers, and from them they derived more exacting rulings, which they called *toledot*, descendants. Later, other laws were added to these fundamental ones. In general, the Sabbath restrictions concern work that involves some form of creating or producing, whether it is creating light through kindling or producing food through planting.

For Jews who delight in the Sabbath, however, the restrictions are part of the day's overall specialness, not confining but providing freedom from the routine crush of living. Each week when Shabbat comes, it turns ordinary time into the sacred and extraordinary. So extraordinary is this day that it is the only one of the week with a name. All others simply bear numbers in relation to it, as in "first day," "second day," and so on. So sacred and spiritually fulfilling is it that the sages pictured it as a foretaste of the world to come, a touch of paradise here on earth.

❖

The Sabbath begins at dusk on Friday evening with the lighting of candles, no later than eighteen minutes before sundown. But preparations—shopping, cooking, cleaning, bathing—start much earlier, and the entire day is referred to as *erev Shabbat*, the Sabbath eve. For the observant, the greeting for Sabbath peace, *Shabbat Shalom*, closes the workweek, just as it opens the Sabbath itself. As candlelighting time approaches, the Mishnah teaches, a tailor should not go out with his needle stuck in his coat, or a writer holding her pen. Work needs to recede now to allow the spirit of the day to take over.

The rabbis told of wondrous things created on the eve of the world's first Shabbat, in the mystical twilight after the sun had set but the stars had not yet appeared. Among them was the rainbow Noah would see after the great Flood, the ram that would be sacrificed in place of Isaac, and a miraculous well that would accompany the Israelites during their long trek in the wilderness.

Candlelighting on the Sabbath eve ushers in its own magic, as a canopy of peace and repose descends on the home. Usually the woman in the household kindles the Sabbath candles, but a man should light them if no woman is present. The lights recall the first act of Creation, the separation of light from darkness. Mystics also saw in them additional souls humans receive for the day, which depart when Shabbat ends. Two candles are lighted, representing the two versions of the Sabbath commandment, to observe and to remember. But more may be lit; some families use one for each child. After the benediction over the candles many women silently add personal prayers.

Two braided *hallah* breads covered with a cloth rest on the Sabbath table, set more formally than at any other time. The word *hallah* comes from a portion of dough set aside for the priests in the ancient Temple, where a bread offering to God was made. Two loaves are used to echo the double portion of manna the Israelites gathered in the desert on Friday to last them through the Sabbath.

Joyous synagogue services known as *kabbalat Shabbat* welcome the Sabbath before the evening meal. They include images that go back to the third century, when the Palestinian sage Rabbi Hanina would wrap himself in a robe on the Sabbath eve and exclaim, "Come, let us go out to meet the Sabbath Queen." Another scholar, Rabbi Yannai, would say, "Come, O Bride; come, O Bride."

Building on those images, the sixteenth-century kabbalists spoke of a mystical union between God the King and the Sabbath Queen. Their beautiful hymn "*Lekhah Dodi*" alludes to that union and ends with Rabbi Yannai's words. As congregants sing "Come, O Bride; come, O Bride," they turn toward the synagogue entrance to receive the Sabbath Queen.

After services, a popular legend tells, two angels accompany people home, one good and one bad. If candles are lit and the home is beautified for Shabbat, the good angel says, "May it be this way on the next Shabbat," and the bad angel must answer "Amen." But if the home is not readied, the bad angel says, "May it be this way on the next Shabbat," and the good one must say "Amen."

The family greets those angels with the Sabbath hymn "Shalom Aleikhem," then bids them farewell. After the singing, parents bless their children, a ritual way of expressing their love and concern. A husband might then pay tribute to his wife by singing from the Book of Proverbs of the "woman of valor," who devotes herself to the care of her family (31:10–31). Increasingly, in egalitarian families, husbands and wives sing the verses together, to each other, just as together they readied their home for Shabbat.

The *kiddush*, recited over a brimming cup of wine, sanctifies the Sabbath before dinner begins. Such Sabbath evening blessings on earth, the mystics said, add sanctity and blessing to the heavenly hosts above. Traditionally, the father recited the kiddush, which opens with the biblical verses that recall God's rest on the seventh day. Today women often lead it, and family members and guests may join in. Afterward, participants ceremonially wash their hands, and the hallah is blessed, cut, and sprinkled with salt, another reminder of the Temple offerings, which were accompanied by salt. The grace after the Shabbat meal is, like the meal itself, the most elaborate of the week. Then everybody lingers around the table singing *zemirot*, lively Sabbath table songs.

Oh, and one more part of this special evening: the sages deemed it of particular merit for husband and wife to have conjugal relations that night, to add to the Shabbat joy.

❖

In the synagogue on Saturday morning, a reader chants a portion from the Torah scroll followed by the *haftarah*, a section from the Prophets. Orthodox and a number of Conservative synagogues read through the entire five books of Moses in a yearly cycle. Many Reform, Reconstructionist, and other Conservative synagogues stretch the reading over a three-year cycle. Certain Sabbaths of the year, named for the Torah portion, are connected with special events, and are discussed in this book in their proper places on the calendar.

A Sabbath custom is to eat three meals during the course of the day. Called *shalosh se'udot*, they were originally a sign of luxury for a people who generally ate only twice a day. Many congregations enjoy a light third meal together between afternoon and evening services, when they also study a sacred text.

The Sabbath ends, traditionally, when three stars are visible in the sky, or, officially, forty-two minutes after sunset, with the ceremony of *Havdalah*, "separation." Instead of the simple white candles with which the day began, a tall multicolored braided candle with several wicks is lighted. In its complexity, it stands for the hustle and bustle of the weekdays now returned. A benediction is said over a cup of wine (or juice), and another over a mixture of spices, whose fragrance represents a last reminder of the loveliness of Shabbat. A third blessing is said over the candle, and a final one emphasizes the many distinctions of life—between sacred time and profane, light and darkness, Israel and other nations, and the seventh day of rest and the six of labor.

The Havdalah service closes with thoughts of a time to come when the beauty of Shabbat will last eternally. It sings of Elijah the prophet, who, it is said, will herald the arrival of the Messiah.

Not content to let go of the Sabbath, the sages instituted a fourth meal at day's end called *Melaveh Malkah*, "escorting the queen." Today Hasidic groups in particular have a long, festive meal on Saturday nights. Folklore gives another explanation for the meal: God told King David that he would die on a Sabbath, but not which one. From then on, the king gave a feast every Saturday night in gratitude for having survived another Sabbath. Hence this meal is also called King David's Feast.

❖

The number seven in mystical thought symbolizes perfection, the orderly creation of the world in six days, with the seventh day of Shabbat—itself perfection. The concept of Shabbat is so essential to Jewish life that it extends beyond humans and animals to the land and beyond days to years. Scripture decrees that every seventh year farmers must allow their land to "rest" by lying fallow. In that sabbatical year poor people and wild beasts may eat freely of the unworked land, and persons in debt are released from their obligations. At the end of seven sabbatical years, a jubilee year must be declared, when indentured servants are freed and all land that has been sold reverts to its original owners.

Later sages modified the laws of the sabbatical and jubilee years so that people would not refrain from lending money to the needy for fear they might lose their loan in the sabbatical year. But the purpose behind the laws stayed constant. The seventh year was a "sabbath of the Lord" (Leviticus 25:4), just as the seventh day of the week is. Both are meant to show concern for others—the slave, the poor, the hungry. Both also are set apart as sacred time when humans relinquish control over nature and one another and acknowledge, in the words of the Psalmist: "The earth is the Lord's and all that it holds" (Psalm 24:1).

Because Shabbat is a day for joy and rest, no mourning or fast may take place on it, except for *Yom Kippur*, the Day of Atonement. For the superstitious there is one other exception. The Talmud discusses the custom for a person who had a nightmare to fast the next day in order to annul its evil effects. Some sages allowed such a fast even on the Sabbath if the bad dream had been on Friday night. But, they ruled, the person had to atone for violating the Sabbath by fasting again the next day!

For all the centrality of the Sabbath, it gives way to the even greater centrality of human life. Shabbat may be desecrated to save a life—not only may be but must be. The Talmud gives the example of a man who sees a door shut on a room in which an infant is alone and may be endangered or simply frightened. He must break down the door to get the baby out, and "the sooner the better," although that may mean violating the Sabbath. What is the rationale for overriding Shabbat to preserve life? Scripture says: "You shall keep the sabbath, for it is holy for you" (Exodus 31:14). That means that the Sabbath was given to *you* but you are not surrendered to the Sabbath, the rabbis explained. Even the sanctity of Shabbat must take second place to the sanctity of life.

❖

The Sabbath was given to the people of Israel, and spread far beyond them. Ancient Roman writers such as Seneca and Tacitus spoke of it contemptuously as a superstitious practice of wasteful idleness. Yet the spirit and beauty of this holy day influenced the general population. The Roman Jewish historian Josephus describes the spread of Sabbath practices throughout the Roman Empire, including the lighting of Sabbath candles. Christianity later incorporated the Sabbath into its theology, but transposed it to Sunday and connected it to the resurrection of Jesus. Muslims observe Friday as a form of Sabbath, a day of assembly, when work is permitted but prayer services are held.

For Jews the seventh day has remained sacred. In the Middle Ages and later in the shtetls of Eastern Europe, families would scrimp on food all week in order to enjoy a Sabbath meal that included a piece of fish or meat. For those who could not afford Sabbath festivities, the community often provided help. That is not to say that Jews have always kept all the laws. As far back as biblical times, the prophet Jeremiah warned against carrying merchandise in and out of the gates of Jerusalem on Shabbat, adding, "But they would not listen . . ." (Jeremiah 17:23). In economically pressing eras, many Jews found restrictions against working on the Sabbath a particular hardship. In our own age of greater affluence but also greater assimilation, many have dropped Sabbath observance. Yet growing numbers do incorporate some ceremony into their lives, such as lighting Shabbat candles or gathering the family together for a Friday evening meal.

And always, the rhythm of the Jewish calendar flows around this day of rest and reflection. In every week of every month of every year, the Sabbath arrives to re-create that moment after Creation when God rested and the entire cosmos was in peace and harmony. Shabbat may be a miracle, as my father taught me. It is also a unique gift only fully appreciated when used.

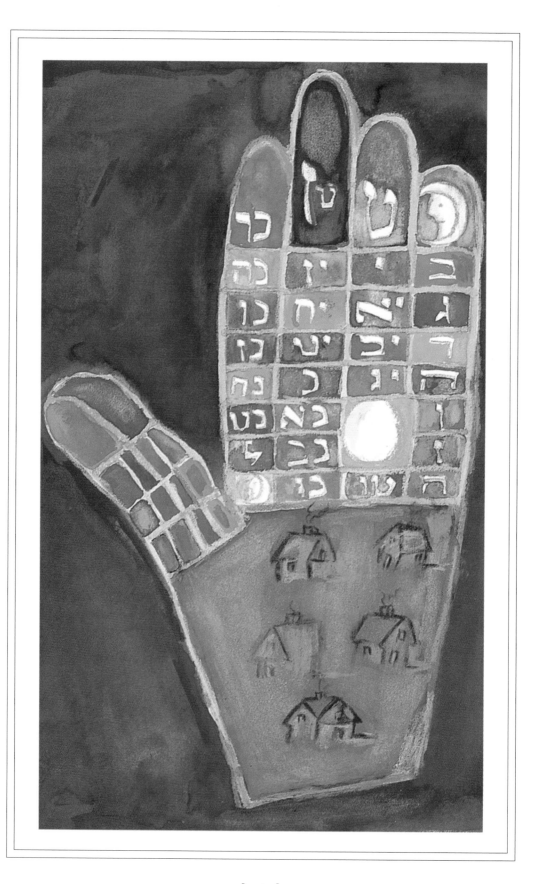

ROSH HODESH

Celebrating the New Moon

WHY DID GOD CREATE THE MOON INSTEAD OF ALLOWING THE SUN TO LIGHT THE EVENING SKY? The sages of the Talmud raised the question and answered it by suggesting that God foresaw that people would worship the celestial bodies as gods. Lest they regard the sun as the all-powerful deity, God created the moon to compete with it and diffuse its influence.

The rabbis knew well that many ancient peoples worshipped both sun and moon. Moon worship was particularly popular in Mesopotamia, the area where the early biblical patriarchs lived and traveled. Abraham came from Haran, which had a great temple dedicated to the moon god, Sin. Jacob worked for his father-in-law, Laban, whose name in Hebrew, *Lavan,* means "white" and is related to *levanah,* the moon. It is a name that hints at an association with a moon cult. As the Bible portrays them, however, Abraham and Jacob and their descendants rejected sun and moon worship and other pagan practices. Instead, they entered into a covenant with a single God who transcends nature and its parts.

In posing their question and answering it as they did, the rabbis were subtly distinguishing between Israel and the peoples around it.

But why did God make the moon smaller than the sun?

Scripture first tells of the creation of "two great lights" on the fourth day (Genesis 1:16). Why then, the sages asked, did one become a "greater light" and the other a "lesser light"? One explanation they gave was that the moon had to be reduced in size because it encroached on the sun's domain by being sometimes visible during the day as well as by night; another, that it was punished by being made smaller because it complained about having to share the universe with the sun. Most important, the rabbis compared the moon to Israel. Though smaller than the sun, the moon is more active. It waxes and wanes and waxes again, ever renewing itself. So Israel will be ever renewed, and one day it will be redeemed and restored to its original brightness. Moreover, just as the moon can be seen by day and by night, Israel has a portion in this world and the next, the world to come.

Rejected as a deity but identified with Israel, and essential to the Jewish calendar, the moon became incorporated into the Jewish year with the festival of Rosh Hodesh, celebrating the new moon, or new month. In biblical times, it was a major festival, when special sacrifices were brought to the Temple. Eventually it receded in importance, becoming a minor holiday recalled mostly through simple synagogue ceremonies. Yet, like the moon itself, the New Moon festival, seemingly faded, has once again been renewed. In our own day, women have rediscovered it, seeing in the moon's monthly cycle a reflection of the cyclical patterns of their own lives.

The biblical Rosh Hodesh was a happy occasion when trumpets were blown and feasts held. Work ceased for the day, and people visited the prophets to hear their teachings. The first synagogues may have developed from such Rosh Hodesh and Sabbath gatherings at the prophets' homes.

In biblical and talmudic times, before the calendar was firmly fixed, a colorful ceremony surrounded the appearance of the new moon. On the thirtieth of the month, members of the high court in Jerusalem would gather to hear testimony from witnesses who had sighted the first sliver of a crescent in the sky. If, after careful examination, the testimony was accepted, the head of the court would proclaim the new moon with the words "It is hallowed!" Then all the people assembled would respond, "It is hallowed! It is hallowed!" The witnesses would be given a lavish meal, and notice of the new moon sent to Jews wherever they lived. If the new moon was not sighted on the thirtieth day, the proclamation would be made on the thirty-first. The elaborate proclamation of the new moon ended when the calendar was established, in the middle of the fourth century C.E.

Though moon worship did not become part of Jewish practice, ancient Jews (even the sages) were not above superstitious beliefs. Some said that an eclipse of the moon was an evil omen for Israel, the result of its sins. Some said there is a man in the moon and he has the face of Jacob, or perhaps of Joshua, who led the Israelites into the Promised Land. Joshua was also believed to have chosen as warriors for his battles against the Amalekites men born in the leap-year month of Adar II, because witchcraft has no power then. As for the months in general, Jews, like other ancient peoples, incorporated the signs of the zodiac into their ideas about the cycles of the year, but gave them uniquely Jewish meanings.

The kabbalists of the sixteenth century introduced new rituals for the moon. They interpreted the moon's disappearance at the end of the month as the exile of the *Shekhinah*, the feminine aspect of God. Accordingly, they fasted on the day before the new month as a way of repenting and seeking God's return. Still observed by some Hasidic Jews, the fast is called *Yom Kippur Katan*, a small Day of Atonement.

Today the standard Rosh Hodesh rituals are just shadows of earlier ones. On the Sabbath before the new moon, during the Torah service, the reader announces the coming month, giving its name and the day or days on which the festival will fall. (One day of Rosh Hodesh follows twenty-nine-day months, and two days are celebrated after thirty-day months: the thirtieth day itself and the first day of the next month.) Congregants stand during the announcement, in remembrance of the original proclamation in Jerusalem. They repeat the month's name aloud and pray that it will be a time of goodness and blessing, of gladness and salvation.

On the day of Rosh Hodesh itself, worshippers include special prayers and recite psalms of praise to God. Fasting is forbidden, and festivities are called for, including housewarmings, dedications, and other cheerful events.

The most charming Rosh Hodesh rite doesn't actually take place on Rosh Hodesh. Between the third of the month and the fifteenth, on an evening when the moon is clearly visible, traditional Jews go outdoors and bless the moon. An air of mystery and mysticism surrounds this ceremony under the skies, reinforced by prayers for a messianic time when the moon will be restored to its former luster and the kingdom of David will likewise be restored to Israel. Called *kiddush levanah*, the "sanctification of the moon," or *birkhat ha'levanah*, the "blessing of the moon," it originated in talmudic times. Toward its end, participants exchange greetings. *Shalom Aleikhem* ("Peace be with you"), they say to each other, and they respond, *Aleikhem Shalom* ("to you peace").

❖

The newest form of Rosh Hodesh observance expresses the vitality women have given the celebration by reclaiming it as a holiday of their own.

Why Rosh Hodesh as a woman's festival? An old tradition holds that women are freed from work on this day although men are not. The freedom and the festivity that accompanies it are rewards for the merit of ancient Israelite women who refused to surrender their jewelry for use in constructing the golden calf.

The tradition probably reflects an older connection between women's monthly menstrual cycles and the cycles of the moon. It also reflects the cycle of marital sexuality in Judaism. According to Jewish law, partners abstain from all sexual activity during a woman's menstrual period and for seven days afterward, until she immerses herself in the *mikveh*, the ritual bath. Then marital intimacy is resumed, as the moon is renewed each month.

Since the 1970s, groups of Jewish women in the United States, Canada, Israel, and other parts of the world have held monthly New Moon celebrations, and the custom waxes stronger with each passing year. There is no set pattern to the celebrations, allowing free rein to the participants' imaginations. Most groups meet monthly, at the new moon or close to it. They may discuss the month's holidays or study a related text. Often they will chant together the prayer for sanctifying the moon, symbolically appealing for women's restoration to their full place in Jewish spiritual life along with the moon's restoration.

Occasionally, these rituals so emphasize women's biology and its connections to the moon that they seem to veer far from traditional Judaism and move close to New Age and other non-Jewish spiritual communities. But for most women who join them, Rosh Hodesh groups offer the opportunity men have always had to pray and study together. And they celebrate in a creative and original way a festival older than the calendar yet one that each month signifies rebirth and the never-ending vibrancy of Jewish life.

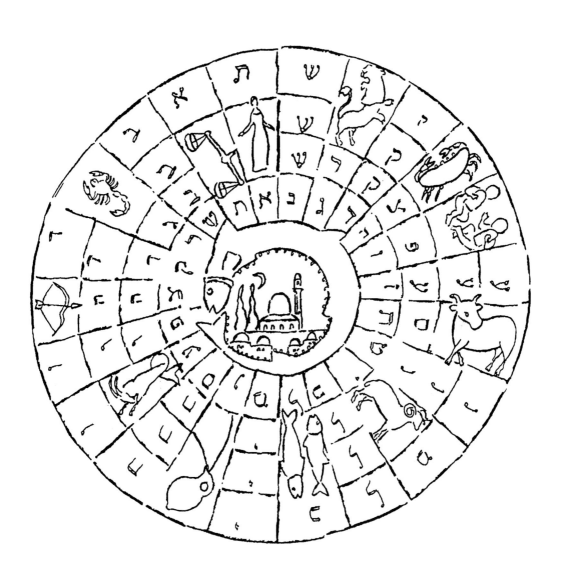

TISHREI

September–October

ISHREI, THE SEVENTH MONTH ON THE HEBREW CALENDAR, ARRIVES WITH A PUZZLE: WHY DO JEWS CELEBRATE *ROSH HASHANAH*, THE NEW YEAR, AT THE BEGINNING OF THIS MONTH AND NOT DURING NISAN, THE FIRST MONTH OF THE HEBREW YEAR? True, that month has its own stately festival of Passover. But why a new year fete in the seventh month, halfway through the year?

The answer has been veiled by time. The holiday has its source in a biblical celebration on the first day of the seventh month of the year, when the *shofar* (ram's horn) was to be sounded and all work cease. Most likely, ancient Jews regarded the seventh month, like the seventh day of the week, Shabbat, as a time of holiness to be observed with more extensive ceremonies than those of other months. Certainly Tishrei includes the greatest number of holy days in the entire Jewish calendar, among them the most awesome of all, Yom Kippur. The beginning of the month, then, may have held a special spiritual significance that set it apart from the historical importance of Nisan, which honors the Exodus of the ancient Hebrews from Egypt.

Like so many festivals, also, the first day of Tishrei was probably connected to an agricultural event. The month falls during the late harvest season in Israel, and its opening days may have been celebrated as the end of one agricultural year and the beginning of the next.

One other explanation: after the Jews were exiled from Judah to Babylonia in 586 B.C.E., they adopted Babylonian names for the months of the year. Before that, as we see in the Bible, they had used simple ordinal numbers, such as "first month" or "second month." The name Tishrei comes from a Babylonian root that means "beginning," and Babylonian custom may have influenced the Jews to adopt Tishrei as the opening of a new year, a new beginning in the fall.

Whatever the ultimate reason, by talmudic times, in the centuries before and after the start of the Common Era, Rosh Hashanah was firmly fixed in the seventh month of Tishrei. But the rabbis gave due respect to both Nisan and Tishrei by explaining that Nisan is the month when our ancestors were redeemed; Tishrei is the month when the people of Israel will be redeemed in a time to come.

The zodiac sign for Tishrei is Libra, with its symbol of a balancing scale, eminently appropriate for a month that Jews see as ushering in a period of divine judgment. All people are judged on the heavenly scales of justice, wrote the scholar Maimonides. Performing even one good deed or fulfilling one commandment can tip the scales in our favor, and through our personal deeds any one of us can bring salvation to the entire world.

The First Day of Tishrei
ROSH HASHANAH—NEW YEAR'S DAY

"Today is the birthday of the world."

Three times during the synagogue services for Rosh Hashanah, a series of shofar blasts are sounded and in unison congregants utter aloud these words. The Creation of the world is one of the major themes the holiday celebrates. Actually, in tradition, Creation began several days before Rosh Hashanah, but it was on this day, the first of Tishrei, that God created Adam and Eve. With their existence, the world as we know it came into being. Rosh Hashanah teaches that it is a world in which humans bear responsibility for their actions but in which they also have an opportunity to look into themselves, take stock of their behavior, and change what they know to be wrong. It is a world formed long before memory, but one that can be renewed each year by each individual through repentance and self-repair.

"Today all creatures everywhere stand in judgment . . ."

Three times congregants chant aloud these words immediately after proclaiming the world's Creation, acknowledging the second major theme of the holiday as a day of judgment. (It is sometimes called *Yom HaDin*, or Judgment Day.) Legend has pictured that judgment as taking place in a heavenly courtroom, where each person's advocates face off against Satan, the accuser, before the throne of the Almighty. The advocates point to every good deed as evidence for the defense, while Satan harps on the bad. But when Satan looks down on earth and sees people earnestly praying for forgiveness, he becomes confused and thwarted in his evil intent.

Imagery aside, Rosh Hashanah and Yom Kippur, which follows it, are the most introspective of all Jewish holidays. Unlike the others, they have little historical content; in fact, they are almost ahistorical. Their purpose is to turn us away from what has been in order to focus on what can be. They are observed more in the synagogue than at home, with prayer and soul-searching.

The shofar's insistent sounds symbolize the holiday themes. Maimonides interpreted those sounds as a wake-up call to stir people toward repentance. To Nahmanides, the thirteenth-century Spanish Jewish scholar and mystic, each note has its own hidden meaning. The short quavering sound called *teru'ah* represents God's attribute of justice. (One other name for the holiday is *Yom Teru'ah.*) The long, plain sound, known as *teki'ah,* stands for the attribute of mercy. The shofar is blown in sets, with the long teki'ah note both preceding and following the short teru'ah. This, Nahmanides said, is to show that God's justice is always surrounded by mercy.

The shofar is sounded a hundred times in all during the synagogue service, unless the holiday falls on a Sabbath, when it is forbidden to blow the shofar. Throughout, majestic prayers and blessings build on the themes of God as Sovereign, Creator, Judge of the world, a God who remembers the deeds of all people and cares enough to judge them in kindness. (Still one more name for Rosh Hashanah is *Yom HaZikkaron,* Day of Remembrance.)

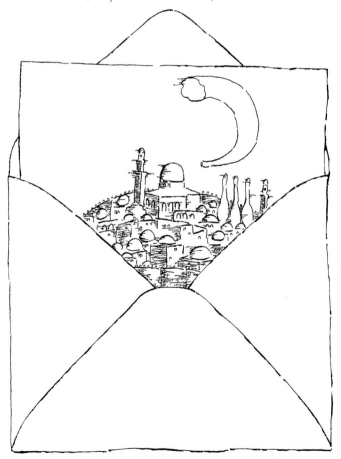

In a softer mode, the same themes appear in the biblical readings of the day through the lives of two women. The Torah portion, from Genesis, tells of Abraham's wife, Sarah. Childless for most of her married life, she gives birth to their son, Isaac, as God had promised, although she is ninety and Abraham a hundred years old. The prophetic reading, from the First Book of Samuel, describes another childless woman, Hannah. God answers her prayers by giving her a son, Samuel, who will become one of the great leaders of Israel.

Both stories assert the absolute sovereignty of God in Jewish thought. No goddesses, no fertility rites, no magic potions, but only God has the power to open a woman's womb, these texts affirm. Only God can create life. In rabbinic lore, just as God created Adam and Eve on Rosh Hashanah, on this day God "remembered" Sarah and Hannah, and also Rachel, Jacob's wife, and formed life within them.

The story of Hannah carries a corollary to God's power that is another part of this holiday's message: the power of human prayer. Hannah prays for a child at a shrine in the town of Shiloh, moving her lips without speaking. At first the priest Eli mistakes her for a drunkard, muttering to herself. After he recognizes the fervency of her prayer—"I have been pouring out my heart," she says (I Samuel 1:15)—he assures her it will be answered. Hannah's prayer, silent, intense, profoundly felt, serves as the model for what all true prayer should be, the sages taught.

❖

The prayer and repentance that dominate synagogue services on Rosh Hashanah morning form the base for a late-afternoon custom called *tashlikh*, which means "to cast." Its source is a phrase in the prophetic book of Micah, "You will cast all their sins / Into the depths of the sea" (Micah 7:19), and it calls for symbolically casting away one's sins in a sea, river, or other place with flowing water. Usually people go in groups and together recite the verse from Micah along with several psalms, often turning their pockets inside out as if emptying them of sin. (If the first day of Rosh Hashanah is a Sabbath, the ceremony takes place on the second.)

Though many rabbis have opposed this custom as smacking of magic and superstition, it has persisted. In part its popularity comes from the social gathering surrounding it, and perhaps in part from the very concreteness of the act—the sense it gives of truly freeing oneself from the sins of the past.

The flowing waters signify washing away those sins. But on a deeper level, the waters represent the essence of the miracle of Creation celebrated on Rosh Hashanah. From out of the waters that filled the cosmos, God separated light from dark and heaven from earth, Scripture tells us. Later, the waters came together again to flood the land and destroy its inhabitants except for Noah and those he saved. When those waters receded, the world seemed to be created anew, with a promise from God that never again would it be destroyed.

The waters of Rosh Hashanah symbolize the Creation of the world and its new beginning, a Creation and beginning that are commemorated and reenacted each year.

Rosh Hashanah is the only holiday in the Jewish calendar celebrated for two days in Israel as well as outside it. Second days were added to other holidays in the Diaspora because of the uncertainty of knowing exactly when they fell, but Rosh Hashanah was considered a two-day festival from early times. The Talmud suggests that the prophets themselves established it that way. More realistically, it was observed for two days because, even within ancient Palestine, authorities found it difficult to establish the precise time of the new moon, when the festival begins. The extra day ensured observance of this major holiday in its proper time frame.

The sages regarded the two days of Rosh Hashanah as one long holy day, and that view led to a challenging question and a lovely custom. The question: Should the *sheheheyanu* blessing that thanks God for keeping us alive and bringing us to this season be recited on the second evening of Rosh Hashanah? It is usually said only at the start of a holiday and on special occasions. The custom: Wearing new clothes or eating a new fruit—not yet eaten that season—which would require the blessing. That way it can be included in the second evening, and the festive feeling of the holiday continues.

Other delicious customs carry over from the first day. Families eat round hallah breads, symbolizing the ongoing cycle of life, dipping pieces in honey to signify the hope for a sweet year. Sliced apples are also eaten with a dollop of honey and a blessing for sweetness ahead.

The distinguishing feature of the second day in the synagogue is the scriptural reading from Genesis, chapter 22. In a passage that shocks and disturbs, no matter how many times one reads it, God commands Abraham to offer his beloved son Isaac as a sacrifice. Abraham binds Isaac to an altar, but as he raises his knife for the kill, an angel stays his hand. A ram suddenly appears in the thicket, and Abraham sacrifices it instead. People often refer to this event as the "sacrifice of Isaac," but the point of it is that the sacrifice is *not* made and Isaac is saved. In Hebrew it is known as the *Akedah,* the "binding" of Isaac.

But what is the meaning behind it? Some commentators have seen it as a lesson to the ancient Hebrews—in the most graphic form possible—to refrain from human sacrifice, a practice common among neighboring peoples. The Bible itself gives no such indication. It portrays the episode only as a supreme test of Abraham's faith. The midrash adds that though God surely knew the outcome of that test, its purpose was to demonstrate to the nations of the world the worthiness of the father of the Hebrew people.

It is an extreme test, a cruel one actually. Critics have wondered why Abraham did not protest it or plead to save his son's life as he had pleaded earlier for the lives of the inhabitants of the evil cities of Sodom and Gomorrah. In traditional Jewish thought, however, Abraham's readiness to follow God's command and Isaac's willingness to give up his life acquired merit for both of them that would forever benefit their descendants. Time and again the Rosh Hashanah liturgy calls upon God to remember the deeds of Abraham and Isaac and apply them on behalf of all the people of Israel.

The shofar connects Isaac's binding with Rosh Hashanah. The ram's horn, preferred for the holiday shofar (although the horns of goats and other animals may be used), is reminiscent of the ram sacrificed in Isaac's place. In the midrash, its piercing sounds recall Sarah's anguished cries after she learned of the excruciating ordeal her son, Isaac, had endured.

Along different lines, the second day's Torah reading is tied to that of the first, and the two together suggest a holiday lesson that is often overlooked. The first reading, from chapter 21 of Genesis, describes Isaac's birth and Abraham's subsequent banishment of his concubine, Hagar, and son Ishmael from his household. Terrified, mother and son wander in the desert with no food or water until an angel shows Hagar a well, whose waters revive her weakened son. The angel promises that from Ishmael's seed will arise a mighty people.

Isaac and Ishmael grow up apart from each other, leading totally different lives. Yet there is a hint in these two days' readings of more in common than meets the eye. Each as a child suffers a terrible trauma: Ishmael cast out from his father's home and almost dying in the wilderness; Isaac almost slaughtered at the hand of that same father. Each is rescued by an angel of God, and each receives a promise to be the forebear of a powerful nation. Many years later the two brothers, separated throughout their lives, come together to bury their father, Abraham.

An underlying theme of Rosh Hashanah, which becomes a major motif of Yom Kippur, is of forgiveness among individuals. These holidays stress repentance not only for sins against God but also for those against other persons. The narratives of the two brothers show that even in polarities there can be samenesses; even in disparity, eventual reconciliation among all people.

The First Ten Days of Tishrei
DAYS OF AWE—TEN DAYS OF REPENTANCE

Three books are opened in the heavens on Rosh Hashanah, legend says. In the first are recorded the names of thoroughly righteous people; the second lists the thoroughly wicked; and the third holds the names of those who are neither completely righteous nor completely wicked. The righteous, in the first book, are instantly inscribed for life in the year to come. The wicked, in the second book, are instantly inscribed for death. Those not totally righteous or wicked (meaning most of us) have their verdict suspended between Rosh Hashanah and Yom Kippur. If they repent of their sins and bad deeds and are found worthy, they will be inscribed in the book of life. If they are unworthy, their fate will be death.

The days beginning with Rosh Hashanah on the first of Tishrei until Yom Kippur on the tenth of the month are known in Hebrew as *Aseret Yemei Teshuvah*, "Ten Days of Repentance," and spoken of as "Days of Awe." The rabbis tie the ten days to the Ten Commandments, which the Israelites took upon themselves and which serve as their advocates while their fate is being entered in the heavenly books.

The concept of books of life and death has its origin in an intense biblical scene. In it Moses pleads with God to forgive the Israelites the sin of the golden calf. If not, he says, "erase me from the book which You have written" (Exodus 32:32). God responds that only those who have sinned will be erased from the divine book. As translated into popular usage, the image of books of reckoning brought out on Rosh Hashanah expresses the fragility people feel as the new year opens into an unknown future. It is an image that underlies the season's greeting, "May you be inscribed and sealed for a good year," and dominates the most moving hymn of the Rosh Hashanah synagogue service, "*U'Netanneh Tokef*," "And We Acclaim."

"On Rosh Hashanah it is written and on Yom Kippur it is sealed," congregants sing in a solemn refrain as they ponder together how many will leave this world and how many will be born into it, who will live and who will die, and how the life of each person will be affected by the new year. "But penitence, prayer, and good deeds can annul the severity of the decree," the hymn proclaims at the end.

The hymn and the symbols of books of life and death are not meant to imply that death comes only as punishment for sin. Though life is sacred and good in Jewish thought, death is also accepted as part of the divine plan. The purpose of connecting death with sin during the Days of

Awe, however, is to drive home as strongly as possible each individual's responsibility for his or her own behavior. There are consequences to our deeds, this season emphasizes. The choices we make *do* count in our bearing toward God and one another.

But this idea of personal responsibility, so inherent in these days, raises another issue that runs through much of Jewish thinking. How, in fact, can individuals be held accountable for their actions if God is all-powerful and all-knowing? Isn't each person's fate predetermined, and if not, how can we speak of God as omniscient and omnipotent?

The answer held throughout the tradition is that while God knows the future, that knowledge does not influence the decisions we as individuals make. We have the free will to choose our own paths, regardless of God's foreknowledge, and that freedom allows us the opportunity to repent and, in that sense, shape our fate. In the words of the great sage Rabbi Akiva, "Everything is foreseen, yet freedom of choice is granted."

The reasoning may not be wholly satisfactory from a philosophical point of view, but it explains the importance given to repentance, particularly during the ten days from Rosh Hashanah to Yom Kippur. In the synagogue during these days, congregants recite *selihot,* penitential prayers; and at home, people often give extra amounts to charity. But true penitence goes beyond prayer or philanthropy, the tradition teaches. It calls for stringent self-examination that leads to regret for sins committed and a determination to change. Lest anyone think, however, that "sins" refers only to religious observance or blatant misbehavior, Maimonides explains that the deepest and most difficult form of repentance demands rejecting such everyday impulses as anger and hostility toward others, jealousy, greed, and the inordinate pursuit of money and honor.

The word *teshuvah,* for repentance, actually means "return," a turning back from wrongdoing. The term has also been associated with *ba'alei teshuvah,* Jews who had been distant from Jewish teachings and returned to them. In modern times thousands of such returnees, many of them young people, have become religiously observant.

Rabbi Akiva himself was a returnee of sorts. An illiterate shepherd, he began studying Torah at the age of forty at the urging of his wife, Rachel, who suffered extreme poverty for years in support of his studies. He became one of the most influential scholars of the talmudic period and died a martyr's death at the hands of the Romans. One legend places that death on Yom Kippur eve. Akiva taught that God rules the earth with mercy but also in accordance with the good and bad in human behavior. The Ten Days of Repentance are meant to bring out the good inclination in humans and the attribute of mercy in God.

The Third Day of Tishrei
THE FAST OF GEDALIAH—A KINGDOM LOST

In the year 586 B.C.E., King Nebuchadnezzar of Babylon conquered Jerusalem, capital of the ancient kingdom of Judah, destroyed its great Temple, and exiled its most influential citizens. For years earlier, the prophet Jeremiah had warned of the oncoming slaughter, portraying Nebuchadnezzar as God's instrument in chastising the Jews for their moral degradation. Jeremiah opposed any resistance to Nebuchadnezzar, correctly predicting that the Judeans were too small and too weak to take on the mighty Babylonian empire. His prophecies brought upon him enraged accusations of treachery from the Judeans. But when the disaster he foresaw did strike, the sorrowing prophet offered his people hope that in years to come the exile would end and they would return to their homeland.

For many Judeans, one small symbol of that hope was Nebuchadnezzar's appointment of Gedaliah, son of Ahikam, as governor of the remnants of Judah who had not been exiled. Many of these people came from the poorer classes and had been allowed to stay behind because they were not considered a threat to the conquerors. Other Judeans who had fled to neighboring lands after the Babylonian conquest returned and gathered around the new governor.

Gedaliah came from a family that had been prominent during the last days of Judah; his father, in fact, had used his influence to save Jeremiah from the people's wrath. He made his headquarters at Mizpah, site of an old shrine, and Jeremiah joined him there. Like the prophet, the governor sought to accommodate to the Babylonians and in that way maintain some hold on the land of Judah.

The Book of Jeremiah relates that in the seventh month of the year one Ishmael, son of Nethaniah, a man of royal Judean descent, came with ten of his men and murdered Gedaliah and dozens of others at Mizpah. Gedaliah had been warned about Ishmael, but, a trusting and dedicated leader, he refused to believe the reports of danger. Ishmael seems to have been in a conspiracy with King Baalis of neighboring Ammon to overthrow Babylonian rule. Although some of Gedaliah's followers sought revenge, Ishmael escaped to Ammon.

Gedaliah's assassination effectively destroyed the last vestige of self-rule in Judah for decades to come. No Jewish governor replaced him, and many survivors of the violence fled to Egypt, fearing they would be blamed for Gedaliah's death. They took Jeremiah with them against his will, leaving behind in Judah only a small number of poor, demoralized, and leaderless Jews.

Almost twenty-six hundred years after Gedaliah's assassination, another head of a Jewish state, Prime Minister Yitzhak Rabin of Israel, was gunned down by another extremist, this one opposed to his policies of making peace with the Palestinians. As with the murder of Gedaliah, Rabin's assassination stunned and grieved the Jewish people at large. The date was November 4, 1995, 11 Heshvan 5756. Since then thousands of persons have come to his tomb in Jerusalem to pay tribute to him.

In memory of Gedaliah's death, traditional Jews observe the Fast of Gedaliah on the third of Tishrei, the day after Rosh Hashanah. It is one of four fasts connected with the destruction of the First or Second Temple, the most significant of them being the fast of the Ninth of Av. The Fast of Gedaliah is a minor one, observed from dawn to evening of the same day. But it needs to be maintained, the sages said, to show that "the death of the righteous is placed on the same level as the burning of the House of our God."

Shabbat Shuva—the Sabbath of Return

Falling between Rosh Hashanah and Yom Kippur, the Sabbath of Return highlights the holiday themes of repentance and repair. The Hebrew name, *Shabbat Shuva*, comes from a verse in the portion of the prophets read that day that begins: *Shuva Yisrael . . .*, "Return, O Israel, to the Lord your God" (Hosea 14:2). People sometimes speak of the day as *Shabbat Teshuvah*, the "Sabbath of Repentance," because it falls within the Ten Days of Repentance.

Even in ancient times, the Sabbath of Return was an occasion for rabbis or scholars to preach lengthy sermons that included impassioned exhortations to listeners to repent. Included in those sermons were parables built around biblical verses designed to capture the audience's attention while helping them connect lofty concepts to their everyday lives.

A popular parable from early rabbinic sources used time and again by preachers tells of a prince who was far away—a hundred days' journey—from his father. His friends said to him, "Return to your father." He answered, "I cannot. I do not have the strength." Whereupon his father sent word to him and said, "Go as far as your strength will carry you and I will come the rest of the way to meet you." Similarly, the parable continues, the Holy One says to Israel, "Turn back to Me, and I will turn back to you" (Malachi 3:7).

But the length and intensity of sermons given on the Sabbath of Return also often reflect the frustration rabbis feel as they try to stir their congregants to inner change. The eighteenth-century Rabbi Ezekiel Landau expressed the sentiments of many others when he confessed to his congregants, "My words have not been successful, nor borne fruit, for you have not accepted my ethical instruction. Worse than this: the more I continue to chastise, the more the dissoluteness grows."

Despite such rabbinic discouragement, Shabbat Shuva serves both rabbis and congregants as a prelude to the most important day in the Jewish calendar. When it ends, thoughts turn immediately to the long, demanding Yom Kippur fast.

The Ninth Day of Tishrei

YOM KIPPUR EVE—USHERING IN THE DAY OF ATONEMENT

For a little while on the eve of the Day of Atonement, synagogues throughout the world assume the characteristics of a courtroom. Congregants gather in the sanctuary before sunset to enact a two-part legal ceremony that begins the holiday. The ark is opened and the cantor stands on the *bimah,* the podium, flanked on either side by a distinguished member of the congregation holding a Torah scroll. The three together re-create a *bet din,* a religious tribunal empowered to make legal decisions. The proceedings get under way in daylight because Jewish courts do not meet at night.

The cantor opens the first part of the ceremony with a declaration: "By authority of the court on high and by authority of the court below, with divine consent and with the consent of the congregation, we hereby declare it permitted to pray with those who have transgressed."

Nobody knows the origins of the declaration or the transgressors to whom it refers. Many scholars attribute the statement to the thirteenth-century Rabbi Meir ben Baruch of Rothenburg, who, they believe, wished to include in the community people who had fallen away from Judaism or been excommunicated. Some connect the statement to the *Marranos,* the hidden Jews of Spain in the fourteenth and fifteenth centuries who had officially renounced their religion but longed to join in communal prayer on this holiest night of the year.

But much earlier, Rashi (Rabbi Solomon ben Isaac), the renowned eleventh-century French commentator on the Bible and Talmud, referred to the necessity of counting sinners among worshippers. He pointed out that along with all the fragrant spices used to make incense for the ancient Tabernacle, the Bible lists a foul-smelling one called *galbanum.* This inclusion, he said, shows that on our fast days and in our worship we must allow sinners—the unpleasant spices—to pray along with the sweetly pious.

Implied in Rashi's comment is a view of the community as a mixture, like the mixture of incense spices, in which sinners cannot be singled out from the rest. That view suggests that we are all offenders in one way or another, and the permission granted to the congregation to pray with sinners is permission granted to all of us to pray together as sinners.

The second part of the legal ceremony is longer, more familiar, resonant with the emotions of centuries of history. The words are simple: *Kol Nidrei*—"All vows," it begins, and goes on to nullify the vows each person will make and not keep from this Yom Kippur to the next, and by implication those made and unkept during the past year. The vows annulled are not those contracted with another person; in Jewish law, abrogating such oaths requires the consent of both parties. These are the vows people make to themselves or to God, ethical obligations undertaken unwittingly or personal promises an individual may be unable to carry out.

Why precede the holiest day of the year with this courtroom ceremony? As usual, the answer lies buried in the past. We know that the Kol Nidrei declaration is more than a thousand years old—Babylonian Jewish scholars of the eighth century referred to it in their writings. It is in Aramaic, the vernacular of ancient Jews, and may have been composed in early Palestine. Over the centuries, it changed form several times, and many Sephardic (Spanish) congregations still use a slightly different version from the Ashkenazic (Germanic) one. The Talmud refers to a ceremony in which individuals absolved themselves of vows in front of a religious court on the day before Rosh Hashanah, a practice continued today in modified form in Orthodox synagogues. The ceremony may have been moved to the eve of Yom Kippur, when large numbers of people attend services, and expanded to include the entire community of worshippers.

With time, the Kol Nidrei took on a meaning of its own. Persecuted in many lands, often forced to convert, Jews poured their deepest feelings into a statement that in their hearts nullified vows of apostasy, at least before God.

On a spiritual level, the Kol Nidrei courtroom setting creates the atmosphere for all that will follow. In the heavens on high, a court of a different order is in session, popular belief holds. On this day, final decrees are being passed on the fate of each person. The holiday greeting no longer speaks of being inscribed in the book of life but of being sealed into it, ending the Days of Awe with a sense of fulfillment. The court on earth parallels the heavenly one. Words spoken unthinkingly and pledges made in haste take on heightened significance now. They need to be rendered null and void, as each person faces the final reckoning with as clean a slate as possible.

With the congregation joining in, the cantor chants the Kol Nidrei three times in a beautiful, haunting melody of unknown origin but powerful impact. The first time the chant is soft, in the manner of people entering a sovereign's court, fearful of how they will be received. By the third time, the chant becomes strong and loud, reflecting joy and the confidence of being accepted.

Some of that joy and confidence begins to appear earlier in the day, during the home preparations leading to the evening service. In a mood of excitement, people rush home to eat the final meal before beginning a fast that will not end until the next night. The sages taught that eating a festive meal before the holiday is as important as the fast itself, for that meal honors the day to come.

Many people dress in white for the synagogue, to resemble the angels. Some wrap themselves in a *kittel,* similar to the white shroud the dead are buried in. It symbolizes purity along with a recognition of human frailty and mortality. Both men and women often wear canvas instead of leather shoes because leather was a sign of luxury in early days. (Perhaps, also, it does not seem appropriate on this day to wear the skin of an animal slaughtered for human pleasure.) In the synagogue, congregants put on the *tallit,* the prayer shawl, which they otherwise wear only during morning prayers.

The fast officially begins after the meal, when candles are lit and a blessing recited, similar to the lighting of the Sabbath candles. The candles stand for the light the holiday sheds and its position as the *Shabbat Shabbaton,* the Sabbath of complete rest. Many people also light memorial candles to recall the dead. In some homes, parents bless each of their children before the family departs for the synagogue.

Most important, in the hours before the holiday, climaxing the days leading up to it, people ask forgiveness of one another for the hurts they may have imposed during the year. One of the most fundamental teachings of this festival is that fasting, repentance, and prayer may effect atonement only for sins against God. For offenses committed against another human being one must ask that person's forgiveness. Example: proneness to malicious gossip may be considered a sin against God. Spreading a rumor that damages another's reputation is a sin against that person, and pardon must be requested. The tradition urges people who are asked forgiveness to grant it, and not to hold grudges.

There are other things fasting and praying on Yom Kippur cannot do. If a person says, "I will sin and Yom Kippur will atone," Yom Kippur will not atone, for, the sages taught, Yom Kippur brings atonement only for those who truly repent.

❖

True repentance and God's forgiveness are the themes that will dominate the rest of the evening and the next day's services for Yom Kippur. As the cantor completes the Kol Nidrei formula and the sun goes down, the courtroom scene closes. Together the cantor and congregation chant words of hope and comfort from the Torah:

"And all the community of Israel shall be forgiven, as well as the stranger who dwells among them, for all the people acted in error" (Numbers 15:26).

The Tenth Day of Tishrei

YOM KIPPUR—"A SACRED OCCASION"

The humorist Shalom Aleichem captured the mood of more than one person as the Yom Kippur fast stretches on. In his short story "The Search," he wrote of a major disgrace in the mythical town of Kasrielevky. Toward the end of daylong Yom Kippur services, a wealthy stranger, a Lithuanian, accuses the townspeople of having stolen eighteen hundred rubles he had hidden in the synagogue during the holiday. A search of all the congregation turns up no money. But in the pockets of the town scholar, son-in-law of its richest man, it does turn up—by forcibly holding him down after he refuses to be searched—recently gnawed chicken bones and still-moist prune pits. The learned scholar had been secretly eating on Yom Kippur! It's a scandal no one will soon forget.

Yom Kippur is no laughing matter, to be sure. The Bible decrees it to be "a sacred occasion" when "you shall practice self-denial" (Leviticus 23:27), and the Talmud interprets "self-denial" to mean no "eating, drinking, washing, anointing, wearing shoes, and marital intercourse." Yet built into this most solemn day on the Jewish calendar is also a spirit of optimism and hope. On Yom Kippur afternoon in ancient Jerusalem, young women dressed in white would dance in the vineyards with an eye to attracting male suitors, and the rabbis not only condoned the practice but spoke of it as adding to the gladness of the occasion.

One source of that gladness is the tradition that on the tenth of Tishrei, Moses descended from Mount Sinai carrying the second tablets of the Law. He had destroyed the first in fury at discovering the golden calf the people had built during his stay on the mountaintop. With the second tablets he brought them forgiveness for their sin and reconciliation with God. That reconciliation holds within it the promise of pardon for other sins at other times. Behind the prayers of Yom Kippur lies the conviction that this time, too, forgiveness will be forthcoming.

Another cause for happiness on this sacred day was its position in early times as the occasion for announcing a jubilee year. In that year—every fiftieth according to biblical counting—slaves and bonded servants were set free and lands returned to their ancestral owners. "You shall proclaim liberty throughout the land" (Leviticus 25:10), Scripture declares of the jubilee year, the proclamation to be made with a great blast of the shofar on the Day of Atonement.

The mixture of joy and solemnity that characterizes Yom Kippur has its counterpart in the mixture of ritual observance and ethical teaching that gives the holiday its meaning and texture.

Ritual is prevalent throughout. The festival centers on the synagogue—there are no home customs after the final meal on the eve of Yom Kippur—and the sequences of prayers and poems are the longest of any during the year. Fully ten times, beginning on the holiday eve, congregants recite a formal confessional, an alphabetical listing of sins. The Torah portions of the day concern ceremonies and regulations, including sacrifices brought to the Temple and rules of sexual behavior. (Rabbis like to say that the latter are included to perk people up in the midst of so much prayer.)

Capping it all is the high priest's *Avodah* service, a dramatic expansion on the morning's Torah reading. Through the prayer book, worshippers reenact the high priest's activities as he entered the Holy of Holies, the inner sanctum of the ancient Temple. Only he was permitted into that sanctuary and only on one day of the year, Yom Kippur. With sacrifices and prayer he made atonement for himself, other priests, and all the people of Israel.

In one of the most powerful moments of the ceremony, the high priest symbolically transferred the sins of the nation onto a scapegoat chosen by lot. He would bind a thread of crimson wool around the goat's horns, lay his hands on its head, and confess the people's transgressions. A priest would then lead the goat off to the wilderness of Azazel. The Talmud relates that when the goat reached Azazel, another thread of crimson tied to the Temple entrance would turn white, a sign that the sins had been forgiven, in keeping with the verse "Be your sins like crimson, / They can turn snow-white" (Isaiah 1:18). Later that Temple thread was discontinued because the people would become despondent if it remained crimson.

The entire ceremony was primitive, critics say, too close to magic for comfort. Some argue that the mysterious-sounding Azazel was not a place but a wilderness demon, a carry-over from pagan beliefs. Yet many people still find this ritual deeply moving, evoking forgotten emotions. (In my grandparents' home on Yom Kippur eve, my brother and I, like all our relatives, would wave a live chicken around our heads while reciting Hebrew verses that transferred our iniquities onto it. Our ritual was an echo of the Temple scapegoat ceremony, as thrilling as it was frightening. The chicken served as a *kapparah*—from the same root as *Kippur*—an atonement to ward off evil from us. In later years we replaced the chicken with money to be donated to charity, a practice many observant Jews still follow, although a few continue to use live chickens.)

There is something in the scapegoat imagery that makes the concepts of sin and repentance so real, so immediate, so difficult to avoid that we remain riveted, and never mind primitiveness.

❖

For all the drama of ritual, however, for all its color and emotion, it never overshadows the ethical content of the holiday. The ideas behind the long confessionals, for example, represent Jewish thought at its highest. None of the misdeeds confessed deal with ritual laws, not even the laws of the Sabbath. Each treats a matter of conscience—the sin of betraying a neighbor and the sin of disrespecting parents and teachers, the sin of bribery and the sin of haughtiness. As important, the listings are in the plural. Judaism has no human intermediaries to whom individuals can confess sins and be absolved from them. The community confesses as a whole, equals before God. In those public confessions each person assumes some responsibility for the actions of others, but privately each can also find his or her own place on the list and seek forgiveness.

The day's prophetic readings reinforce its moral concerns. "Is such the fast I desire, / A day for men to starve their bodies?" demands the prophet Isaiah in the morning portion read. "No," he replies, "this is the fast I desire: / To unlock the fetters of wickedness . . . / To let the oppressed go free . . ." (Isaiah 58:5–6). Misinterpreted by some people as a negation of all religious observance, the prophet's words negate only practice without purpose, performance that has lost its moral core. The Yom Kippur fast, the prophet insists, is not for the sake of going hungry but for the sake of spiritual cleansing and reawakening.

A different kind of spiritual rebirth lies at the heart of the Book of Jonah, chanted in its entirety in the late afternoon, the only time of the year when a full Torah service is held in the afternoon as well as the morning. Jonah is a reluctant prophet. His name means "dove," and like the dove from Noah's ark that could find no dry land upon which to rest its feet, Jonah is restless, running away from God and from his mission to preach to the pagan city of Nineveh. Through his own suffering—being swallowed by a huge fish, among other things—he learns lessons about God's compassion. And from the Ninevites' acts of contrition, he—and we—learn of the power repentance can wield.

❖

By early evening of this long day, people begin to look at their watches and fantasize about the meal they hope to indulge in when the holiday ends. Then *Ne'ilah*, the last service, begins, and a new energy grips everyone. The name Ne'ilah means "closing": as the sun sets and prayers draw to an end, the gates on high through which supplications have entered all day are being shut, and with them the great books that hold each person's fate. The spirit of joy and solemnity, the ritual acts and ethical teachings that marked the entire day come together now in final prayers, final appeals for mercy along with justice, final reckonings within oneself.

The ark is kept open during the entire Ne'ilah service, like the last opening of the heavenly gates, and the tradition is to stand throughout. The service ends with the words "The Lord is God" chanted seven times and a loud blast of the shofar, reminiscent of the shofar sound that proclaimed liberty in a jubilee year. With that, congregants cry out, "Next year in Jerusalem." (In Israel they say, "Next year in Jerusalem rebuilt.") Yom Kippur and Passover are the only two holidays that conclude with these words, both holding out the possibility of redemption for the Jewish people.

The Fifteenth Day of Tishrei

SUKKOT—THE FEAST OF BOOTHS

When the Pilgrims at Plymouth colony wanted to create a thanksgiving celebration for their first harvest, they turned to the Bible—which they revered—for their model. There they found instructions to the Israelites to hold a great annual harvest festival, called *Hag HaAsif,* the "Feast of Ingathering," beginning on the fifteenth day of the seventh month. But the implications of the festival extended beyond the people of Israel. According to later rabbis, the seventy bulls to be sacrificed during the holiday were meant to secure blessings for the seventy nations of the world known to the ancients. Moreover, the prophet Zechariah foresaw a time when all peoples would make a yearly pilgrimage to Jerusalem to observe this feast and "bow low to the King Lord of Hosts" (Zechariah 14:16). The Pilgrims' three-day thanksgiving feast (the source for Thanksgiving in the United States) was their way of "bowing low" and translating Zechariah's vision into their own lives.

For the Israelites, the harvest festival, which celebrates the end of the agricultural year in Israel, was so important that it became known simply as *HeHag*, "the festival." But the name most often used for it is *Hag HaSukkot*, the "Feast of Booths." It is a name that connects this festival to the most pivotal event in Jewish history, the Exodus from Egypt. Jews are commanded to live in booths for the seven days of the holiday as a reminder of the makeshift huts the Israelites dwelt in when they wandered in the desert. The word *sukkah*, a single booth, derives from a Hebrew root meaning "to cover over," and the branches used to form the roof of a sukkah are known as *s'khakh*, a covering.

There is a historical problem, however, in linking Sukkot with the Exodus. That event forms the core of the spring festival of Passover, separated from Sukkot by a full six months. How do autumn booths tie in with springtime's unleavened bread?

Some commentators explain that although the Exodus took place in the spring, the Israelites' hardship of living in booths is intentionally reenacted in the fall because this is a harvesttime. Living in fragile booths reminds people not to take for granted the bountiful fruits and vegetables they have gathered but to see them as God's miracle, like the booths the Israelites lived in, like the Exodus itself.

The talmudic sages also connected the Sukkot booths to the clouds of glory that hovered over the Tabernacle the Israelites built in the wilderness and led the way for them through all the seasons of their wanderings. Some went further and described seven clouds of glory that descended on the people when they came to the town of Succoth, the first stop on their journey. From there on, the clouds enveloped them like a sukkah—one under their feet to protect against thorns, one above their heads to provide shade, four hovering in front, behind, and on each side of the camp, and a seventh to show the way.

Contemporary scholars suggest that the booths actually are unrelated to the Exodus but reminiscent of the huts farmers built when they flocked to Jerusalem to celebrate the harvest feast. Sukkot is one of three pilgrimage festivals prescribed by the Bible, when people brought sacrifices to the sanctuary (the other two are Passover and Shavuot). Because the harvest was already in and farmers could leave their fields, this holiday probably drew the largest crowds of pilgrims, and with them the need for temporary housing.

The festival lasts seven days. In Israel the first day is a holiday when work is forbidden; in the Diaspora the first two days are. An eighth festival day, *Shemini Azeret*, is separate from but still connected to Sukkot. Jews are expected to take all their meals in the sukkah during the festival unless it rains or they experience other discomfort. It is a special obligation to eat there on the first night.

The work of building a sukkah begins immediately after Yom Kippur. The sukkah may not be higher than twenty cubits (about ten yards) or lower than ten handbreadths (about forty inches), dimensions that make it comfortable to live in but with a sense of impermanence. Its three sides may be of any material, but its roof must be of the s'khakh, whose materials were grown in the ground and then detached from it, such as branches or cane. The s'khakh rests on the sukkah in a way that provides more shade than sunlight, a reminder of God's protection of the Israelites from the burning heat of the desert. The covering should also allow occupants to see the stars at night so that they may be aware of their vulnerability in the vast universe, and also their closeness to the Divine.

As it is with many Jewish laws, the obligation to dwell in a sukkah falls on men, not women. Yet a woman of the first century set a precedent that has been an example for others. She was Helena, queen of the ancient kingdom of Adiabene in northern Mesopotamia, who converted to Judaism and became scrupulous in observing the law. On a trip to Judea, she had a large sukkah built for herself in the town of Lydda, and the rabbis showed their approval by spending time in it. Many women today keep the sukkah commandments along with the laws concerning four different plants that form the other major symbol of the festival.

They are called the four species. The Bible describes them as the "product of *hadar* [goodly] trees, branches of palm trees, boughs of leafy trees, and willows of the brook" (Leviticus 23:40). The exact meanings of the biblical Hebrew words is unclear. Rabbinic rulings interpreted the hadar to mean a citron, in Hebrew *etrog*. The branch of palm became known as the *lulav* (literally, a young shoot); the boughs of leafy trees are *hadasim*, or myrtle leaves; and the willows are called *aravot*.

Although the four plant varieties represent the holiday's agricultural ties, they also have symbolic meanings. Some sources describe the etrog as the forbidden fruit Adam and Eve ate in the Garden of Eden. Some connect all the species to the human body—the tall lulav is the spine, the myrtle the eye, the willow the mouth, and the etrog the heart. Together they give meaning to the biblical words "All my bones shall say, / 'Lord, who is like You?'" (Psalm 35:10). Some relate the species to four heroes of biblical history: Abraham, Isaac, Jacob, and Joseph; and some identify them with the four matriarchs Sarah, Rebekah, Leah, and Rachel.

Worshippers carry the species to synagogue (except on the Sabbath) and wave them while reciting *Hallel*, Psalms 113 to 118, praising God. The rule is to hold the lulav with the hadasim and aravot in the right hand and the etrog in the left and with hands together to shake them on certain verses toward the east, south, west, north, above, and below—to show that all corners of the earth belong to God. (It should be said that gripping the species while keeping track of how many shakes are made in which direction and on what verses is not the easiest task.) Later, congregants walk in procession around the synagogue with the species in hand chanting prayers for deliverance. This procession is a reminder of the one that took place around the Temple altar in ancient times. In itself it is also a beautiful and emotional moment of communal worship.

❖

Behind all the Sukkot symbols lie the themes of rejoicing and thanksgiving, for the abundance of the harvest, for the Exodus from Egypt, for the continuity of the tradition. A poignant moment in that continuity appears in the Book of Nehemiah. About the year 428 B.C.E., some hundred years after groups of Jews had returned from exile in Babylonia, the people assembled in Jerusalem to hear the scribe Ezra read aloud from the Torah scrolls. Among the passages he read were those giving the laws for the feast of Sukkot. The people were so moved that they gathered the plants decreed and built sukkot on their roofs and in their courtyards. Not since the days of Joshua, when the Children of Israel first entered the land, had the holiday been celebrated so wholeheartedly. Now the "whole community that returned from the captivity made booths and dwelt in the booths . . . and there was very great rejoicing" (Nehemiah 8:17).

The Sixteenth Day of Tishrei

SUKKOT, THE SECOND DAY

The Mishnah records a mysterious incident. On "one occasion," it says, a "certain person" poured water over his feet during a ceremony in the Second Temple and the people pelted him with citrons. What was the occasion? Who was the man? And why did the people hurl their citrons—their *etrogim*—at him?

The Roman Jewish historian Josephus sheds some light on the event. It took place on one of the days of Sukkot, possibly the second morning, when Alexander Yannai, both king and high priest of Judea, was to conduct a water libation ceremony in the Temple. Yannai, who lived in the first century B.C.E., was a descendant of the Hasmonean family whose defeat of the Syrians in the previous century is celebrated in the festival of Hanukkah. The family line had become corrupt, with much fighting among its members and with the Judeans. In Yannai's day, also, bitter discord existed between two Judean sects, the Pharisees, the rabbis and scholars whose teachings were later gathered into the Mishnah and Talmud, and the Sadducees, mostly aristocratic and priestly classes, who rejected the Pharisees' teachings and recognized only the written Torah.

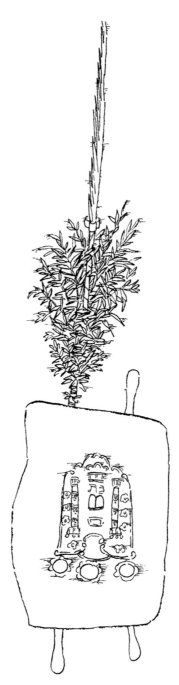

Yannai inclined toward the Sadducees, and to show his disdain for the Pharisees, he mocked the libation ceremony they regarded as religious law. The ceremony called for the priest to pour water from a silver bowl onto the altar in a symbolic prayer for rain in the months ahead. Instead, Yannai poured the water over his feet. Enraged at his arrogance, the crowd of worshippers hit him with the citrons they had carried with them to the Temple and denounced him as unworthy of the priesthood. He, in turn, called out an army of mercenaries, who slaughtered thousands of Judeans.

Eventually the Pharisees made peace with Yannai, and on his death they gave him an elaborate burial. That reconciliation may have led to the omission of his name from the cryptic Mishnah passage.

The water libation ceremony Yannai had derided was part of one of the most colorful Sukkot practices at the time of the Second Temple. On the festival mornings, a procession would make its way to the spring of Shiloah, which was probably near present-day Siloam, outside Jerusalem. There a golden flask was filled with water. At the Temple, a priest would transfer the water to a silver bowl from which it could be poured on the altar as a libation.

From the second night on, a great celebration would take place in the women's court outside the Temple. Priests would light four huge golden menorahs, or candelabra, and the people would revel in the holiday with dancing, singing, acrobatics, and feats of torch-throwing that often lasted through the night. Though the festivities took place in the women's section, it's unlikely that women participated in them, but they could watch from a balcony surrounding the court. The celebration ended when loud blasts of either a shofar or a trumpet announced a new day.

The entire festive ceremony was called *Simhat Beit HaSho'evah,* "Rejoicing at the Place of the Water Drawing," its name probably derived from a verse in the Book of Isaiah, "Joyfully shall you draw water / From the fountains of salvation" (Isaiah 12:3).

It is not surprising that water should be at the heart of Temple ceremonies. The festival of Sukkot coincides with the beginning of the rainy season in Israel. The sages taught that the water libation was necessary because this festival was a time of heavenly judgment for rain, when the season's rainfalls were determined, and therefore an occasion to ask for the blessing of water.

Some rabbis associated the four plant species carried during Sukkot with the centrality of water. The palm trees from which the lulav comes, they said, grow in valleys where there is plenty of water. Willows and myrtles both thrive near the water, and the etrog needs more water than any other plant to grow.

Modern critics connect the Temple water libations to magical rites of other ancient peoples, who would pour water on the ground to stir the gods to deliver rain. Regardless of their origins, however, the water ceremonies became distinctly Jewish events, dominating the Sukkot festival.

The ceremonies ended when the Second Temple was destroyed. Although Jews could practice the rituals of the etrog and lulav anywhere, the water libation ceremonies were too closely connected to the Temple to be transferred. They can be counted among the many other losses Jews suffered when the Temple no longer stood. For, the rabbis said, "Anyone who has not seen the Rejoicing at the Place of the Water Drawing has never seen rejoicing in his life."

The Seventeenth through the Twentieth Days of Tishrei

SUKKOT, THE DAYS BETWEEN

Along with family and friends, a parade of spiritual guests may come to inhabit a sukkah. These are no ordinary spirits but ancient leaders of Israel. Nor do they slip in unobtrusively. They are invited in to grace the sukkah, called forth with special words of greeting.

The custom comes from the mystics, and the guests are known as *ushpizin,* from an Aramaic word. Traditionally, there are seven: Abraham, Isaac, Jacob, Joseph, Moses, Aaron, and David. On the first day Abraham heads the list, with the others behind him; on the second day Isaac; and on in order until the seventh day, when King David leads the rest. Some families add biblical women, among them Sarah, Rebekah, Leah, Rachel, Miriam, Hannah, and Esther, or later ones, including poets and political leaders. All the ushpizin are welcomed with a formula that begins: "Enter, exalted honored guests."

As desired as these invisible visitors from above are, the tradition encourages Jews to supplement them with earthly guests, specifically the poor who cannot afford their own sukkah.

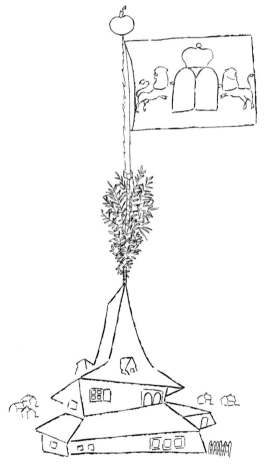

Seemingly far removed from the spirits of patriarchs past or the plight of the present-day poor is the Book of Kohelet, or Ecclesiastes, usually read on the Sabbath after the first days of Sukkot. The narrator dwells on the futility of all human pleasures and urges that we simply enjoy what we have, for soon it will be gone. With poetic imagery he depicts the degradations of growing old, and with deep pessimism he sees little hope for change in the world. There is a season for everything, he says in the most famous passage of the book, including "a time for being born and a time for dying" (Ecclesiastes 3:2), and we have no control over our fate.

No mystical toying here, no playfulness; Kohelet is one of the most disturbing books in the Bible, yet one that sparks a quick sense of recognition in readers. It is one of the "five scrolls," the shortest books in the Writings, the last section of the Hebrew Bible (the others are the Song of Songs, Ruth, Lamentations, and Esther). It has been ascribed to King Solomon because the author identifies himself as "Kohelet, son of David, king in Jerusalem" (1:1). Tradition says that Solomon wrote the lyrical Song of Songs in his youth, the practical book of Proverbs in his middle years, and the despairing Kohelet in old age. But the book's language has led scholars to date it much later than Solomon's time.

Why this book has become Sukkot reading is an unanswered question. One traditional explanation is that a verse in it directing us: "Distribute portions to seven or even to eight" (Ecclesiastes 11:2) refers to the seven days of the festival along with the eighth day of Shemini Azeret. A second is that Kohelet's view of the transience of all possessions reinforces the idea of human fragility symbolized by the holiday booths. With the attribution of the book to King Solomon, the fact that the First Temple, built by him, was dedicated during Sukkot also ties the book and the holiday together.

But there is one other bond between Sukkot and Kohelet to consider. The festival follows a period of the most intense self-scrutiny Jews undertake all year, and in fact, some of that scrutiny is revisited on its seventh day, Hoshana Rabbah. The writings of Kohelet are the musings of a man wrestling with himself and with the large issues of existence: How does God function in the universe? Does life have meaning beyond its everydayness? What purposes do we serve on earth? All are questions of the holiday period beginning with Rosh Hashanah and continuing through Sukkot. None has a definitive answer known to humans, but, like Kohelet, we continue to go about our activities, enjoy our festivals, be swept up in the coursing of time—and seek meaning behind it all.

The Twenty-first Day of Tishrei

HOSHANA RABBAH—A CRY FOR SALVATION

In English the word *hosanna* means great praise, as in "She received hosannas for her beautiful voice." It's a word that has become widely known through the New Testament. Jesus is described there as entering Jerusalem before Passover, shortly prior to his death, and being greeted by crowds of people carrying palm branches and calling out "Hosanna." It is less well known that *hosanna* comes from a Hebrew word which is actually a contraction of two words together making up a cry for salvation. The Hebrew word is *hoshana*, and it is taken from *hoshi'ah na*, meaning "O save." Every day of Sukkot, worshippers march in procession around the interior of the synagogue—in a ceremony called *hoshanot*—chanting hymns that ask for God's help and salvation. After each verse they repeat the refrain, "Hoshana." On the seventh and last day of the festival, the procession makes its circuit seven times, giving the day its name, *Hoshana Rabbah*, the Great Hosanna.

(Some scholars have suggested that the hosannas and palm branches that accompanied Jesus' entry into Jerusalem indicate that he actually arrived there during the Sukkot festival. It was then that throngs would fill the streets carrying their palm branches, and then that priests led hoshanot processions around the Temple altar. The entry may have been transposed to Passover in its retelling to make the narrative consistent with the events leading to his death.)

The daily Sukkot procession in the Second Temple would include the chanting of a verse from the Psalms: *Ana Hashem hoshi'ah na*, "O Lord, save" (118:25). Some rabbis substituted other, more obscure words for these, and those substituted words have become standard in today's liturgy along with the others. They read in Hebrew: *Ani va'ho hoshi'ah na*, which can be translated loosely as "I and He, O save." The letters of the words have the same numerical value as the verse in Psalms (in Hebrew, each letter has its own value), and the phrase as a whole seems to have a hidden, mystical significance. The commentator Rashi identified the words *ani va'ho* as two mystical names for God, part of a series of seventy-two such names, each made up of three Hebrew letters. But the phrase may symbolize something broader, a partnership between humans and God—an "I and He"—that both acknowledges suffering and leads toward salvation.

❖

Mysticism, and some magic, mark much of the Hoshana Rabbah ceremonies and customs. The practice of circling the Temple altar during the hoshanot may have held traces of an early use of circles to create magical space from within which to ward off evil spirits. In legend, for example, the sage Honi received the nickname "the circle-maker" because he would draw a circle on the ground around himself and pray for rain. Miraculously, his prayers were usually answered. With time, any connection between magical circles and the circular processions on Sukkot was forgotten; the processions simply added to the pageantry of the holiday.

A custom peculiar to Hoshana Rabbah is "the beating of the willows," again originating in Temple practices. In those days, the people would go as a group to cut willow branches with which they decorated the altar. At the end of the hoshanot processions they would beat a bunch of willow sprigs against the ground, a practice that continues in synagogue services today. The willow, which grows near water, represented fertility to many early peoples, and beating willows may have been a ritual designed to induce fruitfulness. In the Hoshana Rabbah service, however, it became one more symbolic way of asking for rain, a request repeated in many forms throughout Sukkot.

The number seven, so significant in Jewish ritual, has particular importance on Hoshana Rabbah. It is the seventh day of Sukkot, which falls during the seventh month of the year. The four species carried during the hoshanot actually have seven elements—the etrog, the lulav, two willow branches, and three myrtle branches. The processions circle the synagogue seven times, a reminder of the seven guests—the ushpizin—symbolically invited to the sukkah on each night of the festival. The seven circles are reminiscent also of the seven circuits Joshua made around the city of Jericho on the seventh day before bringing down its walls.

The most blatantly superstitious of all the day's customs is the belief that a person who stands in the moonlight on the night of Hoshana Rabbah and does not see the shadow of his or her head will die during the coming year.

❖

But the association between Hoshana Rabbah and death has a more serious and ethical side. In tradition, the books of life and death opened on Rosh Hashanah and closed on Yom Kippur have their final, irrevocable sealing on the seventh day of Sukkot. When this day ends, according to the kabbalists, the period of atonement ends and the heavenly decrees are set in motion. Consequently, the day carries an air of solemnity, a touch of Yom Kippur, although it is not treated as a holy day but as one of the intermediary days of the festival, when work is permitted.

At night, observant Jews may stay awake studying passages from Scripture, similar to a custom more widely practiced on the festival of Shavuot. A special anthology, called a *tikkun,* holds a variety of texts to be studied, and the practice of study is called *tikkun leil Hoshana Rabbah,* "tikkun for the night of Hoshana Rabbah." The word *tikkun* also means "repair" or "perfection," which in this case can come through study. During the morning synagogue service the reader wears the kittel, the white robe that symbolizes purity, as on Yom Kippur.

This last day of Sukkot is also the last time for taking up the lulav and etrog and the last time the blessing for the sukkah is said when eating in it. (People might have a snack in it the next day, without saying the prayer.) A pleasant custom is to save some of the lulav ribs until Passover, to be used instead of a feather in the search for leavened bread. The saved lulav ties one holiday to the next and one passage in Jewish history to another.

The prophet Isaiah envisioned a time to come when God will protect the righteous of Israel under a great sukkah (4:5–6). Legend elaborates that in the end of days a huge sea monster called Leviathan will be destroyed and from its skin God will create a great sukkah in which the righteous of Israel will sit and feast on its meat. On leaving their sukkah for the last time of the year, some people recite a prayer asking that they merit the privilege of dwelling in the sukkah of Leviathan.

The Twenty-second Day of Tishrei

SHEMINI AZERET—A SOLEMN GATHERING

A parable gives a reason for the holiday of Shemini Azeret: A king invited his children to a feast for a certain number of days. When the time came for them to depart, he said, "My children, I ask you to tarry with me one day longer. It is difficult for me to part with you." So it is with God. The long Sukkot festival has ended, but God wants to detain the Children of Israel a little longer and enjoy them, so an eighth day, Shemini Azeret, has been added.

It's as good a story as any, told by Rashi to help explain this peculiar festival: peculiar because it is considered independent of the seven-day Sukkot feast, yet its name literally means the "Eighth

Day of Assembly." The Bible lists it as a separate celebration, a "solemn gathering" and holy day when work is forbidden and the sacrifices offered are different from those of Sukkot (Leviticus 23:36). But even as a day of gathering or assembly, it has an obscure significance, and in practice it has become more like an appendage to Sukkot, the eighth day of a seven-day holiday.

The major distinction of Shemini Azeret in the synagogue is that after all the symbolic requests for rain during Sukkot—the waving of the four species, the beating of the willows, the ancient water libation ceremony—its liturgy includes a direct prayer for rain. In addition, from this day until Passover, the words "who causes the winds to blow and the rains to come down," referring to God, are inserted in the prayer service as a further incentive for rain. Answered prayers having the potential for problems as they sometimes do, the sages may have held off outright requests for rain until this day after Sukkot lest it arrive too early and prevent enjoyment of the sukkah.

Actually, there is something quite wonderful about the fact that wherever Jews live, they recite prayers for rain now, whether or not the countries they inhabit need rain at this time. The liturgy links them to one another and to the land of Israel, where the rainy season will soon start.

❖

Historically, Shemini Azeret seems to have been a true day of national assembly on one occasion. That was in the tenth century B.C.E., at the end of a fourteen-day celebration and dedication of the First Temple in Jerusalem that began a week before Sukkot and lasted through the seven days of the holiday. King Solomon had built the Temple, called the House of the Lord, in a vast enterprise that took seven years to complete and involved the labor of thousands of Israelite and foreign workers.

The Temple served as the embodiment of all that was unique about the people of Israel, a public display of its belief in One God. Tradition says that it stood on the very spot where Abraham had bound Isaac in a demonstration of his absolute faith. That place became known as the Temple Mount and, later, was also the location of the Second Temple. Today two Muslim mosques stand on the site.

The Temple building boasted magnificent courtyards, carved walls, and furnishings of gold, but its most sacred object was the ancient Ark of the Covenant, which held the stone tablets of the Ten Commandments. During the dedication ceremonies the Ark was placed in a room of its own, the Holy of Holies. The High Priest would enter that room just once a year thereafter to perform the rites of atonement.

In mystical thought, the Temple on earth reflected the likeness of the Temple in the world above, and when it was constructed, the two worlds were in perfect harmony. Legend tells that no tools touched the Temple stones. Instead a tiny insect or worm, called a *shamir*, shaped them to size. So strong that it could cut through the hardest diamond, the shamir had been created during the mysterious twilight on the sixth day of creation specifically for use in building the Temple. Solomon sent an eagle to carry it from the Garden of Eden, where it was hidden, to Jerusalem to perform its task. When the Temple was destroyed, the shamir disappeared.

At the dedication ceremonies, Solomon made a moving speech before the masses of people who had come to Jerusalem for the occasion. The first part of it is read in the synagogue on the second day of Sukkot, and the last part, including the blessing Solomon gave the nation, on Shemini Azeret. In his dedication, Solomon pictured the Temple as a place of universal worship for people of many lands. "Thus all the peoples of the earth will know Your name and revere You," he proclaimed (I Kings 8:43). Later, the prophet Zechariah would echo that thought in his vision of international pilgrimages to Jerusalem during Sukkot.

The Book of Chronicles relates that when Solomon finished his dedication, a miraculous fire from heaven came down and consumed his sacrifices, as it had for Moses in the wilderness Tabernacle (II Chronicles 7:1). On the eighth day after the festival, Solomon held a "solemn gathering" of all the people, then sent them home the next day, "rejoicing and in good spirits over the goodness that the Lord had shown to David and Solomon and His people Israel" (7:9–10).

Ironically, the king who went to such lengths to construct the Temple became later in life an idol worshipper. According to the Bible, he had wed seven hundred wives, many from neighboring lands, in order to secure his empire. In his old age these foreign wives "turned away Solomon's heart after other gods" (I Kings 11:4), to which the sages said, "It would have been better for Solomon to have cleaned sewers than to have such a verse written of him."

The Temple remained standing for nearly four hundred years before King Nebuchadnezzar of Babylon destroyed it. Prophets and poets have written many beautiful words of sadness and praise for it, but a brief interpretation of a biblical verse serves well to summarize its place in Jewish thought. The verse reads: "And for the house he made windows, broad and narrow" (I Kings 6:4). The fourth-century scholar Rabbi Avin the Levite explained:

"When a person makes openings for windows, he makes them broad on the inside and narrow on the outside. Why? So that they allow in the greatest amount of light. But the windows in the Temple were broad on the outside and narrow on the inside. Why? So that the light would stream out from the Temple and illumine the world."

The Twenty-third Day of Tishrei

SIMHAT TORAH—REJOICING IN THE LAW

Anyone who has ever attended a *Simhat Torah* service as a child will probably have memories of parading through the synagogue aisles carrying a blue-and-white cloth or paper flag adorned with a star of David and topped with an apple holding a candle. Or, for some, the flag may have been multicolored and decorated with the signs of the twelve tribes of Israel.

Anyone who has ever witnessed Hasidim celebrating the holiday will have a mental image of black-frocked men clutching Torah scrolls and dancing ecstatically, while women push against one another in the balcony or behind screens, trying to grab a moment's glimpse of the excitement.

Anyone who remembers the oppression of Jews in Russia before the Soviet Union collapsed may also remember newspaper photos of thousands upon thousands of Jewish men and women pouring into the streets near synagogues on Simhat Torah eve, celebrating this above all other festivals as their holiday, a time to proclaim their Jewishness no matter how distasteful to the reigning regime.

Simhat Torah, the festival of "Rejoicing in the Law," is celebrated mostly with noise, laughter, dancing, and singing. But the nub of all that is a thread of seriousness—an unbroken tie that connects the Jewish people to the Torah, and therefore to its own history and beliefs.

More than any other day of the year, Simhat Torah resembles the Jewish calendar itself, with its cycle of holidays leading one into the next. On Simhat Torah the cycle celebrated is the reading in the synagogue of the Torah, which ends with the death of Moses in the last verses of Deuteronomy, then begins immediately with the Creation of the world in the first verses of Genesis. All the noise, laughter, dancing, and singing are about that ending and beginning.

In Israel, Simhat Torah is combined in one festive day with Shemini Azeret. Reform Jews also observe only one day for the two feasts, but Orthodox and Conservative Jews outside Israel commemorate Simhat Torah as a holiday in its own right.

The main feature of the holiday celebration in the synagogue is a series of processions, called *hakafot*, or "circuits," in which congregants carry Torah scrolls in procession around the synagogue, much the way they carried the four species on Sukkot. Now they make seven circuits—again the symbol-laden number seven. Children march along, holding their flags—whose candles symbolize the light of the Torah—and everyone sings, shouts, dances, and reaches out to kiss the scrolls. The total effect is chaos, but with some internal order.

The order is this: On the holiday eve, all the Torah scrolls are removed from the ark and congregants take turns parading and dancing with them in the processionals. In liberal synagogues, women participate with men in the Torah circuits. In some Orthodox synagogues, women hold their own services with their own scrolls. In others the women may mingle with the men in the men's section—the only time of the year when this is permitted—although they don't carry the scrolls. The women in Hasidic communities usually watch the proceedings from behind a screen. At the end of the processions, a reader chants some passages from one of the scrolls, usually parts of the concluding portion of Deuteronomy, but not the very last verses. Those are saved for the next day.

On that day of Simhat Torah the seven circuits with the scrolls take place again. The Torah reading is arranged so that all congregants receive an *aliyah*, the honor of reciting the blessings over the Torah. (In most Orthodox synagogues only men receive the honor.) Shortly before the final reading, all the young children present go to the podium for a group aliyah. Congregants spread a large prayer shawl over the children's heads like a canopy, and an adult leads them in the blessings. When they finish, the entire congregation blesses them and showers them with candy.

Marriage symbolism runs throughout the day's ceremony. The person called to bless the Torah for the final reading in Deuteronomy is known as the groom of the Torah, or the bride, if a woman. The person who blesses the Torah for the opening reading in Genesis is called the groom—or bride—of Genesis. Both are usually people the community wishes to honor. Ushers often escort them up to the Torah, where songs of praise greet them. (In eighteenth-century Italy, the wives of men chosen for these honors were themselves called brides and enjoyed the same respect as their husbands.) Even the seven circuits of the synagogue are reminiscent of the custom at many traditional wedding ceremonies for the bride to circle the groom seven times.

The wedding imagery is not unusual in Judaism. The sages interpreted the Song of Songs as a love poem between God and Israel; a "marriage" of the people to the Torah is another expression of that love.

For all the fun and commotion of the holiday, one of its best moments is also one of its gentler ones. As the first chapter of Genesis is read, the congregation chants aloud in Hebrew, "And there was evening and there was morning, a first day," which is then repeated by the reader, and on through all the days of Creation. The chanting is a reminder of the participation of humans in the act of Creation, a participation that, like the cycle of Torah reading, never ends.

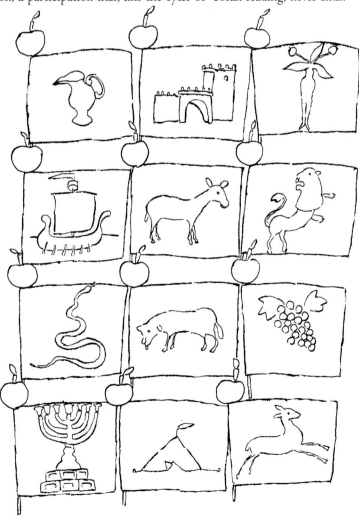

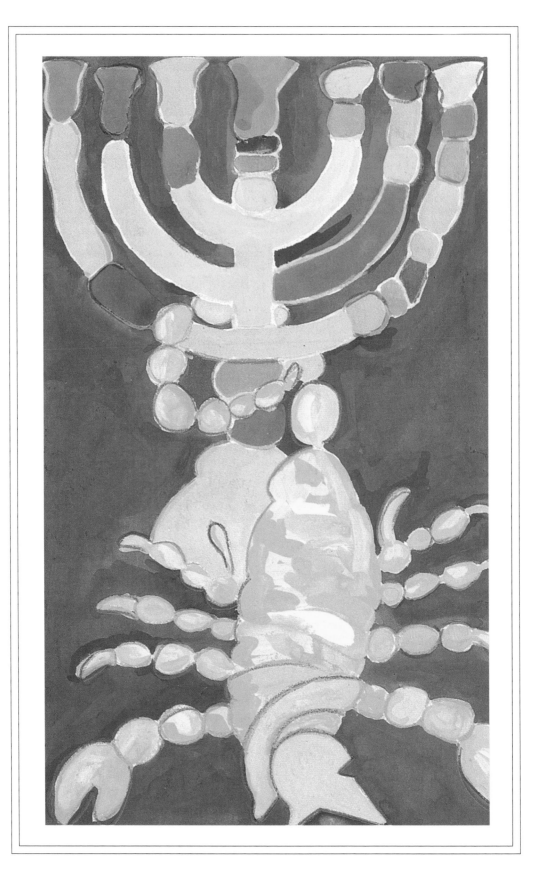

HESHVAN

October – November

THE NAME *HESHVAN* IS AN ABBREVIATION OF *MARHESHVAN*, WHICH COMES FROM THE ASSYRIAN AND MEANS "EIGHT MONTH." When the month of Tishrei is counted as the seventh month, Heshvan is the eighth, although it is the second month of the religious year that begins with Tishrei. The biblical name for Heshvan is *Bul*. It appears in the Book of Kings, which reports that Solomon's Temple was completed in the "eleventh year, in the month of Bul—that is the eighth month" (I Kings 6:38). A year would go by before the completed Temple would be dedicated during the following Tishrei.

Ignoring their literal meanings, tradition has given both alternate names other interpretations. The *mar* in *Marheshvan* is said to stem from a Hebrew root that means "bitter," and to refer to the bitter fact that this month has no holidays. The biblical *Bul* has been connected to the Hebrew word *mabul*, meaning "flood," and in that way to the great Flood, believed to have started in Heshvan. Some also say that before the Temple was built, torrential rains would begin in Heshvan and soak the Land of Israel for forty days, the length of the Flood. The year the Temple was completed, the destructive rains stopped, and have never returned.

The astrological sign for Heshvan is Scorpio, in Jewish thought symbolic of a dangerous desert scorpion mentioned in the Bible, and in rabbinic tradition signifying Greece. It is an ominous sign, for, according to legend, those persons whose sins were found in the previous month to outweigh their good deeds are punished now by being sent to the nether regions, where serpents and scorpions abound. If we want to stretch a point, however, we can find a more comforting legend for the sign of Scorpio, which is that all the time the Temple stood, not one person in Jerusalem was harmed by a scorpion!

The Eleventh Day of Heshvan

RACHEL, MOTHER OF THE JEWISH PEOPLE, DIES

Five lines make up one of the most moving passages in Scripture: "A cry is heard in Ramah— / Wailing, bitter weeping — / Rachel weeping for her children. / She refuses to be comforted / For her children, who are gone" (Jeremiah 31:15).

The words refer to Rachel, wife of Jacob, who died in childbirth on the road between Bethel and Ephrat as the family journeyed through the land of Canaan. Jacob buried her at the place of her death instead of in the family burial cave at Machpelah, and Jeremiah, prophet of the Babylonian exile centuries later, portrayed her weeping as bands of captives passed her grave after the fall of Jerusalem.

There are two ironies in this portrait of Rachel as the quintessential mother bewailing her suffering children. The first is that Rachel herself suffered greatly before having a child, almost giving up hope that she would ever become a mother. The Bible presents her as childless for years, while her sister, Leah—also married to Jacob—bore one child after another. She had cried to Jacob in desperation, "Give me children, or I shall die," only to be rebuffed with an angry reply, "Can I take the place of God . . . ?" (Genesis 30:1–2). Finally she had two children, Joseph, and then Benjamin, whose birth led to her death. Yet it is she, more than the fecund Leah or the two earlier matriarchs, Sarah and Rebekah, who is seen as the comforting mother of her people. Her own suffering may have earned her that special position in the nation's folklore.

The second irony is that the exiles to Babylon, whose fate Rachel laments, came from the kingdom of Judah, composed of the tribes of Judah and Benjamin. The remaining ten tribes, descendants of Jacob's other sons, had made up the northern kingdom of Israel. They were exiled by the Assyrians about a hundred and fifty years earlier and never heard from again. Rachel's son Benjamin was the progenitor of the tribe of Benjamin, and her mythical sorrow over its exile is understandable. But the tribe of Judah, the dominant one in the kingdom, descended from Leah's son Judah, and it is through that tribe that Jews today trace their heritage. Rachel competed with her sister, envied her, ultimately lost out to her in establishing the line that would become the Jewish people. Still, in prophecy and popular thought, Rachel weeps for that people.

What that picture tells us is something the Bible does not, at least not directly: the bond between Rachel and Leah went deeper than competition. Both grew together to become mothers of an entire family and eventually matriarchs of an entire people. The image of Rachel grieving over the Babylonian exiles is also an image of her grieving over *all* the exiles, from the kingdom of Israel as well as Judah, from the tribes attributed to her as well as those attributed to Leah. Her path to that image included many twists and turns, and always it wound around that of her sister.

❖

We first meet Rachel in the Bible as a shepherdess and object of Jacob's instant love. Entranced by her, he agrees to work seven years for her father, Laban—his uncle—for no other wage than her hand in marriage. We hear nothing of Rachel's feelings for Jacob. We learn only that on her wedding night her father tricks Jacob by substituting her older sister, Leah, for her in the bridal bed. A beautiful midrash teaches that Rachel colluded in the substitution, not wanting to humiliate Leah by having Jacob discover the ruse and reject her. It continues that because of that act of kindness, she alone among all the ancestors was able to win God's promise that ultimately the Jewish people would be restored to their land.

Even when polygamy was still permitted, Jewish law prohibited a man from marrying two sisters simultaneously. But after agreeing to work without pay for another seven years, Jacob marries Rachel—the usual explanation being that the law was given after his time. The sisters compete bitterly about having children, but they also learn to cooperate by organizing their husband's marital behavior. Rachel trades Leah her night with Jacob for some mandrake plants—regarded as an aid to infertility—that Leah's son Reuben had found, while Jacob remains a passive bystander in the transaction. Jacob shows no interest in the sisters' burning desire for offspring, and takes no part in naming his sons. Each sister gives her children names that reflect her own feelings, Leah's as the unloved wife, Rachel's as the long-barren one.

After Rachel finally conceives and gives birth to Joseph, Jacob decides to leave his uncle's home and return to his homeland, Canaan. He consults the sisters, and in one voice they agree with him, describing themselves as "outsiders" in their father's house. Despite their rivalries, the women have created a family together, loyal to their husband and more connected to each other than to their father. As the family departs, Rachel steals her father's household idols, hides them beneath her, then lies to him when he searches for them. Her reason for taking the idols is unclear, but her break with her father comes through unequivocally.

When Laban seeks his idols, he first accuses Jacob of stealing them. Unaware that Rachel has them, and believing that Laban is fabricating the theft, Jacob replies that "anyone with whom you find your gods shall not remain alive!" (Genesis 31:32). That unthinking curse, the sages said, would lead to Rachel's early death.

She does die after the family leaves Bethel, where God blesses Jacob. Part of that blessing is a promise that kings would descend from him. In fact, Saul, the first king of Israel, would come from the tribe of Benjamin, descendants of the son whose birth takes Rachel's life. As she lies dying, Rachel names that son Ben-oni, meaning "son of my sorrow" (Genesis 35:18). Jacob later changes the name to Benjamin, which may mean "son of the south," referring to his birth in Canaan, south of the area where the other sons were born. It may also mean "son of my right hand," a symbol of power.

Jacob buries Rachel near Bethlehem, another name for Ephrat, and sets a pillar over her grave. The midrash adds that he chose that spot because he foresaw that the exiles to Babylon would pass it. Scholars are uncertain of the actual location of Rachel's burial place, but tradition has placed it between Bethlehem and Jerusalem, where over the centuries the tomb that stands there became a highly popular pilgrimage site, particularly for women. In 1841, Sir Moses Montefiore donated funds to renovate the tomb into its modern, domed structure and had a mausoleum designed for himself in the same form in Ramsgate, England. In 1948, when the Jordanians gained control of that region, they converted the area around the tomb into a Muslim cemetery. After the 1967 Six-Day War, Israel restored the tomb as a shrine.

Although the fifteenth of Heshvan has generally been accepted as a major pilgrimage day to the tomb, tradition places Rachel's death and Benjamin's birth on the eleventh of the month.

❖

After Rachel dies, we learn nothing more in the Bible about Leah except that she is buried at Machpelah. It is as if her life came to an end along with Rachel's, so tied were they to each other, as sisters, as rivals, as joint wives and mothers.

We learn a great deal about Rachel's elder son, Joseph. His brothers sell him into slavery, jealous that their father favors him, the son of his favored wife. He rises to become a powerful minister in Egypt, and when the brothers seek food there during a famine they do not recognize him. Eventually he reveals himself and reassures them that he will not punish them for what they had done to him. "Can I take the place of God?" he asks (Genesis 50:19), in the same words his father had used with his mother years earlier. But now the phrase is not harsh. It's a statement of acceptance and reconciliation.

Rachel's son draws his broad family together into the beginnings of a nation. Rachel weeping in her tomb remains the symbolic mother of that nation, her tears sustaining its people through centuries of exile.

Kristallnacht is not a "Jewish day" as such. It was a day inflicted on Jews, a time of terror and destruction in Germany and Austria, a prelude to the more widespread devastation to come. But Jews mark this event, as they do other calamities in Jewish history, with acts of remembrance intended to prevent the evil from being forgotten and to honor those victimized by it. In this case, the secular date, November 9, is commemorated. In 1938, the year of Kristallnacht, that day fell on the fifteenth of Heshvan.

It was a pogrom more brutal and widespread than any the Jews had suffered in Czarist Russia. Beginning on the evening of November 9 and through the day of the tenth, the Nazis smashed thousands of windows in Jewish houses and storefronts all over Germany and Austria—hence the name Kristallnacht, night of the broken glass. They murdered dozens of people, destroyed more than eight hundred shops, and set fire to close to two hundred synagogues. The government, which instigated the action, later pretended it had been a spontaneous demonstration against the Jews. Yet in the course of the violence, the police arrested more than thirty thousand Jews—about one in ten of the Jewish population—and sent them to concentration camps. The government itself fined the Jewish community one billion marks, sadistically holding it responsible for the outrage against it.

The tyranny had been triggered by the assassination of a German diplomat by a Jew, and that, in turn, had resulted from Nazi policies begun earlier to drive the Jews from Germany. In October the Germans had rounded up about seventeen thousand Polish-born Jews living in Germany and sent them, in sealed cars, to the Polish border. But earlier, in March, the Polish government, anticipating the German action, had taken its own steps to keep those Jews out of Poland. It passed a law annulling citizenship of Poles living abroad for more than five years unless they received a special stamp from the Polish consul, then made it almost impossible for Jews to obtain that stamp. The Jews deported from Germany became stateless, driven from the land they had inhabited for years and refused entry into their homeland. They were kept at the Polish border under horrendous conditions in the small town of Zbaszyn, living in temporary shelters built with funds supplied by the Polish Jewish community. Only months later, under international pressure, did the Poles allow the Jews in.

Among the deported Polish nationals in Zbaszyn was a family named Grynszpan, who had lived in Hanover for more than twenty years. The eldest son, seventeen-year-old Hershl, was studying in Paris at the time. Hearing of his family's plight and in despair, he went to the German embassy in Paris and shot Ernst vom Rath, third secretary. The shooting took place on November 7. Two days later vom Rath died, setting off the Kristallnacht rampage.

With Kristallnacht, the German war against the Jews escalated beyond abuses already committed toward open barbarism. Before that night Jews had been pushed out of their jobs, Jewish business firms given over to "Aryan" owners, and Jewish community activities placed under the control of the police. Now the government prohibited Jews from all public places and barred their children from public schools. From there it was a short step to forcing them to emigrate from Germany. In fact, some of the people sent to concentration camps during Kristallnacht were released and their lives made so intolerable they felt pressured to leave the country. Tragically, as the terror increased and more and more Jews tried to leave, few of the world's nations would accept them. With the Nazi invasion of Poland and the outbreak of World War II in September 1939, the forcible Jewish emigration became, instead, deportation to the death camps.

Among the many synagogues burned and destroyed during Kristallnacht was the Oranienburgerstrasse synagogue in Berlin, completed in 1866 in a Moorish revival style. It was the largest synagogue in the world at the time, seating more than three thousand people. More than anything else could, it symbolized the confidence Jews had in themselves and in their lives in Germany. Today it remains just a shell of a building in the former East Berlin, a testament to the betrayed sense of security of Germany's Jews.

The Seventeenth Day of Heshvan
THE GREAT FLOOD BEGINS

The massive Flood that Noah and his family survived marked a profound divide in the history of the world, according to the biblical account.

Before the Flood, humans and animals appear to be vegetarians. God gives Adam "every seed-bearing plant . . . and every tree that has seed-bearing fruit" as food, and the animals are permitted "all the green plants" (Genesis 1:29–30).

After the Flood, Noah is told, "Every creature that lives shall be yours to eat" (Genesis 9:3), an indication, tradition says, that for the first time humans had permission to consume meat. Some commentators consider that permission a concession to human desire, still less acceptable than vegetarianism. A hint that this may be so comes from the laws given Noah that prohibit eating the flesh or blood of a live animal. They reflect a respect for animals and a sensitivity to their suffering even though humans have dominion over them.

Before the Flood, society has no systematic rules to regulate human behavior. When Cain kills his brother Abel, God condemns him to be a wanderer on earth but does not require him to pay with his own life. Five generations later, Lamech, Noah's father, boasts of slaying a man and a young lad and not suffering any retribution (Genesis 4:23–24).

After the Flood, the absolute inviolability of human life is established. "Whoever sheds the blood of man, / By man shall his blood be shed," the Bible proclaims (Genesis 9:6), laying down the principle from which will stem all future laws of homicide.

Before the Flood, the world was created out of chaos, with a "wind from God sweeping over the water" (Genesis 1:2).

After the Flood, the world is created anew. In many ways the pattern of this creation follows that of the original act. A wind from God makes the flood waters subside, and the creatures of the earth swarm out of Noah's ark in almost the same order in which they had been created: "birds, animals, and everything that creeps on earth" (Genesis 8:17). God blesses Noah in words that echo the blessing given Adam: "Be fruitful and multiply . . ." (Genesis 9:1). Yet a crucial difference exists between the two creations. The second does not begin from nothingness—all the original species on earth have been preserved, most important among them the species of humans. The new civilization is built on the old one, and despite the vast social changes that follow the Flood, a basic link exists between those who came before it and those who come after. All remain descendants of Adam and Eve, and therefore, as the rabbis taught, no person may say, "My ancestors were greater than yours."

❖

Why did the Flood happen? The Bible relates only that the earth had become corrupt and filled with lawlessness. The rabbis were more specific. They imagined that as well as being deceitful the people had become sexually dissipated, appearing naked in public and engaging in various unchastities, including bestiality. As to the knotty question of why, if humans were evil, the animals on earth also had to be wiped out, some argued that the animals had become impure themselves, recklessly cross-copulating with one another. Others said that since animals were created for the sake of humans, it would not be right for them to survive the human destruction. Some contemporary scholars view the obliteration of all life as necessary in biblical terms to wash away the earth's corruption and start over.

We do know that the Flood story in the Book of Genesis resembles stories in many other Near Eastern cultures, particularly the Babylonian epic of *Gilgamesh*. There may have been some cataclysmic flood in the distant past which overwhelmed parts of civilization, and which many peoples preserved in memory. But it is also clear that the biblical story has strong ethical overtones the others lack. Whereas we learn little about the gods' motives in *Gilgamesh*, in Genesis God causes the flood because of the world's evil. Throughout, God dictates events, guiding Noah's ark (other stories have a boatman) and determining when to end the rains (in others, the gods themselves become overwhelmed). As for Noah, he is not singled out for survival simply at some god's whim but because, Scripture emphasizes, he is a moral man.

But just how moral Noah was is another matter, and one that many Jewish thinkers have pondered. The text describes him as "a righteous man . . . blameless in his age" (Genesis 6:9), and the question arises: Was he a righteous man only in comparison with the evildoers of his time, or would he have been even more righteous surrounded and encouraged by other good people?

No one can say. Certainly Noah does not measure up to Abraham, who when informed that the wicked cities of Sodom and Gomorrah were to be destroyed argued the people's case before God. Noah remains silent when told that the entire universe he inhabits will be blotted out, as if all that matters is that he and his family will be saved. He remains silent again when, emerging from his ark, he faces the devastation around him. Not a word of sympathy or pain or even guilt at surviving do we hear from him. One of his first acts after the deluge is to plant a vineyard and get drunk, so drunk, perhaps, that he can push aside all memory of the disaster he did not try to prevent.

Still, Noah has many admirable traits. In tradition, he invented the plow and other agricultural tools that eased people's lives. His name means "rest" or "calm" or possibly "comfort," and he brought a calm strength to his work. The rabbis portrayed him as suffering greatly from the cold in the ark, but still lovingly caring for the creatures within, feeding the diurnal animals by day and the nocturnal ones by night. They also elaborated on his faith, saying that he followed God's commands about building the ark meticulously, though his neighbors laughed at his warnings of a destructive flood to come. Then he entered the ark in full daylight to affirm before all his belief in God's words.

❖

The ark that Noah builds is about 450 feet long by 75 wide and 45 high. Without rudder or sail, it is steered only by divine protection. Symbolically, its construction hints of the future. Just as this ark will preserve Noah as a new progenitor of humankind, a tiny ark will later save the infant Moses from death at the hands of the Egyptians to become leader of a new nation.

Noah enters the ark and the deluge begins on the seventeenth day of Heshvan, according to tradition. It continues for forty days and nights—another connection with Moses, who spent forty days on Mount Sinai receiving the Torah. When it ceases, the waters remain for another hundred and fifty days, receding only gradually. Twice Noah sends out a dove to test for dry land, and on the second trip it returns with an olive leaf in its beak. The midrash says the leaf came from the Mount of Olives in Jerusalem, for the Holy Land had been spared the Flood. But some claim the leaf came from the Garden of Eden itself, whose gates were opened up to the dove.

By the twenty-seventh of Heshvan, about a year after the rains started, the land is dry enough for Noah and all the species with him to leave the ark. Although we still hear not a word of his feelings, we hear God's words now promising never again to destroy the earth. "Since the devisings of man's mind are evil from his youth" (Genesis 8:21), God says, it is futile to keep destroying and renewing humanity in hope of change.

Instead, laws will be given to curb the evil "devisings." The Bible gives the laws prohibiting murder and eating the flesh of a live animal, and the Talmud expands these into seven rules considered incumbent on all people. Known as the Noahide Laws, they forbid idolatry, blasphemy, bloodshed, incest and adultery, robbery, and eating from a living animal, and they prescribe establishing courts of law. Jewish teaching regards people of all religions who adhere to this fundamental code as moral beings.

As the story of the Flood ends, a rainbow appears in the sky as a sign of God's covenant with Noah and his descendants never again to annihilate humanity. Because of that covenant and the moral laws that accompany it, Abraham, the next great personage in the Bible, will be able to argue with God for justice to all people.

The month of Heshvan has no festivals and several sad days. But it ends with the first glimmers of a rainbow whose radiance will be reflected in the glowing lights of *Kislev*, the month of Hanukkah.

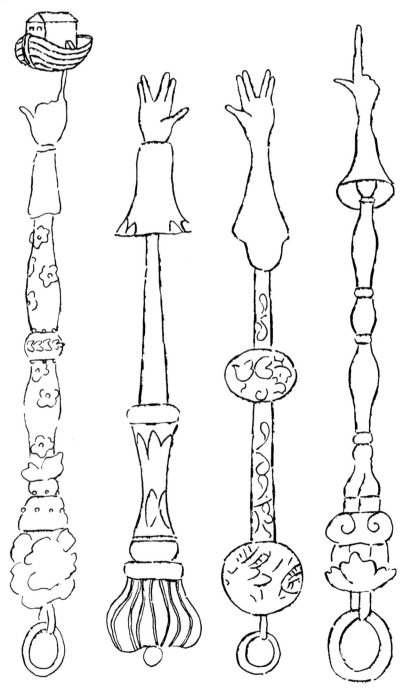

KISLEV
November–December

THE ZODIAC SIGN FOR KISLEV IS SAGITTARIUS, THE ARCHER. In Hebrew, the symbol is called *keshet*, a bow. In the story of Noah and the Flood, which dominates the previous month of Heshvan, the rainbow that glows after the Flood is also called *keshet*. That bow symbolized God's covenant and continued reconciliation with humans. The bow of Kislev is a more warlike one, the archer's weapon, and perhaps God's as well, aimed at defeating Israel's enemies.

In this month the defeated enemies are the Hellenized Syrians who sought to eliminate the Jewish religion and the highly assimilated Jews who would have allowed them to do so. The archers are Judah the Maccabee and his brothers, who saved the nation. Indeed, the prophet Zechariah is said to have foreseen the Maccabean victories when he proclaimed in God's name, "I have drawn Judah taut, and applied [My hand] to Ephraim as to a bow" (9:13).

The days grow short and night arrives early in Kislev. A midrash tells of Adam's fright when he first saw darkness descending earlier and earlier. "Woe is me," he said; "perhaps because I sinned, the world around me is getting darker and returning to chaos and confusion . . ." He fasted and prayed for eight days. But when the winter solstice came and he saw the days gradually lengthening, he said, "This is the way of the world," and he began eight days of festivity.

Those eight days of festivity were the prelude to Hanukkah, whose lights increase in number each day, just as the days will gradually increase in light as Kislev draws to a close.

HANUKKAH EVE—THE FIRST LIGHT

Of all aspects of the holiday of Hanukkah, one image more than any other stands out: the menorah, whose eight lights represent the miracle at the heart of the festival. The miracle was that a small cruse of oil, found in the Second Temple after it had been desecrated by enemies, managed to provide light for eight consecutive days.

It's a wonderful image. The only problem is that of all aspects of Hanukkah, it is the least historical—not just the miracle story but even the special connection between the lights and the holiday. That connection came later, nobody knows exactly wherefrom. No matter. Real or not, on many different levels the image of lights captures in the best way possible what this holiday is about.

The part of the story that has a historical basis is told in the Book of Maccabees, in the Apocrypha, an assortment of works not included in the canon of the Hebrew Bible. In the year 165 B.C.E., Judah Maccabee and a band of Jewish rebels marched into Jerusalem and within a few months cleansed the Temple, which the Syrian rulers of Judea had defiled. They proclaimed the twenty-fifth of Kislev the beginning of an eight-day holiday of rededication. The festival of Hanukkah—the name comes from the Hebrew word for dedication—has been celebrated on that day ever since.

The rebellion had been ignited three years earlier by Judah's father, Mattathias, an elderly priest from the town of Modi'in, not far from Jerusalem. Mattathias had rallied his five sons and other townspeople to oppose Antiochus IV Epiphanes, the Seleucid king of Syria, who prohibited all Jewish religious observance in the land upon pain of death. Antiochus had carried off the most precious objects in the Temple, then used it as a house of worship to the Greek god Zeus, sacrificing pigs on its altar. He had also ordered pagan altars built throughout the countryside. When Mattathias saw a Jew sacrificing on such an altar, he cut the man down and shouted to the people, "Follow me, every one of you who is zealous for the law and strives to maintain the covenant" (I Maccabees 2:27).

Mattathias and his followers fled to the mountains, and from there they waged guerrilla warfare against the Syrians. After he died, his son Judah succeeded him as leader. The family was known as the Hasmoneans, but Judah's fearlessness earned him the name Maccabee, from the Hebrew word for hammer. Later his brothers were also called Maccabees. Judah fought brilliantly, time and again outwitting the far more powerful Syrian forces. When he entered Jerusalem, he chose for his celebration date the twenty-fifth of Kislev, the third anniversary of the desecration of the Temple.

❖

The circumstances behind Antiochus' actions and the Maccabean rebellion were these: About a hundred and fifty years earlier, Alexander the Great had conquered all of the Near East and spread Greek Hellenistic ideas throughout the region. (People often label the enemies in the Hanukkah epic Greeks. They were Syrians, but Greek in the sense of having absorbed Greek culture.) After Alexander's death, his empire split into several kingdoms. Syria and Egypt became rivals in the Near East, and the small state of Judea found itself constantly buffeted between them.

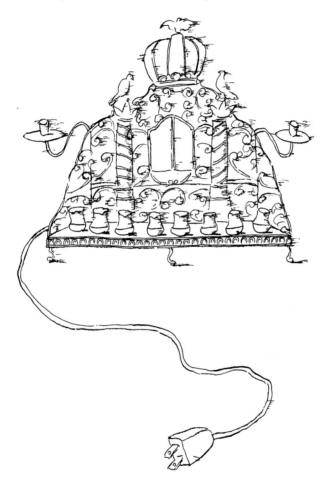

Syria eventually gained control of Judea, and it was partly to keep that control that Antiochus instituted his laws against Judaism. By spreading Hellenistic culture, he hoped to unite the peoples in his realm under one political and religious system and thus strengthen his hand against Egypt. Since Jewish religious practices were unique among the nations, he made them his special target.

Antiochus might not have attempted to enact his laws had he not received strong support from highly Hellenized upper-class Jews within Judea. They assumed Greek manners and dress, built a gymnasium in Jerusalem where they held Greek games, and gave up all Jewish ritual—some even undergoing painful surgery to hide their circumcision. With Syrian help, they won control of the high priesthood, and, in turn, used that office to further the Hellenistic cause.

The battle Judah Maccabee and his warriors waged was also an internal battle against the assimilationists. When they took Jerusalem they routed some of the extreme Hellenists, including the high priest. The Maccabees were helped in their struggle by religious pietists known as Hasideans and by some moderate Hellenists who themselves feared that assimilation had gone too far.

Now this is the point in the story when the miracle is said to have occurred. When Judah and his men began purifying the Temple they found only one unopened, uncontaminated cruse, with enough oil to light the menorah for one day. Miraculously, the oil kept the Temple lit for eight days, until new oil was prepared, and that is the reason why the holiday has been celebrated for eight days.

The Book of Maccabees, however, describes none of that. It does connect Judah's celebration to King Solomon's dedication of the First Temple, when a miraculous fire descended from heaven. It makes a stronger case, however, for linking Judah's festivities to the holiday of Sukkot. During their three years of fighting the rebels had not been able to celebrate that festival properly. Now, rejoicing, "they recalled how, only a short time before, they had kept that feast while they were living like wild animals in the mountains and caves" (II Maccabees 10:6). Modeling their ceremonies on Sukkot, they carried palm branches and chanted psalms of praise, extending the holiday for eight days in imitation of the seven days of Sukkot and its additional day of Shemini Azeret.

No mention is made of lights in relation to Hanukkah until about the year 100 C.E., when Josephus speaks of a "Festival of Lights" commemorating the Maccabean victory. No mention again for almost another hundred years until the name Hanukkah crops up full-blown in the Talmud and the story of the miracle appears, along with discussions about lighting the menorah.

What is the source of the Hanukkah lights? They may have originated in the need for light and hope during the dark days of winter. Or they may have been an adaptation of the great menorahs lit in the Temple court during the ancient Sukkot celebration. Whatever their origin, with time the miracle of the lights grew in importance while the Maccabees fell into and out of favor.

❖

Judah's restoration of the Temple had not ended the struggle with Syria. A bloody battle continued for years, during which Judah and then his brother Jonathan lost their lives. But by the time the last remaining brother, Simon, gained power, the family had won independence from Syria and extended the borders of Judea. With Simon and his son John Hyrcanus it became a dynasty, in control of the high priesthood as well as the government.

The early Hasmonean rulers had great popular support, but, ironically, their descendants became Hellenized themselves and deeply disliked by the people. (As opposed to their forefathers Judah and Jonathan, they had names like Alexander and Aristobulus.) They fought bitterly against one another, eventually losing their dynasty and allowing the nation to fall under Roman rule. For most people the Maccabean victories receded into the past, but the story of the menorah and its lights remained cherished in popular lore.

To the talmudic rabbis, the Hanukkah legends became more real than the warriors' battles.

They viewed the lights and the miracle that led to them as fulfillment of Zechariah's words: " 'Not by might, nor by power, but by My spirit,' said the Lord" (4:6), part of the prophetic portion they assigned for the Sabbath of Hanukkah. For them, God's providence far more than human strength had shaped the events of Hanukkah.

The heroism of the Maccabees has been reemphasized in the modern State of Israel, where their courage has come to stand for the courage of the nation as a whole, pitted as it was for so many years against enemies on all sides. Today, Jews inside and outside of Israel tend to recognize both the national and spiritual aspects of the holiday by celebrating its story and kindling its lights. In doing so, they rejoice in the wondrous victory of the few over the many and the weak over the powerful. They also recall the many other dark periods in their long history that, like the Maccabean era, were illumined by the determination of a small people to remain unique among the nations.

The Twenty-fifth through the Twenty-ninth Days of Kislev

THE DAYS OF HANUKKAH—LIGHTS, LAWS, AND LATKES

The schools of Shammai and Hillel, the two great sages of the talmudic age, had a debate on a point of law: What is the proper procedure for lighting the Hanukkah menorah? The school of Shammai argued that all eight lights should be kindled on the first night and thereafter reduced by one every night. The school of Hillel held that one light should be kindled on the first night and thereafter increased by one every night. The school of Shammai may have based its argument on the original connection between the festivals of Hanukkah and Sukkot. On Sukkot, the priests sacrificed thirteen bullocks on the first day, twelve on the second, and so on, decreasing the number by one each day. The school of Hillel based its argument on a single principle: we increase in matters of holiness, not decrease.

The school of Hillel won (as it usually did). We increase in holiness by lighting one candle on the first night of Hanukkah, two on the second, and on until the menorah glows on the eighth night with all eight lights.

The holiness of each new night shines through again in the way the candles are lit. They are placed in the menorah from right to left—the first candle is farthest to the right as one faces the menorah. But they are lit from left to right. Each night the newest candle is lit first, the second newest next, and down the line to the others.

Although Hanukkah lights may be kindled in the synagogue, the main activities for this holiday take place at home, and most of its laws apply there. Here are the key ones:

The menorah should be placed in front of a window or near a door so that it is visible to the outside. In that way, it fulfills a rabbinic precept to publicize the Hanukkah miracle. (The menorah is also called a *hanukkia* to distinguish it from the seven-branched menorah that stood in the Temple and has become a symbol of Judaism.)

Both men and women are expected to kindle the Hanukkah lights, among the few laws of any holiday equally incumbent on both sexes. The lights, by the way, need not come only from candles. Oil lamps may be used, as they were in early days, with any kind of oil, although olive oil, especially from Israel, is preferred.

The lights must not serve any other purpose than to represent the holiday—they may not be used for reading, for example. In keeping with that, one candle called the *shammash*, or servant, is used to light all the others, because the candles may not even be lit from one another. The shammash rests in a ninth branch of the menorah, placed either higher or lower than the other eight, which should all be on the same level and distinct one from the other.

The candles should be lit just after sundown, but they may be lit later, up until a time when there are no longer people in the street or family members awake to see them. On Friday evening, however, the Hanukkah candles are lit before the Sabbath candles so as not to profane the Sabbath by striking a fire.

Two blessings are recited over the Hanukkah candles, except on the first night, when a third blessing, the *sheheheyanu*, "Who has kept us alive," is added, as it is on the first night of all festivals. Of the two, the first raised some rabbinic eyebrows from the start. Like the benediction for the Sabbath and other festivals, it blesses God, "Who . . . commanded us" to kindle the Hanukkah light. But where is this or any other divine command about Hanukkah? Certainly not in the Bible—the holiday arose after the biblical period. Using various forms of exegesis, however, the sages managed to find hints in the Scriptures that rabbinical decrees, such as celebrating this holiday, can hold the same weight as biblical law. Therefore the blessing becomes God's command.

Nobody had trouble with the second benediction. It blesses God, "Who performed miracles" for our ancestors.

The miracles of Hanukkah take center stage again in a song of triumph, *Al HaNissim*, "For the Miracles," included throughout the holiday in the daily silent prayer and the grace after meals.

During morning prayers, worshippers chant the Hallel, the psalms of praise also recited on Sukkot and other festivals. In addition, the Torah is read every morning.

Along with laws, customs make the festival a pleasure:

Ashkenazic Jews eat *latkes*, or potato pancakes, on Hanukkah, and Sephardic Jews enjoy *bimuelos*, which are fried honey puffs. Why these delicacies? Because all are fried in oil, a reminder of the Maccabees' miraculous little cruse of oil. In Israel, especially, people also eat fried jelly doughnuts, called *sufganiyyot*, for the same reason.

People play cards and other games of chance. Why? There's no special explanation—it's an old custom.

Children play with a holiday top called a *dreidel* (in Hebrew, *sevivon*) marked on each side respectively with the Hebrew letters *nun, gimel, he*, and *shin*, initials for the phrase *nes gadol hayah sham*, "a great miracle happened there." In Israel the last letter is a *pe*, for *poh*, and the phrase is "a great miracle happened here." Dreidel playing is another form of gambling: the child who bets on the letter the top falls on wins; and there are variations.

The best custom of all: children, and adults, too, give and get Hanukkah gifts. The old tradition for this festival was to give money, Hanukkah *gelt*, to schoolteachers, to the poor, and eventually to children. (Throughout my youth I received one silver dollar every Hanukkah. I saved them all in a little leather purse my grandmother gave me. Today some are worth much more than a dollar, but I have no wish to sell them.)

As everyone knows, outside of Israel the competition of Hanukkah with Christmas, which falls in the same season, has upped the ante for Hanukkah giving. Many children expect, and receive, a gift a day for each of the eight days of the holiday, with the parental hope that this will take their minds off Santa and Christmas stockings. Actually, it's not a bad practice in spite of the seasonal sermons and articles in Jewish circles decrying it. If the gifts are relatively modest and children learn about Hanukkah at the same time (granted, these are two big "ifs"), receiving presents simply makes the season festive and fun, a counterpart to the holiday clamor all around.

That Hanukkah falls at Christmastime has been a mixed blessing. This holiday, essentially a minor one on the Jewish calendar, has had to compete with the most celebrated and colorful of Christian festivals. Nevertheless, precisely because of the competition, many Jews who may have little connection to their tradition or knowledge about it have become alerted to their history and identity through Hanukkah.

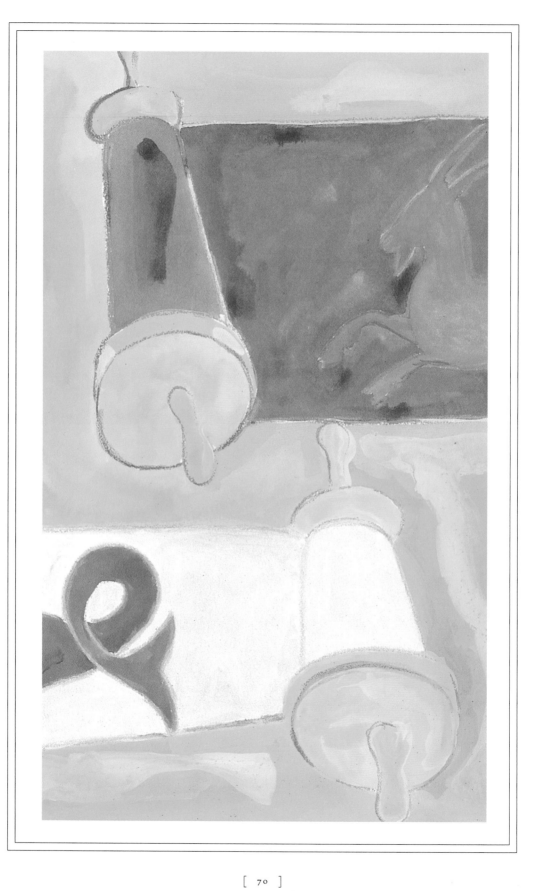

TEVET

December–January

LUCKY FOR *TEVET* THAT THE LAST FEW DAYS OF HANUKKAH FALL WITHIN IT, FOR OTHER THAN THOSE DAYS NO FESTIVALS GRACE THIS MONTH. The days noted here are historical ones. They include the events leading up to the destruction of the First Temple, the anniversaries of the deaths of two great leaders, the scribe Ezra and the scholar Maimonides—each controversial in his own way—and the completion of the first major translation of the Bible from Hebrew into the Greek, the *Septuagint*. Oddly, the rabbis regarded the latter as a catastrophe, the beginning of the misuse of the Bible by other peoples. But legend has softened their dismay and given the Septuagint a miraculous cast.

The name Tevet, like other month names, derives from the Assyrian, but its meaning is unclear. Its zodiac sign is Capricorn, the goat. One interpretation from the mystics connects that sign to those people judged sinful during the High Holidays. Having been punished in *Gehenna*, the netherworld, they are released now during Tevet and emerge so happy that they romp around like young goats. It's an interpretation that adds a touch of whimsy to a month of serious commemoration and some mourning.

The third-century Rabbi Joshua ben Levi said, "Women are obligated to light the Hanukkah lamp, for they, too, were involved in the miracle."

The last days of Hanukkah honor that involvement of women, with some people dedicating the eighth day to the heroism of Judith. (Because the month of Kislev may have twenty-nine or thirty days, that final day of Hanukkah may fall on either the second or third of Tevet.)

Judith's is the tale of a determined woman who has more courage than all the men in her town. It is hard to say how it became linked with Hanukkah, because, as told in the Apocrypha, it takes place centuries earlier, when Nebuchadnezzar ruled Assyria (which Babylonia had defeated). It may have been written during the Maccabean era, however, as a symbol of support for that struggle. Eventually it became incorporated into rabbinic lore, with the Assyrians turned into the Syrians, whom the Maccabees fought.

In the original Apocryphal story, Nebuchadnezzar's commander-in-chief, Holofernes, is on a campaign to conquer Judea. He meets resistance from the Jews in Bethulia (possibly Jerusalem) and lays siege to the town. The townspeople are about to surrender when the beautiful widow Judith steps forward with a plan of rescue.

Taking along only her maid, Judith goes to the enemy camp, where she beguiles Holofernes into believing she can, by praying to her God, help him subdue Judea. She stays with Holofernes three days, leaving each night to pray, and in that way accustoming the commander's guards to allowing her to leave the camp. On the fourth day, Holofernes invites Judith to a banquet. Because he plans to seduce her that evening, he dismisses all his servants. But he drinks himself into a stupor, and alone with him in his tent, Judith takes his sword and with all her might hacks off his head. She and her maid easily leave with the head in a sack and return to Bethulia. When the Assyrian army discovers its decapitated general, it flees in disarray. Israel wins a great victory, and Judith leads the people in dancing and singing praises to God for defeating the enemy "by the hand of a woman" (Judith 16:6).

For Judith's bravery all women are rewarded on Hanukkah by being freed from work while the candles are burning, or, in some traditions, throughout the holiday. Another custom comes from her devoutness. In the Apocryphal telling, she carried her own food to Holofernes' camp because she observed the dietary laws. In other renditions she ate only dairy foods to avoid breaking the laws. She also fed Holofernes salty cheese to make him thirst for wine. So in honor of Judith, many people eat dairy dishes during Hanukkah.

The legend of a second woman has come into its own as feminists have uncovered neglected traditions. In it, the woman (some call her Hannah) was the daughter of Mattathias and sister of the Maccabees. The Syrians had decreed that Jewish brides spend their wedding nights with the local ruler, who raped and shamed them. In rebellion, at her wedding feast this bride stripped naked before all the guests. When her brothers sought to kill her for her wantonness, she, in turn, demanded that they take up arms against the Syrians to save the honor of all Jewish women. Her action sparked their revolt.

The best-known Hanukkah narrative about a woman is of a different form of bravery, the courage of a mother who encouraged her seven sons to die for their faith. The Second Book of Maccabees describes how this woman, "who deserves to be remembered with special honor" (II Maccabees 7:20) was forced to watch while King Antiochus tortured and murdered each of her sons for refusing to eat pork. When the youngest son's turn came, the king urged her to persuade the boy to save himself by breaking Jewish law. Instead, she pressed him to follow his brothers' example and die a martyr like them. With all her sons gone, she, too, died.

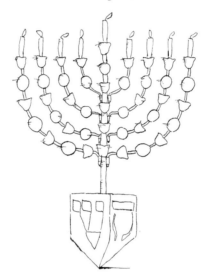

Tradition has also named this woman Hannah, although in the book of Maccabees she is referred to simply as a "mother." In other versions she is called Miriam and the events take place almost two hundred years later, when the Romans ruled Judea.

But whichever version and however the story originated, one legendary passage gets to the essence of Hannah's appeal:

When her youngest son is about to be executed she kisses him and whispers, "Say to Father Abraham, 'Do not pride yourself on having built an altar and offered up your son Isaac. Our mother built seven altars and offered up seven sons in one day. Yours was only a test, but hers was real.' "

Even more than Abraham's intentions, Hannah's sacrifice touched the souls of the Jewish people, and her story has been recalled in every generation in which Jews faced persecutions. In earlier days, special *piyyutim*, liturgical poems, about Hannah and her sons were recited during the synagogue service on the Sabbath of Hanukkah. These martyrdoms also became the model for Christian martyrs persecuted in the early years of the Common Era.

The women's stories add vigor to the last days of Hanukkah, just as the increasing lights add warmth and intensity when interest in the holiday may be waning.

The eighth day of Hanukkah is sometimes called *Zot Hanukkah*, "this is the dedication." The term comes from the day's Torah reading about the dedication of the ancient Israelite Tabernacle, which reads, "This was the dedication offering . . ." (Numbers 7:84). It is an appropriate name for the holiday's conclusion. This was the Hanukkah dedication—this week of reliving the miracle, retelling the tales, and rekindling the lights of national and religious pride.

The Eighth Day of Tevet

THE FIRST GREEK TRANSLATION OF THE TORAH IS COMPLETED, C. 260 B.C.E.

Ptolemy II Philadelphus, a Greek king of Egypt, had a magnificent library in the city of Alexandria consisting of 995 books representing many cultures around the world. "Let us add another five books, to make a thousand," the king said to his minister Aristeas. The minister advised the king to complete his library by having the holy book of the Jews, the Torah, or five books of Moses, translated into Greek. Immediately the king sent messengers to the high priest Eleazar in Jerusalem asking to have translators sent to Alexandria to undertake the task.

Eleazar sent seventy-two elders to King Ptolemy. The king placed the men in seventy-two separate rooms and told each to translate the Torah into Greek. At the end of seventy-two days— Jewish tradition makes it the eighth of Tevet—the elders completed their independent translations. And behold! All were identical. The spirit of God had rested upon the sages of Israel so that though they worked separately, they wrote as one person, with not a single difference among them. Everyone celebrated, and the king sent the elders back to Jerusalem bearing gifts of gold and silver.

Such is the legend of the Septuagint, the earliest translation of the Hebrew Bible into Greek, a legend so extensively accepted that the translation was named for the elders—*septuaginta* in Latin means "seventy." The legend became widely known in the ancient world chiefly through the *Letter of Aristeas*, a document supposedly written by the king's minister to his brother. In reality, the letter seems to have been composed by a Jew of Alexandria whose purpose may have been to show the compatibility of Jewish teachings with Hellenism.

Scholars from the Jewish community of Alexandria probably prepared the Greek translation themselves, and for much the same reasons Jews later translated the Bible into other languages: the people knew little Hebrew. Although the Jews of Alexandria practiced their religion, they spoke and wrote in Greek. The same was true of Jewish communities throughout the Hellenistic world, and Jews of many lands welcomed the Alexandrian Torah translation. Eventually all of the Bible was translated into Greek; in legend, by the same seventy-two elders.

Among its uniquenesses, this first Greek Bible includes the word *Diaspora* several times, and from this translation the term probably came into general use for the settlement of Jews outside the land of Israel. The translators applied it to a number of different Hebrew words that had the connotation of "dispersion."

But for all the enthusiasm that greeted the completion of the Septuagint in its own time, the sages who lived about three or four centuries later viewed it as a tragedy. Although they retold the legend in the Talmud, they designated the eighth of Tevet as a fast day, comparing the completion of the translation to the fashioning of the golden calf. Their objections came partly because the Septuagint text differed in many respects from what by then was the accepted Hebrew one (known as the Masoretic text). More distressing to them, the Greek text had become the standard Scripture of the growing Christian Church, and missionaries used it to preach to Greek-speaking Gentiles and convert them to Christianity.

Said the rabbis, "Just as the golden calf had no substance, yet people worshipped it, so the Greek translation does not hold the true substance of the Torah, yet the Gentiles believe they know the entire Torah through it."

Although other Greek translations of the Bible followed the Septuagint, it remained the most influential. Most of the quotations in the New Testament from the Hebrew Bible are based on it, and it is still the Bible of the Greek Orthodox Church. Over time the rabbinic fast day was generally forgotten or put aside, but the legend of the seventy-two elders and their inspired feat of unity became a cherished part of Jewish folklore.

The Ninth Day of Tevet

THE SCRIBE EZRA DIES, FIFTH CENTURY B.C.E.

The most extreme response to intermarriage in all of Jewish history was that of the scribe Ezra. Arriving in Jerusalem about a century after its population had returned from exile in Babylonia, he discovered that alarming numbers of men had taken wives outside their own faith, from among neighboring peoples. He wept and mourned publicly, appealed to God for forgiveness, and on the twentieth of Kislev called an assembly of all the men in Judah. Religious conversion to Judaism had apparently not yet been developed. His solution to the intermarriages was divorce.

"Separate yourselves from the peoples of the land and from the foreign women," he commanded (Ezra 10:11), calling on those who had intermarried to send their wives back to their own nations along with the children they had borne.

Trembling with fear at Ezra's wrath, the congregation agreed to follow his orders. Over the next three months, files were drawn up on the men who had married "foreign" wives. They ranged across all levels of society, from priests to the city's gatekeepers. The book of Ezra ends with a listing of those names. (No mention is made of women who may have married non-Jewish men.)

Who was Ezra that he had the right to demand such harsh behavior?

We learn about him in the book that bears his name and a second book, Nehemiah, which gives a first-person account of another Jewish leader whose life overlapped Ezra's. The narratives complement each other so closely that the names of Ezra and Nehemiah are always linked.

Ezra received permission from King Artaxerxes I of Persia to go to Judah around the year 428 B.C.E. About a hundred years earlier, Persia had conquered Babylon, and it was the Persian King Cyrus who had permitted the exiled Jews to return to their homeland. Many had remained in Babylonia, however, among them Ezra's priestly family. Ezra had become a highly respected scribe, a teacher of the Bible and leader of the Jewish community. When he left on his journey, fifteen hundred men and unknown numbers of women accompanied him, including priests and Levites who could serve in the newly built Second Temple in Jerusalem.

Whatever his expectations, Ezra found the community of settlers in Judah struggling to maintain itself in the midst of hostile neighbors. He also found the widespread mixed marriages, especially among the upper classes, that led to his severe response. What particularly provoked Ezra was that in Babylon, the place of exile, the Jewish community had been careful to maintain its religious life and its separateness in the hope that the nation would be returned to its land. But once returned, and in the land itself, the people had put aside their distinctiveness and freely intermarried.

Some scholars argue that Ezra saved the Jewish people from disappearing by forcibly dissolving the mixed marriages. Others question whether those dissolutions ever took place. How many men would actually cast out their wives and children? Though the Apocryphal Book of I Esdras indicates that the decision was implemented, neither the Book of Ezra nor that of Nehemiah says so. Ezra's reprimands against intermarriage may have served more as a sobering warning to the returned exiles than a blueprint for action. Nevertheless, his unwavering position must surely have aroused controversy in his own time, as it has ever since.

Far more appealing about Ezra was his role in carrying the teachings of the Bible to all Jews. Nehemiah describes the drama of the New Year's Day, the first of Tishrei, when Ezra read aloud from the Torah scrolls while standing on a podium before thousands of men and women. Beginning at sunrise and continuing for six hours, he read to the people, and they wept for joy at what they were learning and despair at what they had forgotten.

Ezra's reading of the Torah before "men and women and all who could listen with understanding" (Nehemiah 8:2) paralleled in some ways the original giving of the Torah at Mount Sinai. Indeed, the rabbis said, "If Moses had not preceded him, Ezra would have received the Torah." They also said that it was Ezra, a Babylonian Jew, who kept the Torah from being forgotten in the land of Israel. Tradition credits him with the practice, still followed, of reading the Torah in public on Mondays and Thursdays as well as on the Sabbath and with introducing square characters in the Hebrew alphabet, making it easier to read.

Ezra lived after the last great classical prophets such as Isaiah and Ezekiel. The midrash identifies him with the prophet Malachi, but tradition usually places him as the leader of a group of scholars known as the Men of the Great Assembly. They would take over now as expounders of Scripture, developing a process of interpretation that would reach its height with the Pharisees and later sages.

He was, then, Ezra the scribe, a highly learned man deeply devoted to teaching and expounding the law—a devotion so intense that it sometimes interfered with his humanity. A Yemenite legend tells of his insistence that the Jews of Yemen return to Judah after the Babylonian exile. When they refused, he cursed them with lifelong poverty. They, in turn, laid a curse on him that he would not be buried in the land of Israel. Nor would they name a child Ezra, a sign of their anger at him.

Their curse seems to have been fulfilled. Ezra may have died—it is said, at the age of 120—in Babylon or in Jerusalem, but tradition has placed his tomb in Iraq, near Basra. The date generally assigned to that death is the ninth of Tevet, the day on which Nehemiah is also supposed to have died. Despite his human flaws, mainstream Jewish thought regards Ezra as so influential a leader that the highest compliment one can pay a person is that he or she is a "worthy disciple of Ezra."

The Tenth Day of Tevet

FAST DAY—THE BABYLONIANS LAY SIEGE TO JERUSALEM,

588 B.C.E.

Although large numbers of Jews returned to the land of Israel after the First Temple was destroyed and the people exiled to Babylon, although Jerusalem was rebuilt and a Second Temple erected, that first destruction and exile have been carved into Jewish memory as events of unmitigated sorrow.

In the collective dreams and fantasies of the Jewish people, had the kingdom of Judah not fallen and the Temple not been destroyed, Jewish history, possibly world history, might have been different. The demise of Judah represented the end of Jewish independence and sovereignty in the land of Israel. Except for the brief reign of the Hasmoneans about four hundred years later—a reign that lasted less than a hundred years—independence would not be restored for more than twenty-five hundred years, not until 1948, when the State of Israel came into being.

The tenth of Tevet, in Hebrew *asarah b'Tevet*, marks the beginning of the last days of Judah, when the Babylonian army laid siege to Jerusalem. It is a minor fast day, one of four fasts that recall the destruction of the First or Second Temple.

Could that First Temple have been preserved? Could the fall of Judah have been prevented? In classical prophecy and religious thought, the nation's sins led to the catastrophe, and sincere repentance could have forestalled it. The historical perspective is more ambiguous.

The origins of Judah's defeat go back centuries. After King Solomon died, about 928 B.C.E., the nation as a whole declined when his realm was split into two kingdoms—Israel and Judah. The Assyrians conquered Israel and dispersed its population in 722 B.C.E., leaving Judah alone and vulnerable. Gradually the Assyrian empire deteriorated and Babylonia rose to power. The Babylonians warred constantly with Egypt, forcing Judah into becoming a pawn between the two (just as in later years, before the Maccabean rebellion, the small state would be pressed between Syria and Egypt).

Again and again, the prophet Jeremiah preached submission to Babylon as the only way to save the country. But around 601 B.C.E., sometime after Jehoiakim became ruler of Judah, that kingdom joined forces with Egypt in an attempt to repulse the Babylonians. In response, King Nebuchadnezzar of Babylon besieged Jerusalem. Jehoiakim died suddenly, probably by assassination, and his son Jehoiachin was exiled to Babylon along with thousands of the Judean nobility and craftsmen. For some years, Jews dated events in relation to "the exile of King Jehoiachin."

That exile was in 597 B.C.E., a foreshadowing of the later, major one that came during the reign of Zedekiah, whom Nebuchadnezzar had placed on the throne of Judah to replace Jehoiachin. When he also rebelled against Babylonia, with Egyptian aid, Nebuchadnezzar began the final siege against Jerusalem on the tenth of Tevet, 588 B.C.E., that led to its downfall and the destruction of the Temple two years later.

Could, then, the devastation have been avoided? In retrospect, it is obvious that Jeremiah was right and the rulers of Judah should have recognized that they could not possibly withstand the overpowering might of Babylonia. (Jeremiah tried to make that point once during Zedekiah's reign by walking through Jerusalem wearing an ox yoke, symbolic of submitting to the yoke of Babylon.) For those living at the time, however, the longing to throw off the Babylonian yoke and maintain independence must have been so powerful that they ignored the realities. Added to that, army officers and other prophets—whom Jeremiah labeled false prophets—assured the people that Judah could win. The combination made the end almost inevitable.

Once that end became clear, Zedekiah tried to escape. The midrash has it that he ran into a cave that extended from his home in Jerusalem all the way to the town of Jericho. But God sent a deer into the camp of the Babylonian soldiers, and, in pursuing it, they caught Zedekiah just as he emerged from the cave. The Bible describes Zedekiah's cruel punishment. He was made to see his sons slaughtered before he was blinded and led in chains to Babylon (II Kings 25:7).

Zedekiah was the last king of Judah. Looking back at his reign, the rabbis compared Jewish history to the moon's phases. The moon begins to shine at the beginning of the month and reaches its zenith on the fifteenth. Then it starts to fade, until by month's end it is no longer visible. Likewise with the people of Israel. There were fifteen generations from Abraham to Solomon. The light began to shine with Abraham and reached its full power with Solomon, who built the Temple. After that, the light diminished until it totally disappeared when Zedekiah was blinded and the Temple destroyed.

❖

In Israel today, the rabbinate designated the tenth of Tevet a time of *yahrzeit* (memorial anniversary) for Holocaust victims whose death dates are unknown. The major commemoration of the Holocaust, however, is *Yom HaShoah* on the twenty-seventh of Nisan.

The Twentieth Day of Tevet

MOSES MAIMONIDES DIES, DECEMBER 13, 1204

Considering the overwhelming influence the philosopher and scholar Maimonides has had on all of Jewish thought and letters, it is hard to believe there was a time when his works were burned—possibly at the instigation of Jewish scholars—and his teachings banned from Jewish academies. In fact, his writings have probably aroused more emotion and controversy than those of any other Jewish thinker. Here are some reasons why:

A rationalist of the first order, he emphasized the absolute spirituality of God, denying that the Deity could have any physical characteristics—this in an age when many scholars as well as ordinary folk accepted at face value biblical descriptions of God's "outstretched arm" or "strong hand." They also took literally human traits the Bible ascribes to God, such as jealousy or kindness. Maimonides went to great pains to interpret all such references as figures of speech. But he didn't stop there. He declared that anyone who believes God has a physical form is no better than an idol worshipper. To this the French scholar Abraham ben David of Posquières replied angrily, "Men better and worthier than he have held this view."

Maimonides opposed scholars who portrayed the coming of the Messiah as a miraculous time when the laws of nature would be overturned and people would live forever. Instead he pictured the Messianic era in natural terms, a time of peace and goodness, when the people of Israel would live in their own land, free to devote themselves to the study of Torah and an understanding of God. The Messiah himself as Maimonides imagined him would not be immortal but would have children and grandchildren to succeed him.

Maimonides hedged on the idea of resurrection after death. Although Judaism has no absolute dogma about life after death, it does hold a general belief that body and soul will be reunited in the world to come, where the righteous will dwell in God's presence. Maimonides included that belief in his "thirteen principles," a listing of fundamental Jewish doctrines. But his other writings made only vague philosophic references to resurrection, and then only to the immortality of the soul. To critics he appeared to be denying the Jewish views of an afterlife.

In a more practical vein, he insisted that no one should use the Torah as a means of earning money, and the community should not give money to people engaged in the work of Torah, a stance that could hardly go over well with professional rabbis and scholars, and that actually never gained ground. He earned his own livelihood as a physician and not from his scholarship.

Along with all that came his (not unwarranted) somewhat grandiose attitude toward his own work. In the introduction to his monumental *Mishneh Torah*, or *Code of Jewish Law*, he explained that he had systematized all of Jewish law so that the average person need rely only on this work and the Scriptures to live in a Jewish manner. That provoked the attack that he intended his *Code* to replace the Talmud as a source of learning and practice. His other major work, *The Guide of the Perplexed*, written in Arabic and translated into Hebrew as *Moreh Nevukhim*, aimed at harmonizing Judaism with philosophy. That led to the accusation that he was corrupting Jewish belief with Greek thought.

The anger Maimonides aroused grew in intensity after his death, when his works circulated throughout Europe. Some rabbis banned his writings, and in France, almost thirty years after he died, a dispute about him reached such heights that the Christian clergy publicly burned parts of his books. Many historians believe that his Jewish opponents had denounced the works to the Inquisition. The burning sent shock waves through the Jewish community, tempering all future arguments.

At the core of the disagreements about Maimonides lie still-unresolved differences between those who, like him, approach religion from a rationalist point of view and those who take a mystical, less intellectual path. Nevertheless, today all camps acknowledge Maimonides' greatness. His *Guide*, translated into many languages, holds a secure place among non-Jews as well as Jews as a pivotal philosophic work. And the fears that his *Code* would displace the Talmud never materialized. Instead shelves have been filled with countless commentaries on the *Code* itself, an indispensable source of knowledge for Jewish law and ethics.

❖

His full name was Moses ben Maimon, and he became known in Hebrew as the *Rambam*, from the acronym of *Rabbi Moses ben Maimon*. He was born in 1135 in Córdoba, Spain, an important center of Jewish learning, where his father was a highly respected judge and rabbi. When he was thirteen he had to flee the city with his family after radical Muslim Almohads invaded Spain, forcing Jews to choose between conversion to Islam and death. The family wandered for years, moving from

Spain to Morocco and then Palestine, and finally settling in Fostat, the old section of Cairo, Egypt.

By then Maimonides was deep into his first significant work, a commentary on the Mishnah, which he completed at the age of thirty-three. If this would appear an easy feat for a man of his genius, his introduction hints at the toll the years of moving about had taken. "I was agitated by the distress of our time," he wrote, " . . . the fact that we are being driven from one end of the world to the other."

His greatest agitation came later when his younger brother David, a gem merchant who had supported the family, drowned at sea. Maimonides lay ill for nearly a year, and eight years later described in a letter the anguish he still felt: "What can console me? He grew up on my knees; he was my brother, my pupil . . . My one joy was to see him."

To support himself and his family, Maimonides took up medicine, but he continued his writing and scholarship and also assumed the role of leader of the Jewish community in Cairo. He wrote in Arabic, the language of the Islamic world, except for his *Code*, which is in lucid, beautiful Hebrew, designed as it was to stand alongside the Bible as one of the primary texts of Judaism.

The *Code* appeared in 1180. In the midst of its exacting organization and logical discussions, glimpses can be seen of the human side of Maimonides, the side that had revealed itself in his thoughts about his brother. One example of that humanity is his famous description of eight levels of giving charity. With enormous sensitivity to the feelings of a person who must take charity, he describes the highest level as offering a loan or gift or helping the needy find work so they will not have to depend on others. The next highest level is giving so the giver does not know to whom the charity goes and the recipient does not know from whom it comes.

Maimonides completed his *Guide* around 1190. By then, and in spite of opposition, his fame had spread, and he was receiving letters and theological questions from many parts of the world. He had also become a renowned physician to the sultan of Egypt, and had written numerous medical treatises. Later it would be said of him, "From Moses to Moses, there was none like Moses," placing him in a straight line as the spiritual descendant of the biblical Moses. Yet, burdened by his many functions, he wrote to the scholar Samuel Ibn Tibbon, "when night falls, I am so exhausted, I can scarcely speak."

Samuel Ibn Tibbon translated *The Guide of the Perplexed* into Hebrew, but Maimonides didn't live to see that work finished. He died on the twentieth of Tevet, December 13, 1204, and was buried in Tiberias in Israel, where people still make pilgrimages to his tomb. Throughout the Jewish world, communities held public fasts and mourning ceremonies in his honor. In Jerusalem a special reading of Scripture took place. It ended with words from the Book of Samuel: "The glory is gone from Israel, for the Ark of God is taken" (I Samuel 4:22).

SHEVAT

January – February

THE BOOK OF DEUTERONOMY RECORDS THAT ON THE FIRST DAY OF THIS MONTH MOSES BEGAN REVIEWING WITH THE PEOPLE OF ISRAEL ALL THE LAWS THEY HAD RECEIVED AND THE EVENTS THEY HAD EXPERIENCED DURING THEIR FORTY YEARS IN THE WILDERNESS. His teachings led later rabbis to compare *Shevat* to the month of *Sivan*, a time when Israel received the Torah at Mount Sinai. This month, like that one, they said, should be devoted to the study of the Torah and its celebration.

Shevat is also a month of hope, when January thaws can suddenly signal the spring to come. In Israel it's a month when most of the rains have ended and new fruits begin to form on trees. Tradition urges people to pray now for a beautiful etrog, the fragrant citron that will be used during the festival of Sukkot in the following fall.

The zodiac sign for Shevat is Aquarius, the water-bearer. "Why this sign?" the prince of darkness once asked the Holy One. "So that I might use the water-bearer's bucket to splash pure water on humans and free them of all their sins," came the answer.

THE TEN PLAGUES BEGIN IN EGYPT

The Ten Plagues brought destruction and devastation to Egypt, finally convincing its Pharaoh to free the Hebrew slaves. So the Bible tells us. Archaeologists and theologians have speculated for centuries over when and how the plagues happened. Moralists have questioned why they did.

In the biblical account, the Hebrew people first arrived in Egypt when Jacob and his family came there to escape a famine in Canaan. Jacob's son Joseph, powerful as the king's minister, settled his father and brothers in the region of Goshen. Some time later, after the original settlers died out, a new king arose "who did not know Joseph" (Exodus 1:8). He enslaved the Hebrews, and because they continued to grow in number, ordered their newborn sons drowned in the Nile. The baby Moses, saved by being hidden among the bulrushes along the riverbank, would grow up to punish Pharaoh with the plagues and free his people.

One tradition places the beginning of those plagues on the first day of Shevat, lasting ten weeks—one week per plague—until the fifteenth day of Nisan, when the Israelites left Egypt in freedom. Other traditions extend the plagues over an entire year, beginning and ending on the fifteenth of Nisan. Some Bible scholars hold that if the plagues happened at all they may have been natural events extending over the course of several years.

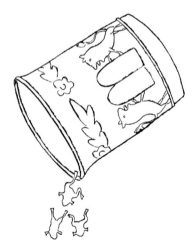

The first plague turned the Nile into a river of blood. The second brought frogs throughout the land. The third was a plague of lice; the fourth, of swarms of insects; the fifth, a pestilence that infected all cattle; the sixth, boils; the seventh, hail; the eighth, locusts; the ninth, a thick three-day darkness; and the tenth, the slaying of the Egyptian firstborn.

Those critics who regard the plagues as natural occurrences have found rationales for each. The river may have appeared bloodied, for example, because heavy rainfalls caused an abundance of sediment from the red earth typical of this area. The hail may have resulted from a severe thunder and lightning storm, unusual in Egypt but not unheard of. But even the most determined naturalists have no feasible explanation for the last plague, the death of Egypt's firstborn—sons, daughters, and cattle as well. The Bible places it outside the realm of nature, a product of divine power unexplainable in ordinary terms and unrelated to the history or mythology of other peoples.

And therein lies the moralists' quandary. Why was this plague—or any of them, actually—necessary? Could not God, so powerful, free the people of Israel from their slavery under Pharaoh without having to inflict such great suffering on all of Egypt?

The rabbis saw the answers clearly: in part, the plagues came as a punishment for Egypt's cruelty. All the Egyptians surely knew of the Israelite hardships, but did nothing to alleviate them. Lowly maidservants, Rashi says, joined with their masters in rejoicing at the affliction of the Hebrews, the only people beneath them on the social scale. Therefore, all were repaid, along with their king, "measure for measure." Thus, the first plague, in which the Nile turned to blood, served as retribution for the drowning of Israel's sons in that river. The final, dreadful plague, in which even the firstborn of the maidservants died, was designed to avenge all that had been done to Israel, whom God spoke of as "My first-born son" (Exodus 4:22).

But the sages taught that the plagues came about also to prove to Pharaoh *and* the Israelites that God reigns supreme over everything in nature and over all the gods of Egypt. Because the Egyptians regarded the Nile as a god, for example, God struck it first. Because they worshipped animals, the firstborn cattle were slain along with the human firstborn. In that way people could not attribute the plagues to their animal gods.

Furthermore, when Moses first approached Pharaoh, the king replied arrogantly, "Who is the Lord that I should heed Him?" (Exodus 5:2). By the end of the last plague, he not only knew who the Lord was but, totally humbled, pleaded with Moses and Aaron to "bring a blessing upon me also" (Exodus 12:32). In legend, Pharaoh never died. He stands to this day at the entrance to hell proclaiming to the kings who arrive there his belief in God and God's sovereignty over the universe.

As for the Israelites, when Moses told them of God's promise to redeem them from slavery, they would not listen to his words. And they remained silent through all the plagues, slaves still fearful of their Egyptian overlords, unsure of Moses and his God. But when the plagues ended, the people "bowed low in homage" (Exodus 12:27), convinced, as were the Egyptians, of God's might and uniqueness.

The plagues achieved their purpose. Nevertheless, the tradition has shown special sensitivity to the plight of the Egyptian people. When the Ten Plagues are recited at the Passover table, participants spill a drop of wine for each, symbolically detracting from the pleasures of victory in memory of the misery it inflicted. The sensitivity extends to the land itself. The Bible relates that Aaron, not Moses, effected the first two plagues, turning the Nile into blood and sending forth swarms of frogs. The reason, the commentators explain, was that the river had protected Moses when he was hidden there as an infant and it would be wrong of him to harm it now.

Still, problems remain. Among the most disturbing is Pharaoh's situation. Twenty times in the course of the plagues narrative, we hear that God will harden or has hardened Pharaoh's heart so that the king will not allow the Israelites to leave. If, then, God determines Pharaoh's actions, why should the king be held responsible for them?

One way around the problem is to note that the text does not portray God as actually stiffening Pharaoh's heart, as threatened, until the sixth plague, boils. Before that, the king's own stubbornness leads him to defy Moses and God. According to Maimonides, in doing so he forfeited his ability to change—and it is in that sense that God hardened his heart. Pharaoh had reached a point of no return, and would now have to see his evil through, unable to reverse his course.

Then, too, in Jewish thought each of us carves out our own path in life. If God has foreknowledge of our behavior, we are not aware of it: we do as we see fit. The same was true of Pharaoh. On a cosmic level, God may have known how Pharaoh would behave, may even have shaped that behavior. But on a human level, Pharaoh made conscious choices, consistent with his character. He may have been no worse than any other king, and, like him, probably no other would have agreed to free a slave people. But had Pharaoh wanted to be different, he could have been.

Taking another tack, the Egyptian Pharaoh saw himself and was seen by his subjects as a god, son of the sun god Ra. From that perspective, the struggle for the Hebrew slaves was an all-out battle between the Egyptian god and the God of the Hebrews. Having God harden Pharaoh's heart was the Scripture's way of demonstrating God's power over every aspect of the king's conduct, his emotions as well as his actions.

The midrash tells us that when the plague of frogs began, only a single frog appeared, but once it started to croak, all its companions came out, inundating the land. It was the same with the other plagues. They began in a small way, as nuisances at first, until they grew and spread to bring desolation throughout Egypt. They came, the Exodus story ultimately wants to demonstrate, to emphasize that the "finger of God" (Exodus 8:15), and not an Egyptian king, was guiding history.

Shabbat Shirah—the Sabbath of Song

The angels in heaven wished to sing a song of praise to God. After fleeing from Egypt, Moses and the Children of Israel had crossed the Red Sea. (In the Bible it is the Sea of Reeds, but tradition has long identified it with the Red Sea.) Miraculously, the sea's waters had parted for them, but now the ocean was closing in on the pursuing Egyptian army, drowning Pharaoh himself along with all his warriors.

"Stop," God said to the angels. "The work of My hands is drowning at sea, and you would sing hymns?" It was a legendary rebuke Jews would cite often as a reminder that all human life—even the life of an enemy—belongs to God and is not to be taken lightly.

Safely on the other side of the sea, their years of servitude and fear of Egypt behind them,

Moses and Israel prepared a song of their own. Again, the angels wanted to chant their praises of God. "Stop," God said to them. "Let My children sing first."

Moses and the Israelite men sang their song, and one more time, the angels began to raise their voices. "Stop," said God. "Now it is the women's turn." The angels complained, "Is it not enough that we have waited for the men? Shall the women sing ahead of us also?" To which God replied, "Without a doubt; that is how it must be." The rabbis later added that even women servants saw more of God's glory at the sea than the great prophet Ezekiel was permitted to see in his entire lifetime.

The angels had reason to envy the singers below, for their song welled up from within them, filling the earth with music and the joyous sounds of their redemption. "I will sing to the Lord, for He has triumphed gloriously," sang Moses, and all the men joined him, "Horse and driver He has hurled into the sea" (Exodus 15:1). Verse after verse they sang, first Moses and then the Israelite men, reviewing the events they had experienced and extolling God for the deeds of splendor that had brought them to this moment.

When they finished, Miriam, Moses' sister, picked up a timbrel and began dancing with it, and all the women danced and sang alongside her. Where did they get timbrels? Miriam and the righteous women had foreseen that God would perform miracles, the sages imagined, so they brought timbrels with them from Egypt.

"Sing to the Lord, for He has triumphed gloriously." Miriam chanted only the refrain of Moses' song, and the women repeated the words after her. "Horse and driver He has hurled into the sea" (Exodus 15:21). It has been said that Miriam's words came first as the source from which Moses' long song grew. It has also been said that Miriam was mocking the Egyptian men in her song. The strong male chariot driver was no better than his horse as they fell into the sea, helpless before God's overwhelming presence.

Shabbat Shirah, the Sabbath of Song, takes its name from the Song at the Sea, which is recited during that week's scriptural reading. The song may be the earliest long poem in the Bible, even older than the prose verses that tell of the crossing at the sea. Although Moses led the Exodus from Egypt, the song says nothing of him, celebrating only God's triumph over nature and humanity. Each of its four sections focuses on a different aspect of that triumph. The first praises God's victory over the Egyptians, the second proclaims the uniqueness of the God of Israel, and the third tells of the fears that surrounding nations will suffer when they hear of the wonders that occurred. The last section looks forward to a time when Israel has its own sanctuary where "the Lord will reign for ever and ever" (Exodus 15:18).

The song is so highly regarded that it is recited during morning prayers throughout the year and chanted aloud again on the seventh day of Passover, the day that commemorates the crossing of the sea. It has its own cantillations and is always written in the Torah scroll in a special manner, what the rabbis called "a half brick set over a whole brick and a whole brick over a half brick"; that is, the words are spaced on each line in such a way that they appear to form a bricklayer's pattern.

The Sabbath of Song usually falls during the first or second week of Shevat, in the heart of winter. On the evening before, children put out food for the birds to give them strength to sing along with the congregation. At morning services, congregants stand throughout the reading of the Song at the Sea and chant portions aloud with the reader. The melody and words brighten that winter Sabbath here on earth, and in the heavens the angels now join freely with the men and women of Israel in their song of exultation.

The Fifteenth Day of Shevat

TU B'SHEVAT—THE NEW YEAR OF THE TREES

Moses heard God speak to him through a bush that blazed with fire but was not consumed by it. In tradition, the miraculous fire appeared in a bramble, one of the lowliest of all plants. From this we learn, Rabbi Joshua ben Korha said, that no place on earth, not even a bramble, lacks God's presence.

The minor festival of *Tu B'Shevat* acknowledges that presence in nature by celebrating all trees. A Jewish Arbor Day, it is closely connected to the land of Israel and marks the season there when the sap begins to rise and new fruit to grow on the trees.

The Hebrew letters for *tu* add up to the number 15; hence the holiday name for the fifteenth day of Shevat. Known as the New Year of the Trees, in early days it signified the time when special tithes on fruits were due to the Temple in Jerusalem. It also served to demarcate the age of trees, necessary because in Jewish law a tree's fruits may not be picked and eaten during its first three years.

Tu B'Shevat is one of four New Year days on the Jewish calendar. The first of Tishrei begins the religious New Year. The first of Nisan is the New Year for kings, a date used for calculating the years of a king's reign. The first of Elul is the New Year for tithing animals, and the fifteenth of Shevat is the New Year for trees. The only New Year to fall on the fifteenth rather than the first day of the month, Tu B'Shevat parallels a midsummer festival of the vineyards, celebrated on the fifteenth day of the month of Av.

Trees hold a distinctive place in the Jewish imagination. Adam and Eve were banished from the Garden of Eden because they ate from the tree of knowledge. Although that tree and the tree of life remained standing in paradise, cherubim and fiery swords guard the portals so that humans can never reenter and achieve immortality. Instead, the Torah itself has come to be seen as a tree of life, offering "length of days" for "those who grasp her" (Proverbs 3:16, 18).

In ecological terms, trees came to embody the great value Judaism places on all plant and animal life. The Bible commands that when soldiers besiege a city they may not destroy its fruit-bearing trees. "You may eat of them," the law states, "but you must not cut them down. Are trees of the field human to withdraw before you into the besieged city?" (Deuteronomy 20:19). From that ruling, the rabbis extrapolated a wide range of restrictions against what they called "wanton destruction," any waste or defilement of nature.

It is fitting, then, to have a holiday that pays tribute to trees. Work is permitted on this day, but observant Jews mark it in a variety of ways. In Israel, children and adults take part in tree-planting ceremonies. Jews in other lands often give donations to plant trees in Israel; and in Hebrew schools, students hold parties at which they eat fruits and nuts from Israel.

Most common among the Tu B'Shevat treats is the fruit of the carob tree, popularly known by its Yiddish name, *bokser*. When fresh, it has a soft, delicious inside; when hard, it can become a jaw-breaker to chew. In English it is known as St.-John's-bread, from a Christian legend that John the Baptist ate this fruit during his years in the wilderness. In Jewish legend, the second-century Palestinian scholar Rabbi Simeon bar Yohai and his son survived on carob fruit for thirteen years when they hid in a cave to escape Roman authorities.

The kabbalists of the sixteenth century introduced a more elaborate way of celebrating the holiday that has become increasingly popular today. They held a seder on the holiday eve for which they adapted symbols from the Passover seder. For example, participants say blessings over four cups of wine in the course of the evening, as they do on Passover, but these wines range from white to pink to rose and finally to red, the changes representing the changing seasons. Instead of the Passover symbols, everyone eats fruits and nuts—some people eat fifteen varieties, for the name of the holiday— based on biblical descriptions of those grown in Israel, such as figs, pomegranates, dates, and olives.

The text used in the Tu B'Shevat seder is called *Peri Ez Hadar*, "Fruit of the Goodly Tree," and it holds rituals, poems, and biblical and talmudic passages. Its name comes from the biblical verse describing the "product of *hadar* [goodly] trees, branches of palm trees, boughs of leafy trees, and willows of the brook" (Leviticus 23:40) used during Sukkot. Both name and verse link the two agricultural festivals.

Aside from its mystical overtones, Tu B'Shevat has become a time for the ecologically minded to urge everyone to recycle the paper they use, whose main source, of course, is trees.

Rabban Johanan ben Zakkai, one of the leading talmudic scholars, advised that if you happen to be holding a sapling in your hand and someone tells you the Messiah has arrived, first plant the sapling and then go out to greet the Messiah. This teaches us that as deep as is the yearning for the Messiah, trees are real, and they need to be tended and nurtured above all dreams and longings. Tu B'Shevat turns our attention to trees and celebrates the continuity of life they represent.

Shabbat Shekalim — the Sabbath of Donations

Synagogues traditionally hold appeals for contributions during the course of services, particularly on Yom Kippur eve, when large numbers of congregants are present. People often complain about those appeals, arguing that monetary discussions do not belong in the synagogue and should not be made on holy days. It should be noted, therefore, that the practice of urging people during services to contribute funds for the upkeep of sacred places has a long and venerable history in Judaism. Its source is the Bible, and it is exemplified by *Shabbat Shekalim*, a Sabbath with an extra Torah reading that draws attention to the requirement for donations.

In the Torah portion (Exodus 30:11–16), God commands Moses to take a census of males over the age of twenty by collecting a tax of half a shekel from each, the money to be used in building the Tabernacle, the wilderness sanctuary that will serve as God's dwelling place. (In biblical times the shekel was not a unit of currency, as it is in modern Israel, but a unit of weight for gold or silver.) Although the tax is described as a one-time contribution, like taxes everywhere, once instituted it remained in effect, becoming a required annual contribution among Jews, to maintain first the Tabernacle and later the First and Second Temples in Jerusalem.

In Second Temple times, Jews outside as well as inside the land of Israel contributed a half-shekel annually for communal sacrifices and other Temple functions. The contributions were due during the month of *Adar*, which follows Shevat. On the first of Adar, a proclamation reminded people of their obligation, and by the fifteenth of the month messengers in each community began collecting the money.

When the Temple no longer existed, the sages ruled that on the Sabbath immediately preceding the month of Adar or on the new moon of that month if it falls on the Sabbath, the biblical passage describing the half-shekel tax was to be read in the synagogue in addition to the regular weekly Torah portion. While the reading recalled the ancient tax, it also reminded listeners of their responsibility to support their own institutions—setting a precedent for the later synagogue appeals.

❖

The Bible describes the original tax as a ransom or atonement, but does not say for what. Some commentators interpret it as expiation for the sin the Israelites committed in worshipping the golden calf. In the midrash, Moses learned what a half-shekel was through God's right hand, for each finger of that hand served to bring about salvation in a different manner. The little finger showed Noah the way to the ark. The finger next to it slew the Egyptians. The middle finger wrote the Ten Commandments on their tablets. And God's index finger pointed out the half-shekel to Moses so that the Israelites could use it for their atonement.

The half-shekel tax was a democratic one, levied on all Jews equally. The poor were not permitted to give less, nor were the rich expected to give more. Today's complex synagogues and institutions, which rely on major contributions from the wealthiest community members, probably could not survive under such a system. But the message still holds: all lives are of equal worth before God, and all people need to bear some responsibility for communal affairs.

❖

Shabbat Shekalim is the first of four special Sabbaths that stretch from the end of Shevat through the end of Adar and sometimes into the beginning of Nisan. The others are *Shabbat Zakhor*, the Sabbath of Remembrance; *Shabbat Parah*, the Sabbath of the Red Heifer; and *Shabbat HaHodesh*, the Sabbath of the Month of Nisan. Each includes an additional Torah portion chanted from a separate scroll, and each highlights a unique theme connected to the season in which it occurs.

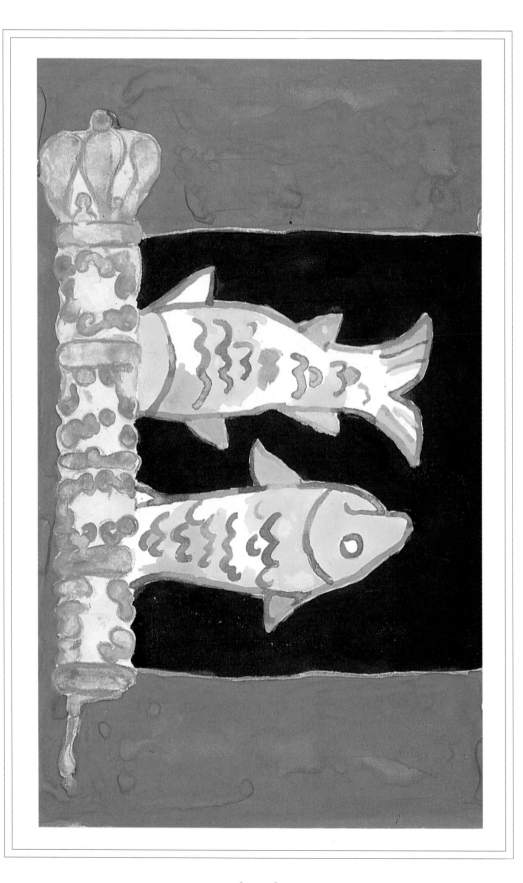

ADAR

February - March

PISCES, THE FISH, IS THE ZODIAC SIGN FOR ADAR. It is an appropriate sign for a month known for fun and frivolity, because, the rabbis said, in joyous ways Israel can be compared to a fish. How so? Just as the evil eye has no power over a fish in water, the evil eye has no power over the people of Israel. Moreover, although fish live in water, when a drop falls from above they catch it thirstily as if they had never tasted water before. So it is with the people of Israel. Although they grow up immersed in the waters of the Torah, when they hear a new Torah lesson they drink it in as if they had never before heard the Torah expounded.

If all this sounds a bit fishy, don't be concerned. We are, after all, talking about Adar, the month in which the holiday of Purim celebrates the defeat of the evil Haman, who set out to destroy the Jews of Persia. As the Talmud says, "When Adar comes, gladness increases." This is a month for masquerades and merrymaking, for parties and parodies, for tall tales and tall drinks that make bodies reel and minds blur as their owners try to distinguish between heroes and villains.

Adding to the gladness but also tinging it with sorrow is the commemoration of both the birth and death of the most towering Jewish leader of all times, Moses. Both have a connection with Purim: the rabbis imagined that when

Haman settled on Adar as the month in which to annihilate the Jews, he believed it to be a time of misfortune for them because Moses had died in that month. What he didn't know was that it was also a time of good fortune, because Moses had been born then.

In some years, this month of cheer comes around twice. These are leap years, when an extra Adar is added to the calendar in order to keep the Hebrew lunar year intercalated with the general solar one. In those years, the months are named Adar I and Adar II, with the second Adar serving as the primary one. Children born in Adar of a regular year, for example, celebrate their bar or bat mitzvahs in Adar II of a leap year. Purim is also celebrated in Adar II, based on a belief that the original Purim took place in the second Adar of a leap year. The Purim date in Adar I is recognized as *Purim kattan,* a minor Purim.

Be happy now. It's Adar!

The Third Day of Adar
THE SECOND TEMPLE IS COMPLETED, 515 B.C.E.

A miracle happened when the priests offered sacrifices on the altar of the newly constructed Second Temple in Jerusalem. An old man had led them to a spot where he remembered seeing an eternal flame from the First Temple buried before the building was destroyed. Instead of fire, the priests found a thick, oily liquid, which they sprinkled over the materials for sacrifice. They waited awhile, and soon the sun, which had been hidden behind clouds, came out and shone on the altar. Suddenly, to everyone's joy, a great fire burst forth and consumed the sacrifice. Some people compared the blaze to the flame that had descended from heaven when King Solomon offered his sacrifice at the dedication of the First Temple.

The prophet Jeremiah himself is said to have hidden the flame from the First Temple. Nobody knew it had turned to liquid, but once it became fire again, it purified all the Temple vessels. Afterward the flame remained on the altar, where priests guarded it so that it would never go out.

The miracle of the flame is part of Second Temple lore, foreshadowing the miracle of lights that three hundred and fifty years later would become part of the Hanukkah story. Yet, in many ways, the greatest miracle of all was the construction of the Temple itself, and the more so because it is history, not legend.

It resulted from the changing fortunes of nations. Babylonia was one of the most powerful nations on earth when it conquered the kingdom of Judah, destroyed its Temple, and exiled many of its inhabitants. But in the course of that exile, the kingdom of Persia grew and prospered, and in the year 539 B.C.E., it defeated Babylon. Cyrus, king of Persia, was a practical and benevolent monarch who believed in keeping his subjects content by allowing them a degree of autonomy and the freedom to worship their own gods. In a stunning turnaround of Babylonian policy, he gave the Judean exiles permission to return to their homeland and rebuild their Temple. He even had the

First Temple treasures, carried away by King Nebuchadnezzar of Babylon, returned to Jerusalem.

The prophets saw the hand of God in these reversals and Cyrus as God's instrument, designated to deliver Israel from its bondage. "I . . . am the same who says of Cyrus, 'He is My shepherd; / He shall fulfill all My purposes!' " exclaims the Second Isaiah, prophet of hope and redemption, speaking in God's name. "He shall say of Jerusalem, 'She shall be rebuilt,' / And to the Temple: 'You shall be founded again' " (Isaiah 44:27–28).

Though many of the exiles chose to remain in Babylonia after Cyrus' decree, thousands of others returned to Jerusalem. Soon afterward they began building a new Temple on the same site—the Temple Mount—where the First Temple now lay in ruins. Zerubbabel son of Shealtiel, governor of Judea, supervised the building project, appointing Levites to oversee the actual construction. On the day the building foundation was completed, the people celebrated with trumpets and cymbals and songs of praise to God. But mingled with the music and shouts of happiness came sounds of loud weeping. Old men who had known the First Temple saw the Second as only a poor reflection of Solomon's magnificent structure and burst into tears for what had been lost and could never be replaced.

The work of building did not go smoothly. Neighboring peoples interfered with it, fearful that Judea might become too cohesive and strong. Fights also broke out between returning exiles and those Judeans who had never left the land. Work was stopped for several years, but, urged on by the prophets Haggai and Zechariah, it was resumed and the building finally completed on the third day of Adar in 515 B.C.E. To the exuberant returnees, the completion of the Temple, just about seventy years after the exile, was the fulfillment of the prophecy of Jeremiah: "When seventy years of Babylon are over, I [God] will take note of you, and I will fulfill to you My promise of favor—to bring you back to this place" (Jeremiah 29:10).

During the years of exile, Jews had created new forms of worship without animal sacrifices, which they conducted at meetinghouses later known—from the Greek—as synagogues. Study and religious services continued in these community houses both within Judea and outside it even after the Second Temple was built. In fact, because they had developed this system of prayer separate from sacrifices, Jews were able to carry their religion with them to whatever lands they went long after that Temple ceased to exist.

While it did exist, the Temple served, as had the first, as the pivot of religious life, an emblem of the unity and faith of the Jewish people. Wherever they lived, Jews contributed to its upkeep, and as often as they could they visited it to offer sacrifices and prayers of thanksgiving.

The land of Israel, the rabbis later said, stands at the center of the earth. Jerusalem is at the center of Israel, and the Temple was at the center of Jerusalem. The Ark of the Covenant, holding the Ten Commandments, had rested at the center of the First Temple, they taught. It had disappeared after that Temple was destroyed, but a foundation stone, known as *even shetiyyah*, had remained, and lay at the center of the Second Temple. The stone had been in place from the days of King

David, the Mishnah states. The midrash goes further. The stone had been in place from the beginning of time, and the entire world had been created from it.

When Zechariah envisioned a future in which peoples of many nations would seek the Lord in Jerusalem, he was expressing the belief the Judeans themselves held that their Temple served as a source of goodness for the entire universe and that God's presence dwelt within it.

Almost five hundred years after the completion of the Second Temple, King Herod, who ruled Judea with the support of Rome, rebuilt it, making it larger and grander than it had ever been. Finishing touches were still being put on the rebuilding when the Romans conquered Jerusalem and burned the Temple to the ground in 70 C.E. The ninth day of Av mourns the tragedy of the Temple's destruction. The third day of Adar hails the miracle of its existence.

The Seventh Day of Adar
MOSES DIES ON HIS BIRTH DATE

The saddest fate of any figure in history may well be the fate of Moses, who led the Israelites out of Egypt toward the Promised Land, but died without ever entering that land himself. Tradition puts his death on the seventh of Adar, considered also the anniversary of his birth one hundred and twenty years earlier.

Why did Moses have to die when he did? What terrible sin did he commit that would prevent him from fulfilling his mission of bringing his people to their homeland? "Because you did not trust Me enough," God says, ". . . therefore you shall not lead this congregation into the land that I have given them" (Numbers 20:12).

But in what way had he not trusted? The traditional answer is that Moses had shown a lack of faith by striking a rock twice with his rod to get water from it when God commanded him merely to speak to the rock to obtain the water. Perhaps. But it has seemed an insufficient crime for such a severe punishment, even to the most respected interpreters of the Bible. After all, in the past Moses had used his rod for any number of miracles. Why not now?

Maimonides argued that Moses' sin lay not in disobeying God but in the uncontrolled anger with which he did so. The Israelites had clamored for water as they wandered in the desert, and, fed up with their constant complaints, Moses had responded, "Listen, you rebels, shall we get water for you out of this rock?" (Numbers 20:10). Such impatient anger, said Maimonides, was a poor trait in a leader and set a bad example for others.

Indeed, along with his greatness, Moses also had a quick temper. As a youth in Pharaoh's court, he had seen an Egyptian striking a Hebrew slave, and, without thinking of the consequences, had killed the Egyptian, an act that forced him to flee Egypt. Later, as leader of the Israelites, he had ascended Mount Sinai to receive the tablets of the Law but smashed them in a rage when he found the people worshipping a golden calf. Now, in a place that would be called *Mei*

Meribah, meaning "the Waters of Strife," he had struck the rock angrily and shouted at the people.

Other commentators have maintained that Moses' problem was less one of anger than of a growing haughtiness. His words "shall we get water for you out of this rock?"—referring to himself and his brother, Aaron—implied that they, and not God, would create the miracle.

Rabbinic interpretation treated Moses more kindly. God prevented him from entering the land, it said, because the generation of people he led from Egypt had been doomed to die in the wilderness. He had to die with them so he could remain their leader in the world to come.

Maybe the simplest explanation is that Moses' only failing was his humanness. He had grown old. He had become bitter because of his people's fickleness. He was unable to change his ways easily—he knew how to brandish his rod but not to speak softly to achieve his ends. The person to lead the people into their land needed to be more vigorous, more optimistic, less burdened by the past, younger.

Or maybe not. "This subject," the mystics said, "is one of the great secrets among the mysteries of the Torah."

The mystery of Moses' death reflects other mysteries of his life. He was born at a time when the Israelites were slaves in Egypt and, to keep them weak, the Pharaoh decreed that all their newborn sons be drowned. Pharaoh's daughter found him as an infant in a basket floating among the reeds of the Nile River, where his mother had hidden him. One might have expected that Pharaoh's daughter, especially, would follow her father's orders. But she saved the child and adopted him as her own son, sowing the seeds of Pharaoh's later downfall. She called him Moses, a name that was probably Egyptian in origin. The Bible gives it a Hebrew derivation: "Moshe," meaning "to draw out," because he was drawn out of the water. It is a name that hints at things to come, when Moses will draw his people out of the Red Sea as they escape Pharaoh's armies. And later he will be punished for the way in which he draws water from a rock.

We learn nothing more about Moses until that moment when he kills the Egyptian and flees to the desert of Midian. There he sees a bush burning with fire but not consumed by it, and he hears the voice of God commanding him to lead the Israelites out of Egypt.

From that command begins Moses' journey to free the Israelites and bring them to Canaan, the land promised to their ancestors. For Moses it is also an inner journey. He begins by refusing his mission, asking that someone else be appointed, but soon becomes unwavering in his determination to fulfill it. He questions the invisible God he hears, seeking proofs, wanting to know God's name. But he grows to become passionate in his belief, delivering to his people the tablets of the Law, teaching them to love their One God with all their "heart and soul" and to utterly reject any form of idol worship. He criticizes and castigates the Israelites for their lack of faith, but he becomes their greatest defender, soliciting God's forgiveness time and again for his "stiffnecked" people.

As the time approaches for Moses to die, he pleads just once to have his sentence revoked. When God rejects his plea, he accepts his fate and appoints Joshua his successor, charging him before all the congregation, "Be strong and resolute" (Deuteronomy 31:7).

In legend, however, Moses was not so acquiescent. With only one hour left to live, he pleaded with God, "Let me become like the beasts of the field that eat grass and drink water, only let me live and enjoy the world." But God refused. "If not," Moses prayed on, "let me become like a bird that flies in every direction." Again God refused. Moses continued to struggle and to hold off the angel of death until a heavenly voice announced, "Enough, Moses; the time of your death has come." Accepting the decree now, he lay down, closed his eyes, and folded his hands across his chest, as God directed. But in one final burst of rebellion, his soul would not leave his body. "God kissed Moses and took away his soul with a kiss of the mouth," the legend concludes. "And God wept."

The Bible portrays Moses in his last moments silently climbing Mount Nebo, where God shows him the sweep of land the people will inhabit. There he dies and there God buries him; "and no one knows his burial place to this day" (Deuteronomy 34:6).

❖

Moses was Israel's supreme prophet, the only one ever known as "our teacher," the only one singled out to speak with God "face to face." Yet his burial place is unknown, tradition says, so that he himself would never be worshipped. For the same reason his name is mentioned only once, and only in passing, in the Passover *Haggadah*, which tells of the Exodus from Egypt. The miracles Moses performed were God's miracles and the lessons he taught were God's lessons. He remains Moses the teacher, the prophet, the man of God, but never a god himself.

The sages arrived at the seventh of Adar as the anniversary of both the birth and death of Moses by comparing various biblical dates. The date has become the traditional time for burial societies, which prepare the dead for ritual burial, to hold banquets and elect new officers. In Israel it is also the day when people pay tribute to soldiers fallen in battle whose places of burial, like that of Moses, remain unknown.

The Tenth Day of Adar

THE FIRST PRINTED AND DATED HEBREW BOOK IS PUBLISHED, ITALY, FEBRUARY 17, 1475

It was not necessarily the most important Hebrew book ever printed, and possibly not even the first. But it was the first Hebrew book printed that had the date and place of publication and the printer's name, and that in itself makes the book significant and the date worth acclaiming.

The book was Rashi's commentary on the Five Books of Moses, printed alone, without the biblical text it commented on. The colophon—the inscription at the book's end—states that it was printed by Abraham ben Garton ben Isaac in Reggio di Calabria, Italy, on 10 Adar, 5235. It is the only book known to have been issued from his press, and only one copy of it exists, in the Palatine Library in Parma, Italy. Scholars have little information about Abraham's life. He may have come from Spain and settled in Italy. His city, Reggio di Calabria, later became a haven for Jews expelled from Spain in 1492, but still later fell under Spanish control, forcing the Jews to flee. Abraham's family may have been among those who left.

Modern printing began in Germany about 1440, when Johann Gutenberg developed movable type. Italy, however, became the first center for Hebrew book printing because German Jews, excluded from the printing guilds, could not learn the new techniques. Italian Jewish typesetters studied under immigrant German printers, and may have produced books, now lost, even before Abraham's edition of Rashi.

Printing revolutionized Jewish intellectual life, as it did general cultural life. Until then scribes painstakingly copied manuscripts by hand, and few people could afford them. Now multiple copies of books made Jewish texts and literature available to everyone. The scribes vehemently opposed printing at first because it cut into their livelihood, but nothing could stop its development. Soon Jewish leaders began referring to it as a holy craft.

Books printed before 1501 are known as *incunabula* and are extremely rare today. The Library of the Jewish Theological Seminary of America has the largest collection of Hebrew incunabula in the world. The earliest of these books had no title page—the text began immediately on the first page—and were generally large, folio, sizes. As printing spread to various Italian cities and then to other lands, typographers designed elaborate title pages and ornamental initials to open the books and border patterns to decorate the inside. One of the most popular title page designs, beginning in the sixteenth century, showed a portal, with the book's title and date in its center. As Jews found themselves persecuted in many lands, printers also learned to make small pocket-sized editions, particularly of the Bible, that could be easily carried from one location to another.

The best known and most prolific of all Jewish printers was the Soncino family, which originated in Germany and moved to Italy, to the town of Soncino, from which it took its name. The Soncino press printed the first complete Hebrew Bible, with vowels, in 1488 and the first pocket edition of the Bible in 1495. Gershom Soncino, the family's most active member, seemed to show up in one country after another gathering manuscripts, establishing presses, and issuing some of the most beautiful printed books in Hebrew, as well as in Greek, Latin, and Italian.

But it was a Christian printer, Daniel Bomberg, who created the format for the rabbinic Bible with commentaries—the *Mikra'ot Gedolot*—and the layout and pagination for talmudic texts that became standard throughout the world and are still used today. An Antwerp merchant, Bomberg set up his press in Venice around 1516. Recognizing the demand for Hebrew books not only among Jews but also among Christian scholars, he devoted himself to Hebrew printing, hiring Jewish assistants as editors and proofreaders. Bomberg printed the first complete edition of the Talmud (the Soncinos had published individual tractates) in 1520–23. His Hebrew typography was of such a high quality that for years Jewish printers copied his "Bomberg type" in their own works.

Compared to the great achievements of Bomberg, Soncino, and other major printers, the first dated book of Rashi's commentary on the Pentateuch seems primitive and insignificant. Yet this book established a precedent of its own. The typeface used in it was a form of italic, based on the style of handwritten Spanish manuscripts. That print style became so identified with Rashi's commentary that it is often known as "Rashi script" and is still used for all Rashi texts. Rashi, who lived in the eleventh century, didn't invent it or even use it himself. It made its first printed appearance in his commentary issued on the tenth day of Adar, 1475.

The people of Amalek, the focus of the Sabbath of Remembrance, became synonymous in Jewish thought with Israel's most ruthless assailants. Haman, Hitler, and others before and after them, all viciously bent on annihilating Israel, have been seen as Amalek, enemies of the Jewish people and at war with God.

Amalek is first mentioned in the Book of Genesis as an individual, son of Eliphaz and grandson of Esau, Jacob's brother and competitor. The Bible identifies Esau with Edom, a tribal foe of Israel, and rabbinic tradition later identifies Edom with Rome, destroyer of the Second Temple.

We next read of Amalek as a nation, the first to attack the Israelites as they flee Egypt. It is a surprise attack and an insidious one, launched from the rear against the weakest members of the Israelite camp at a time when all the people are weary and famished after their flight. Because of that attack, the Bible proclaims: "The Lord will be at war with Amalek throughout the ages" (Exodus 17:16) and commands Israel: "Remember what Amalek did to you on your journey" (Deuteronomy 25:17).

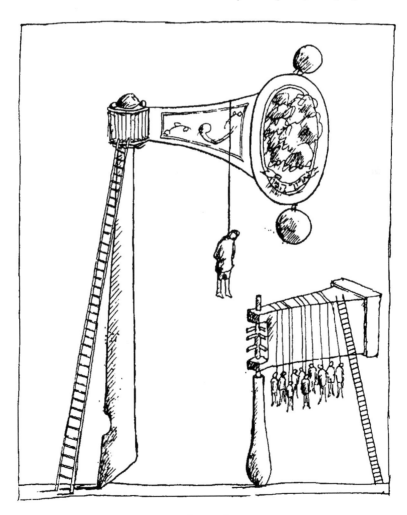

That command is added as a special reading on the Sabbath before Purim, called Shabbat Zakhor from the Hebrew word for "remember." The villainous Haman forms the link between Purim and Amalek. Named an "Agagite" in the Scroll of Esther, he is considered a descendant of Agag, king of Amalek.

But there is more to the command than remembering. It includes an admonition to "blot out the memory of Amalek from under heaven. Do not forget!" (Deuteronomy 25:19), and many people have found that charge morally vexing: Remember, and blot out the memory of. Do not forget cruelty, and mercilessly destroy the cruel. But should enmity be clutched forever? Should an entire people be wiped out because of the actions of its ancestors?

The problem seems most pressing in a gory scene in the book of I Samuel, the prophetic portion read on the Sabbath of Remembrance. King Saul disobeys Samuel's order to destroy all of Amalek's people and possessions in a battle he is about to wage. Instead, he spares King Agag and takes as booty the best of Amalek's cattle to use as sacrifices to God. In cold anger, Samuel has Agag brought to him in chains and proceeds to slash him to pieces. For his disobedience, Saul loses his throne.

Martin Buber questioned whether Samuel had correctly interpreted God's will. It seemed inconceivable to him that God would demand the total annihilation of a people. The rabbis were more supportive of Samuel's insistence on strict obedience to divine command, but they also showed sympathy for Saul. The Talmud pictures him justifying his behavior to God by saying, "If humans sinned, what evil did the cattle do? If adults sinned, what did the little ones do?"

The questions remain unanswered.

Other sources turn away from Amalek's wickedness and emphasize Israel's faults, suggesting that Amalek served as a "strap of chastisement" for it, like a strap used to punish a child who has misbehaved. In the wilderness, each of Amalek's attacks came after Israel had lost faith in God and Moses, and the memory of those attacks is meant to remind the people of their own sins.

In the same vein, one passage in the midrash connects Haman's savagery to the wrongful behavior of Israel's ancestor Jacob. In the Bible, when Jacob cheated his brother Esau out of their father's blessing, Esau "cried a loud and bitter cry" (Genesis 27:34). Esau's retribution for that painful cry came generations later through his descendant Haman from the line of Amalek. For in the Scroll of Esther we read those same words, but this time it is Mordecai, the Jewish leader, who "cried a loud and bitter cry" (Esther 4:1) after Haman decreed death to all the Jews.

Such interpretations and rationalizations notwithstanding, Amalek abides in Jewish consciousness as the prototype of wickedness. Ironically, the memory of the real Amalekites has indeed been blotted out, for no trace of them remains today. They are not mentioned outside the Bible, and even there, they seem to disappear as a people during the reign of King Hezekiah of Judah, in the late eighth century B.C.E. For Jews, however, the name Amalek continues to stand for all who have lashed out against them, attacking them when they were weak and weary. And who is to say that after generations of suffering at the hands of such attackers, refusing to forget their evil is not an appropriate response?

The Thirteenth Day of Adar

TA'ANIT ESTHER—THE FAST OF ESTHER

When I was a child (and my daughter after me), every little girl in Hebrew school wanted to dress up as Queen Esther for the Purim holiday. What could be better than pretending to be the beautiful queen who manages to save the Jewish people in her realm from annihilation? It meant wearing rouge and lipstick, high-heeled shoes, and a crown that shone with sparkles.

Then a funny thing happened. As an adult I found myself, along with other Jewish women, suddenly uneasy with that schoolgirl idealization of Esther. She was, after all, a beauty queen. She had been chosen in a beauty contest from among all the maidens in the land of Persia to be consort to King Ahasuerus. All she seemed to have was good looks, and those alone, we had decided, were no longer enough to gain a woman admiration. To make matters worse, Esther was the quintessential "good Jewish girl," following the advice of her cousin and guardian Mordecai—not much of a model for women trying to assert themselves in a world long dominated by men.

A more exciting model was the king's first wife, Vashti, often ignored in the holiday fun and fantasy. As the Purim story goes, King Ahasuerus gave a seven-day feast for all the men in his capital city of Shushan. Vashti held a separate banquet for women, but on the seventh day, the king, heavy with wine, ordered her to appear at his party. He wanted to flaunt her beauty (some say in the raw) before his subjects. Vashti refused to show, and the incensed king had her deposed (some say beheaded).

Vashti became our ideal because she had pride and the gumption to stand up for herself, even before a king. Not only that, her act of defiance so threatened male authority that the king sent word of her punishment throughout his empire to teach all wives to respect their husbands. How could sweet, submissive Esther hold a candle to this strong-minded woman?

Well, she could, some of us have more recently decided. Over time, we've tempered our reactions. While we're pleased to have reclaimed Vashti as a feminist hero, we're ready to reinstate Esther as Purim hero—not because of her beauty but because of her braininess and courage.

The test of Esther's character began when Ahasuerus appointed Haman prime minister of Persia. Haman expected everyone to bow down to him, but as a Jew, Mordecai refused to do so. In retaliation, Haman convinced the weak-willed king to issue a decree of destruction against all the Jews in his realm. "There is a certain people . . . whose laws are different from those of any other people" (Esther 3:8), Haman had warned the king, in an anti-Jewish diatribe that has been repeated many times in history and in many lands, like Persia, in which Jews thought themselves safe.

Devastated by the king's decree, Mordecai looked to Esther to intercede for her people.

Esther risked her life to do so. On Mordecai's orders, she had never revealed her Jewish identity to the king, lest he reject her. She knew also that anybody who entered the king's presence without being summoned was subject to death. That she hesitated to approach him was understandable. That she was able to devise and implement the plan she did was remarkable.

"If I am to perish, I shall perish!" Esther said, as she went about her mission of salvation (Esther 4:16). She began by asking Mordecai to call a three-day fast for all the Jews of Shushan. The midrash relates that the fast was scheduled for the thirteenth, fourteenth, and fifteenth of Nisan. Mordecai objected that it would coincide with the first day of Passover, to which Esther wisely responded, "Old man, if there is no Israel, why should there be a Passover?" The fast took place.

Now Esther set a trap for Haman that would have made Machiavelli proud. She invited the king and Haman to two banquets. Later sages conjectured that she hoped to arouse the king's jealousy by including the minister at the feast. She was also lulling Haman into complacency, making him too self-satisfied to suspect a thing. In this she followed the lead of Judith, who managed to cut off the head of Holofernes by cleverly gaining his confidence. Women may not have had much power in ancient times, but they knew how to use their wits to win the day.

Esther won a great victory with her plot. At the second feast, she denounced Haman to Ahasuerus as a schemer set on destroying her people. In what may be the most amusing scene in all of Scripture, we see the king, furious at Haman, step out of the room. Haman prostrates himself over Esther's couch, pleading with her for his life. The king returns and in a jealous rage (as Esther planned), believes Haman is trying to rape his wife. Within seconds, the king orders Haman hung on the very gallows he had prepared for Mordecai.

In memory of Esther's trial, the thirteenth of Adar, the day before Purim, was declared a fast day, *Ta'anit Esther*, the "Fast of Esther." It displaced an earlier holiday that celebrated Judah Maccabee's defeat of a Syrian general, Nicanor.

For her courage and cleverness, also, Esther had an entire book named for her, *Megillat Esther*, the Scroll of Esther. Only one other biblical book bears a woman's name, the Book of Ruth, which tells of yet another decisive, directed woman—but that is a tale for a different holiday.

The Scroll of Esther is read in synagogue on Purim eve and again the next morning, and all—men, women, and children—are obligated to hear it. Children stamp their feet and twirl their *graggers*, noisemakers, whenever Haman's name is mentioned, and they dress in costumes, as original as their imaginations dictate. But mostly, every little girl still prefers to be Queen Esther.

The Fourteenth Day of Adar

PURIM—THE FEAST OF LOTS

Purim is named from the Hebrew word *pur*, meaning "lot," after the lots Haman tossed to choose the month in which to destroy the Jews. In ancient times the holiday was also called the Day of Mordecai, because, along with Queen Esther, Mordecai is a hero of the story.

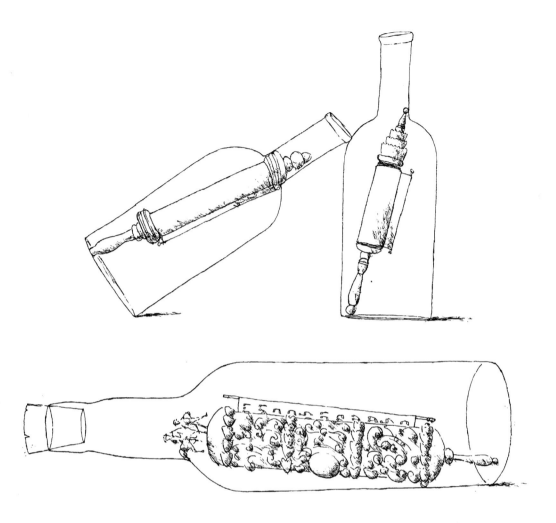

Mordecai son of Jair, from the tribe of Benjamin, descended from King Saul and later Jews who were exiled to Babylon. He himself rose to become a courtier and consultant to King Ahasuerus of Persia. After Esther's parents died, he became her foster father.

It was Mordecai's idea for Esther to hide her identity when she became queen, and it was to Esther as queen that he went after he overheard two men plotting to assassinate the king. Esther gave the information to Ahasuerus, the men were executed, and the incident, with Mordecai's name, was inscribed in the king's annals.

In some respects, Mordecai's struggle with Haman was an extension of the ancient Israelite war with Amalek. Mordecai's ancestor Saul had spared the life of the Amalekite King Agag. Mordecai refused to bow to Agag's descendant Haman, and Haman, in turn, tried to avenge himself by planning to exterminate the Jews of Persia.

Mordecai won on every score. First, King Ahasuerus, unable to sleep one night, chanced on the record of Mordecai's good deed on his behalf. Next, as a reward, the king ordered Haman, of all people, to parade Mordecai through the streets of Shushan on a royal horse, proclaiming, "This is what is done for the man whom the king desires to honor!" (Esther 6:11). Finally, Haman lost his life after Esther denounced him to the king, and Mordecai, of all people, replaced him as minister.

But wait! Did any of this Purim story really happen? Plenty of historians say it didn't. They point out that while King Ahasuerus may have been the Persian king Xerxes I, who reigned from 486 to 465 B.C.E., no references to the events described in the Scroll of Esther exist in Persian sources. Furthermore, the names Esther and Mordecai sound suspiciously like those of the Babylonian gods Ishtar and Marduk, making it likely that our story is a retelling, maybe a parody, of some ancient folktale or myth. Some scholars argue that the whole megillah was invented, possibly during the Second Temple era, to give a Jewish slant to an old, popular spring festival.

The sages had their own problems with the Purim saga. What was this Jewish woman doing in a Persian king's harem, changing her name from Hadassah to Esther, paying no attention to dietary laws, and hiding her identity? Worse still, why is there no reference to God in the entire Book of Esther—not a prayer for salvation when Esther calls for a public fast, not a prayer of thanksgiving when salvation does arrive?

They argued the matter back and forth and finally agreed to accept Purim as a legitimate festival, although a minor one, on which work is permitted. They concluded that though the book appears to be secular, it was actually divinely inspired, perhaps more than any other biblical book. The only reason God is not mentioned in it is because God's presence is hidden, working behind the scenes. How else explain the remarkable victory of the Jewish people than through divine providence, which shapes all events without our awareness? Why, even the thorn tree, on which Haman the "thorn" was hanged, had been created for that very purpose from the beginning of the universe.

So be joyful on Purim, the rabbis commanded, and be sure to follow the practice Esther and Mordecai instituted of sending gifts to one another, known as *mishlo'ah manot*, and especially of distributing food and money to the poor.

Without worrying about the holiday's origins, Jews have accepted the rabbinic injunction and celebrated in high spirits, with carnivals, masquerades, and *Purim shpiels*—plays and poems that satirize the story and its characters. Even cross-dressing, men as women and women as men, is permitted on this day. Families gather on Purim afternoon to eat a Purim *se'udah*, a hearty meal that in Ashkenazic homes may include triangular meat-filled pastries called *kreplah*, and end with the festival's favorite delicacy, *hamantaschen*. Loosely translated as "Haman's pockets," these are small three-cornered cakes filled with poppy seeds or jellied fruits. Like the kreplah, they mock the three-cornered hat Haman supposedly wore. A Sephardic Purim meal might feature fine egg noodles tossed with lemon sauce and known as "Haman's hair," and fried cookies called "Haman's ears," or *oznei Haman* in Hebrew.

In the synagogue, readers chant the Megillah in a melody of its own, folding the scroll like a letter, unlike the Torah scrolls, which are unrolled. The folding is a reminder of letters Esther and Mordecai sent to the Jewish community creating the holiday.

The highest spirits of all come from a saying by the fourth-century Babylonian sage Rava that it is a duty to get so drunk on Purim that you cannot distinguish between the phrases "Blessed be Mordecai" and "Cursed be Haman." Naturally, that idea has won many followers (despite a few hand-wringing rabbis who worry about excesses), but it actually raises some sobering questions. Should one truly try to forget the difference between the good Mordecai and the evil Haman? And isn't this supposed to be a holiday of remembering and not forgetting?

But perhaps what Rava advocated was something else: Purim offers a moment of total victory, rare in the Jewish past. Why not put aside our anger, even our memory, for that moment and simply be happy? Then, too, Jewish tradition teaches us not to gloat over the destruction of our enemies. The Megillah reader, for example, chants the names of Haman's ten sons, who are also killed, in one breath so as not to dwell in detail on their deaths. It may be that melding Haman's name to Mordecai's for a while is a way of preventing ourselves from gloating even while cheering success. It may also be that drinking to oblivion is the only way to quell the pain of a history of Haman-like hatreds.

Purim carries another serious message that makes it resonate with meaning far beyond the day itself. In the story, Esther hesitates at first about approaching the king, knowing that she is putting her life in jeopardy. Mordecai says, "Do not imagine that you, of all the Jews, will escape with your life by being in the king's palace. On the contrary, if you keep silent in this crisis, relief and deliverance will come to the Jews from another quarter, while you and your father's house will perish . . ." (Esther 4:13–14).

It is a statement of connectedness—of Esther to the Jewish people, of Jews to one another, and, ultimately, of all people to all others. Nobody is safe no matter how exalted his or her position, Mordecai is saying, unless people assume responsibility for one another. For so long as even one monster is allowed to remain out there casting lots, who knows who will be the next victim?

The Fifteenth Day of Adar
SHUSHAN PURIM—THE EXTRA DAY

RIDDLE: When is Purim not-Purim and not-Purim is Purim?

ANSWER: When celebrated in cities in Israel that had walls around them in the days of Joshua.

QUESTION: What? Does this have anything to do with being so drunk, you can't tell the difference, etc. . . . ?

ANSWER: No, no. It makes perfect sense. In walled cities, Purim is not celebrated on the fourteenth of Adar, as it is everywhere else, but on the fifteenth. The reason is that in the Megillah, when the Persian Jews defended themselves against their enemies at the king's orders, the fighting continued in the fortress city of Shushan one day longer than anywhere else. From that the custom arose to observe the holiday in walled cities a day after other places. Later rabbis defined such cities as those in Israel that had built walls at the time of the early settlement under Joshua, son of Nun.

Today, inhabitants of Jerusalem, once a walled city, celebrate on the fifteenth of Adar, not the fourteenth. Anyone who wants a double dose of festivity can enjoy Purim in Tel Aviv one day and have a second holiday in Jerusalem the next. The extra day is called *Shushan Purim*, after the city where it began.

Like everything else about Purim, however, even this peculiarity of days, with its extra occasion for partying, has a thought-provoking side. Many commentators have been troubled by the last chapters of the Book of Esther, which describe how the Jews slew thousands of people in fighting their foes. Esther herself receives the king's permission to continue the killing for an additional day in Shushan, giving rise to Shushan Purim.

Haman had already been defeated, the critics claim, so why did this bloodshed have to occur?

The Megillah provides at least a partial explanation. At Haman's instigation, Ahasuerus had issued an edict of extermination for the Jews in his realm. In ancient Persian law, a king's decree could not be revoked once it was sealed, even if the king wished to do so, as in this case. The only solution, then, was for Ahasuerus to permit the Jews to fight in self-defense against those who would slaughter them. This they did, winning mightily, and hence all the killing. (Notice, incidentally, how readily the Persians took up arms against the Jews, without protesting the king's orders.)

But why the extra day of fighting in Shushan? Possibly because it was the king's residence, with more heavily armed troops for the Jews to defeat. Possibly because in this story, which slips in and out of fantasy, the dream of an extra day of triumph—of really hitting back for all time—was too good to leave out.

Possibly, also, all the battles described relate to the ancient strife between Israel and Amalek, seen in miniature in the clash between Mordecai and Haman. This time, the text implies, Saul's mistake would not be repeated. Agag's descendant Haman would be killed so that *he* could not have descendants like himself. With him would be destroyed all the Amalekites—all who would destroy the Jews. Furthermore, Saul had saved the Amalekites' cattle to take as loot, against the prophet Samuel's orders. This time, the Book of Esther emphasizes, the Jews "did not lay hands on the spoil" (Esther 9:15). This victory comes to complete what Saul had left unfinished, to fulfill the command to remember what Amalek did to the Israelites as they straggled wearily in the wilderness.

Despite the violence at the end of the Megillah, and notwithstanding the critics' reservations, the celebrations of Purim and Shushan Purim as they have come down through the ages have centered less on revenge than on deliverance, on the salvation and survival of Persia's Jews. Because of that underlying theme, in later years Jewish communities throughout the world created "second Purims" to recall their own escapes from danger or persecution. They composed scrolls to narrate their events, and marked the dates with fasts and prayers of thanksgiving.

It was also in that spirit that the sages, who had been reluctant at first to accept the Purim holiday, finally embraced it fully. When the Messiah comes, they said, even if every other festival is abolished, Purim will still be observed—an eternal symbol of salvation.

Shabbat Parah – the Sabbath of the Red Heifer

Shabbat Parah is the third special Sabbath in a series of four that includes an extra Torah portion in the synagogue reading. This portion (Numbers 19), one of Scripture's most obscure, concerns an archaic purification rite for people who have been defiled by contact with a human corpse. In Jewish teaching, although the body of a dead person is to be treated with utmost respect and care, it is a source of ritual uncleanliness. That distinction may have arisen in response to the Egyptian practice of worshipping the dead. Jewish tradition honors the dead, but it emphasizes the centrality of life.

The rite begins with finding a red heifer, a young cow (*parah*, in Hebrew), that has no blemishes and has never been yoked for field work. The color red—which refers to a red-brown heifer with no other coloration—associates the animal with blood, a life-force. A priest supervises while people assigned to the task slaughter the heifer and burn it in its entirety, afterward mixing its ashes with fresh spring water. Persons or objects that have been contaminated by the corpse are purified by being sprinkled with the ash-water mixture.

The process sounds clear enough until one learns of a basic contradiction: whereas the ash solution purifies the unclean person, whoever comes into contact with the heifer or its ashes—the priest, the person who slaughters and burns the animal, the one who sprinkles the cleansing waters—becomes ritually unclean himself. Or, in the words of the rabbis, the ashes "purify the defiled and defile the pure."

Sages and scholars have turned themselves inside out trying to unravel that paradox. Some modern scholars have tied the ritual of the red heifer to a "sin offering" sacrifice decreed by the Bible, in which the animal sacrificed purifies a sinner by absorbing the person's impurity and in that way becoming impure itself. Thus the ashes of the red heifer can cleanse the defiled, but in doing so become contaminated. There are enough differences between the two rituals, however, to have prevented the early rabbis from making the same connection. Instead they devoted an entire tractate of the Mishnah to laws about the red heifer, and also managed to come up with inventive ideas about the ceremony itself. Here are some examples:

A female animal was used in this ceremony and not a male, as in most sacrifices, because, like a mother who cleans up after her child, the red heifer atones for the sin of her "child," the golden calf the Israelites fashioned in the wilderness.

In all of Jewish history only nine heifers were ritually burned, because each yielded enough ash to be stored for the future. Moses performed the first rite, the scribe Ezra the second, and seven others after that, until the Second Temple was destroyed and animal rituals ceased. When the Messiah comes, he will burn the tenth heifer.

The number seven is significant in this rite, as it is in so many others, for the biblical portion about the heifer mentions seven things seven times—seven mentions of a heifer, seven of burning, seven of sprinkling, seven of washing, seven of uncleanness, seven of cleanness, and seven of priests (if one includes Moses and Aaron).

Even the wise King Solomon didn't understand the meaning behind the red heifer. He wrote in the book of Ecclesiastes, which tradition ascribes to him: "I said: I will get wisdom; but it was far from me" (7:23). Those words refer to the section on the red heifer.

Even Moses, some say, did not understand. He inquired of God how the ashes can purify, and God replied, "Moses, it is a statute and I have made a decree, and nobody may transgress my decree." That is why this section opens with the words, "This is the ritual law that the Lord has commanded" (Numbers 19:2).

In the end, God's answer to Moses is the answer the rabbis accepted and used as a lesson for all divine laws. Jews must observe these laws in the knowledge that there is meaning behind them even if the human mind does not yet comprehend it.

For all the strangeness of its ritual, the Sabbath of the Red Heifer at the conclusion of Adar prepares the way for the ceremonies and rites of purity that will become all-absorbing in the next month, when Passover arrives.

Shabbat HaHodesh — the Sabbath of the Month

The special Sabbaths leading to the month of Nisan culminate in Shabbat HaHodesh, the Sabbath immediately before the beginning of Nisan or the first day of that month if it is a Sabbath. No other month in the year is so honored with a Sabbath that heralds its arrival.

The extra Torah portion for this day begins with the words, "The Lord said to Moses and Aaron in the land of Egypt: This month shall mark for you the beginning of the months; it shall be the first of the months of the year for you" (Exodus 12:1–2). As it continues, the reading includes the first laws of the Passover festival and the eating of unleavened bread. These laws are also the first that God gives Moses for the entire community of Israel, and they are given in Egypt. All other laws would be delivered after the Exodus, as the people made their way in the wilderness.

The midrash insists that these rules concerning the month of Nisan were so important that God had to make sure Moses fully understood them. So God took Moses outside at twilight and pointed with a finger to a new moon, explaining to what extent it must be seen in order for a new month to be declared. "When the moon becomes new again," God taught, "it will be for you the beginning of the month." That is what is meant by "This month"—the month through which God instructed Moses.

Further, in designating this month as the beginning of months, God was now entrusting Israel with reckoning its own calendar and festival times. In this God was like a king with only one son who had storehouses filled with gold, silver, and precious stones. While the son was small, the king guarded all the treasures himself, but when the son grew up the king said to him, "Now that you are an adult, I hand everything over to you." Thus, while Israel was enslaved, God guarded all the seasons, but with freedom Israel was ready to assume responsibility for fixing the new moon and observing religious holidays.

The reading for Shabbat HaHodesh reminds Jews that Passover is fast approaching. At the time of the Temple, that meant planning for the most important pilgrimage of the year, when people would go to Jerusalem to bring their paschal sacrifices on the fourteenth of Nisan, Passover eve. Today the announcement of the new month of Nisan introduces a flurry of excitement and activity (for some people, frenzy) as preparations for this all-consuming national holiday get under way.

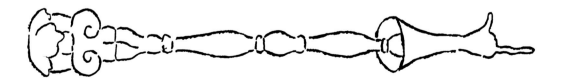

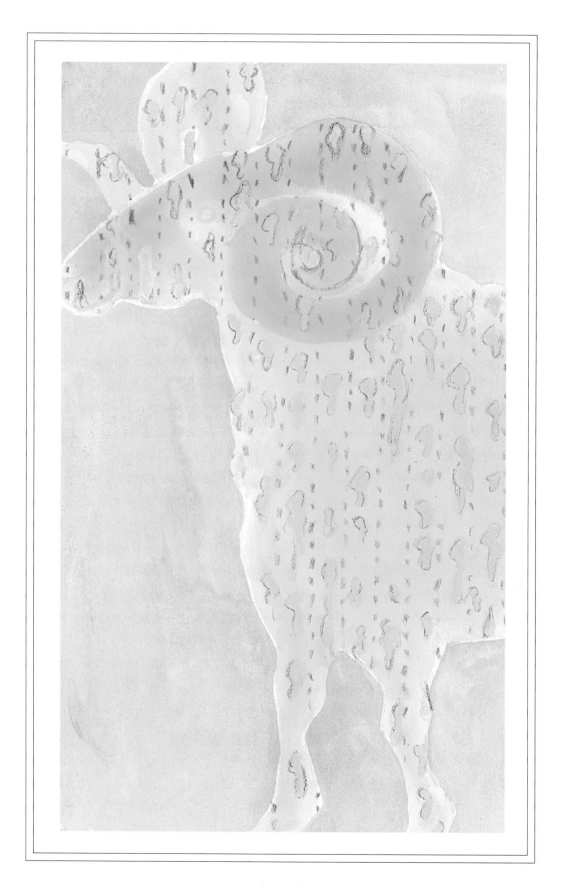

NISAN

March – April

I N NISAN THE ANCIENT ISRAELITES WENT FROM SLAVERY TO FREEDOM AND FROM THE LAND OF EGYPT TOWARD THEIR OWN LAND. That journey makes this month so sacred and celebratory that throughout it eulogies may not be given at funerals and public mourning may not be held.

The name Nisan comes from *Nissanu,* the first month on the Babylonian calendar. But the Bible doesn't use that name. It simply speaks of the first month as the head of all other months and numbers those others in relation to it, just as the days of the week are numbered in relation to the Sabbath. Because of that, the medieval commentator Nahmanides explained, every month reminds us of the first and the redemption that occurred then, as the weekdays remind us of the Sabbath. Even Tishrei, so special in its own right as the beginning of the new year, is still the seventh month on the Hebrew calendar, sixth after Nisan.

Nisan has another name in the Bible—*hodesh ha'aviv,* the month of spring—and symbols of spring appear throughout the Passover ritual.

The zodiac sign for Nisan is Aries, the ram, which tradition connects to the paschal lamb Israelite families ate on the eve of their departure from Egypt. The ram of Nisan also represents the merit of Isaac, who allowed himself to be offered as a lamb for sacrifice and was saved by the ram that appeared in the thicket. His deed has redounded to the benefit of Israel ever since, and in honor of it, the mystics believed, God could not destroy the Temple in this month.

Tradition places Isaac's birth in the middle of Nisan, one more sacred spark in a month of abundant holiness.

The First Day of Nisan

THE ISRAELITES ERECT THE TABERNACLE IN THE WILDERNESS

It must have been a spectacular sight, the raising of the Tabernacle that would be a divine sanctuary during all the years the Israelite tribes journeyed through the wilderness. It had taken months to build, its blueprint, in the Bible, dictated by God to Moses. It had an outer court with an altar upon which the priests made sacrificial offerings and an inner court that held a seven-branched menorah of pure gold with cups shaped like almond blossoms. It had coverings made of blue, purple, and crimson yarn and of goats' hair and dolphin skins. Deep in its Holy of Holies, its innermost section, it had an Ark of acacia wood overlaid with gold, and in the Ark the tablets of the Law that Moses had received on Mount Sinai.

The craftsman most responsible for constructing the Ark and much of the sanctuary was Bezalel son of Uri son of Hur from the tribe of Judah. Thousands of years later an art school in modern Israel would be named for him. He exceeded everyone in his ability to design in precious metals and to carve in wood. Oholiab son of Ahisamach from the tribe of Dan assisted him by carving the furnishings and decorating the curtains and priestly vestments.

All the precious materials used in building the Tabernacle came from the people. As it turned out, they donated so much gold, silver, copper, and other goods that Moses finally had to call a halt to the contributions. (Rabbis ever since have envied Moses' position—no modern building campaign *ever* received too many contributions.) Many commentators have noted the parallel between the Israelites' readiness to contribute to the building of the golden calf and their readiness to contribute to the Tabernacle, suggesting that the latter may have been in atonement for the former.

On the first day of Nisan, the Tabernacle was completed and erected. "Moses set up the Tabernacle," Scripture says (Exodus 40:18), and the rabbis, wondering how one man could possibly have executed such a complicated operation, suggested that Moses had only to put his hand on the structure and God made it rise of its own accord.

The pageantry didn't end with the Tabernacle in place. For twelve days Israel's twelve tribal chiefs brought offerings to its altar. On the first day came Nahshon son of Amminadab of the tribe of Judah bearing a silver bowl and silver basin, both filled with flour and oil, a gold ladle holding incense, and various animals for sacrifice. In legend, he had the honor of that first offering because, wholly trusting in God's salvation, he was the first person to jump into the Red Sea when the

Israelites fled Egypt. Each day after that, another chieftain brought his offering, until, on the twelfth day, Ahira son of Enan of the tribe of Naphtali concluded the dedications.

❖

Soon after the erection of the Tabernacle, Moses consecrated it and ordained his brother, Aaron, high priest of the Israelites, and Aaron's four sons to serve in it. The colorful and joyous ceremony of ordination lasted a week. Then, on the eighth day, a strange and terrible incident occurred. As two of Aaron's sons, Nadab and Abihu, approached the Tabernacle altar, a fire that came "from the Lord" suddenly burst out and consumed them. The only explanation Scripture gives is that they had offered "alien fire" at the altar. That may mean they brought a sacrifice that was not prescribed, most probably one reminiscent of pagan ways. Or they may have moved too close to the inner sanctum, where they were not permitted. But within a split second, these two young priests were dead.

Heartrending in those deaths is their father's reaction. Moses turns to Aaron—one imagines in horror—and speaks briefly. But "Aaron was silent," unable to say a word, overwhelmed by the tragedy. The text itself is silent on their mother's response (Leviticus 10:1–3).

The midrash offers various justifications for the deaths, pointing to other sins the brothers may have committed, but none is convincing. The priests' deaths remain unexplained, fearsome testimony to the mystery and awe of this sacred structure, dwelling place of the Deity.

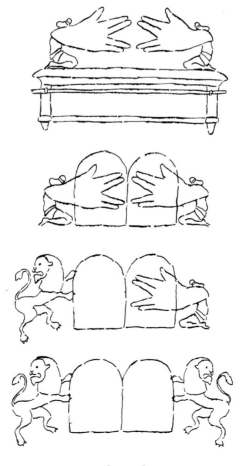

But how can a religion that believes in an invisible and transcendent Deity have such a dwelling place? The text is subtle in describing the Tabernacle's purpose. "And let them make Me a sanctuary that I may dwell among them," it says (Exodus 25:8), implying that God's presence will dwell *among* the people, not *in* the sanctuary. Or, in Rashi's words, the sanctuary will be a house of holiness for God's Name, a symbolic rather than an actual dwelling place for the Divine.

Some commentators have seen the sanctuary as a concession to a human wish for a concrete home in which to envisage God. A midrash pictures Israel appealing to God that the kings of all nations have grand palaces and why shouldn't their King have the same? Though God replies that the King of the universe does not require what flesh-and-blood rulers do, they insist. Finally God gives in and allows them to build the sanctuary, but only as a token of affection, not because of need.

Another midrash compares the Tabernacle to a cave by the sea. If the sea becomes stormy the cave fills with water, yet the sea is not diminished. Similarly, the splendor of God's presence filled the Tabernacle, yet that presence in the world was not lessened.

Still, the rabbis felt deeply moved by the Tabernacle's sacredness. Its wood, they said, came from paradise, carried out by Adam when he was driven from there. Abraham gained possession of it and gave it to Isaac, who gave it to Jacob, who took it with him to Egypt. When the Israelites left Egypt they transported it to the desert to be used in the Tabernacle.

Moreover, the construction of the sanctuary corresponded to the Creation of the world: as God created the sky to cover the world, the curtains served to cover the Tabernacle. As the sun and moon gave light to the universe, the golden menorah illuminated the sanctuary. And as God blessed the seventh day when Creation had ended, so Moses blessed the people when they completed their work on the Tabernacle. The Tabernacle was like the world in miniature, built according to God's will.

Through the Tabernacle, God communicated with Moses. Its Ark had a golden cover, a *kapporet*, from whose sides extended great winged creatures called *cherubim*. Later biblical literature imagined the space above the Ark as God's invisible throne, with the Ark itself as the divine footstool. From that space, between the wings of the cherubim, Moses would hear God's voice.

The Tabernacle stood in the midst of the Israelite camp, with the tribes stationed around it—the priests and Levites closest to it and the others behind them. When it was stationary, the cloud that represented God's majesty covered it by day and by evening appeared as a flame of fire. The people would journey only when the cloud lifted, the priests carrying the Ark on four poles and the Levites wheeling wagons filled with the curtains and carefully wrapped furnishings. When the cloud rested they would set up camp again.

Along with its many other meanings, the Tabernacle foreshadowed the future of the Jewish people. Just as the Israelites carried it with them wherever they went, their descendants would carry their religion with them in all their exiles, always in the belief that the clouds of glory hovered above them, showing them the way.

The Third Day of Nisan

THE GHETTO IS ESTABLISHED IN VENICE, ITALY, MARCH 29, 1516

The word *ghetto* encapsulates centuries of Jewish life in Europe marked by poverty and perse-cution, by state-imposed isolation and self-imposed determination to sustain Jewish culture and customs regardless of circumstances.

The ghetto was named in Venice, Italy. There, on March 29, 1516, Jews were ordered to live apart from the rest of the city on an island once occupied by the *geto nuovo*, the "new foundry." The Hebrew date was the third of Nisan, 5277. Walls and gates were erected around the region to isolate the Jews from their surroundings lest they "contaminate" neighboring Christians. About twenty-five years later, the *geto vecchio*, the "old foundry" region, was incorporated into the area, and some time later twenty new buildings, called the *geto nuovissimo*, were added. After that the Venice ghetto remained unchanged for almost three hundred years.

Jews had long chosen to live in quarters of their own in the villages and towns of lands they inhabited. But the Venice ghetto was different: this was compulsory separation under orders of the Christian Church. All Jews, whether natives of the city or refugees from persecutions in other lands, were forced into the ghetto district. Although they might go out during the day provided they did not mingle too closely with Christians, nobody was permitted to leave the ghetto after midnight, when its gates were shut tight and guarded by Gentile watchmen—whose wages the Jewish commu-nity had to pay.

Directed by the Pope, the Venetian ghetto model spread to Rome and other Italian cities and soon to other lands, including France and Germany. In the eighteenth and nineteenth centuries, Czarist Russia permitted Jews to settle only in certain provinces, the entire region known as the "Pale of Settlement." There and in other parts of Eastern Europe, Jews were confined to small towns, or shtetls, not unlike the ghettos, but they were not walled in as the ghetto Jews were. Although the ghettos differed according to region, all had some things in common: severe overcrowding, poor ven-tilation, inadequate sanitation, and numerous restrictions on the Jewish community.

Behind the ghettos of Venice and other cities lay a compromise between the desire of the Church to segregate and degrade the Jews and the desire of princes and rulers to benefit from their commerce. Instead of expelling the "infidels," as had Spain and Portugal, the Italians and Germans were able to shut them out of Christian society by enclosing them in ghettos, while still adding to the princely coffers. The ghetto Jews were heavily taxed, with the few wealthy among them provid-ing funds to sustain the rest of the community.

Many of the wealthier Jews in the ghettos came from families that had made money through trade, banking, or moneylending, and they managed to continue these activities. Most other people lived in poverty, eking out their living as shopkeepers, pawnbrokers, or dealers in secondhand goods.

Shops and pawnbrokerages usually occupied the first floor of ghetto buildings, with living quarters above them. As the population increased, new stories were added to the buildings, and so much weight placed on wobbly foundations that they sometimes collapsed.

A visitor to the old ghetto quarters of Venice today can still see these early "skyscrapers" with their uneven stories and windows cut almost haphazardly into the walls. Synagogues usually occupy the top floors. Though some are lavishly decorated inside, they are almost hidden from the outside, originally designed to be protected from Christian harassment.

Within the ghettos, people lived lives as normal as possible, celebrating the Sabbath and holidays and attending synagogues and study halls. Venetian Jews became highly organized in their ghetto, with numerous societies to care for community needs. Roman Jews suffered greater hardships, located as they were under the watchful eyes of the papacy.

Later, some people romanticized the ghettos as a positive force that insulated Jewish life against incursions from the outside. Indeed, when ghetto walls began to fall, there were rabbis who shook their heads in dismay, fearing that open contact with non-Jews would dilute Jewish observance and practice. Many of their fears did come true, of course, but the new freedoms Jews enjoyed also led to new bursts of creativity that had been impossible within the oppressive confines of the ghettos.

The Venetian ghetto came to an end in 1797, after French forces under Napoleon invaded Italy and tore down all ghetto walls. The Roman ghetto was rebuilt after Napoleon's defeat in 1815, but finally abolished with the end of papal rule in 1870.

When less than a century later the Nazis resurrected the walled ghetto in Europe, they used as precedents some of the dress codes and humiliating restrictions of earlier days. But the German ghettos had a much more sinister purpose—not to confine Jews to one area but to herd them together as a first step toward liquidating them. Compared to them, the Venice ghetto seems almost benign. Yet a thin line connects one to the other, both motivated by contempt for Jews.

The Tenth Day of Nisan

MIRIAM THE PROPHETESS DIES

The Miriam we encounter in the Bible is an elusive figure, emerging from the shadows at crucial moments in Israel's history, then disappearing again. Those few appearances, however, set her apart so radically from other women in the five books of Moses that some critics believe they are based on a more fully developed tradition about her that was lost over time. In tantalizing hints we see Miriam as her brother's protector, as the leader of women in song and dance, and as a prophet of influence. We may never retrieve the narrative of her life, but as if to compensate for the loss, the midrash surrounds her story with rich interpretations and warm fantasies. At its most beautiful, it connects Miriam with a miraculous well that nurtured the Israelites throughout their long trek in the desert.

The legends stretch back to her early years before the birth of Moses, in fact, giving Miriam credit for that birth.

The biblical story opens with the words "A certain man of the house of Levi went and married a Levite woman" (Exodus 2:1), referring to Moses' parents, Amram and Jochebed. "Where did he go?" asked Rabbi Judah ben Zebina, and answered, "He went and followed the advice of his daughter." What was that advice? After Pharaoh decreed that all newborn males must be drowned in the river, Amram and other Hebrew men despairingly divorced their wives to avoid having children. Miriam chastised her father, saying that his decree was even harsher than Pharaoh's, for Pharaoh's edict affected only males, whereas Amram's affected males and females. Miriam also prophesied that one day her mother would have a son who would redeem Israel.

Urged by his daughter, Amram remarried Jochebed, and Miriam and her brother Aaron danced at the wedding. Moses was born from the remarriage.

The biblical narrative picks up: Jochebed hides Moses in a basket among the reeds of the Nile and his sister stands at a distance to watch over him. When she sees that Pharaoh's daughter has discovered the child, she offers to find a Hebrew nurse to suckle him. The nurse, of course, is her mother, and as a result of Miriam's intervention, Pharaoh's daughter ends up paying Jochebed to nurse her own son.

Miriam protects her brother at the Nile River, and years later she joins him in a song of triumph at another body of water, the Red Sea. The Israelites have crossed that sea safely, and now the waters close in on the Egyptians pursuing them. Miriam takes a timbrel and leads the women in a victory dance, singing aloud the refrain Moses and the men had sung a few minutes earlier. Here, for the first time, Scripture refers to her as "Miriam the prophetess," a personage in her own right (Exodus 15:20). The juxtaposition of Miriam's singing with her title as a prophet has led modern critics to believe that women's prophecy often took the form of song and poetry. They also suggest that Miriam's refrain became the foundation upon which the entire Song at the Sea was built.

Unfortunately, Scripture gives us no details about Miriam's prophetic skills, but they seem to be at the root of the darkest period in her life, for in her next appearance she is vying in prophecy with Moses. She and Aaron have been whispering to each other, first against the "Cushite" wife Moses married and then against his leadership. "Has the Lord spoken only through Moses?" they say. "Has He not spoken through us as well?" (Numbers 12:2).

Their complaints about Moses' wife are unclear. Zipporah, the wife we know of, came from Midian, not Cush, which is usually identified as Ethiopia (although some sources do place Cush within Midianite borders). Their criticism seems to have an ethnic edge, for the Cushites were black, yet in other places both the Bible and Talmud identify blackness with beauty and specialness.

Enter the midrash. Here the talk is not directed against Zipporah but in her favor. Zipporah has told Miriam that from the day Moses descended from Mount Sinai, filled with holiness, he has not had sexual relations with her. Worried that her brother will stop procreating, Miriam speaks to Aaron about the situation. Thus the text says, "Miriam and Aaron spoke . . ." (Numbers 12:1), placing Miriam's name first and using the feminine form of the verb in Hebrew to indicate that she instigated the discussion. As she did with her parents, Miriam concerned herself once again with strengthening her family's domestic life.

But in this account the midrash ignores the second, more significant part of the siblings' grumblings, their protest against Moses' privileged position in relation to God. That complaint suggests that they did not wish to be subservient to Moses, for they were also recognized among the people as prophets. It is another hint that Miriam held a more prominent position as an Israelite leader than the Bible spells out.

For her jealousy and criticisms of Moses, God punishes Miriam with leprosy—and women through the ages have objected to that one-sided punishment that strikes Miriam but not Aaron, her partner in talebearing. Aaron pleads with Moses for help from God for their sister. (*His* punishment may be his need to entreat his younger brother—whom he addresses as "my lord"—rather than speak to God directly himself.) Moses utters a poignant short prayer, "O God, pray heal her!" (Numbers 12:13), which the rabbis considered a model of what a short prayer should be. But God only partially relents.

The episode ends with Miriam, shamed, staying outside the camp with other lepers, while out of respect for her the people do not resume their journey until her illness heals and she returns. The midrash softens the scence by adding that because Miriam had waited at the riverbank years earlier to guard her infant brother, she is rewarded in her time of trouble by having all of Israel wait for her.

The exuberant Miriam who danced with her timbrel at the Red Sea is gone. Her name, sometimes associated with the Hebrew word *mar*, for "bitter," may refer to the bitterness she suffered because of her humiliation. The biblical narrative tells us nothing more except that she dies and is buried at a place called Kadesh. Tradition places her death on the tenth of Nisan.

Immediately following Miriam's death, we learn that the Israelites have no water and blame Moses for their situation. Once more the midrash moves in to enlarge the picture, this time to tie Miriam's death to that lack of water. For Miriam's sake, the sages said, a wondrous well was created in the magical twilight of the eve of the first Sabbath at the end of Creation. It resembled a rock in the form of a beehive, and it accompanied the tribes wherever they went, watering the desert lands they inhabited. From it came all the good things the Israelites enjoyed—fruits, vegetables, trees, even wine. But on the day Miriam died the well dried up, leaving the people without water.

Rashi goes a step further. In the biblical text, Moses strikes a rock to get water from it, disobeying God's command to speak to the rock, and thereby forfeiting his right to enter the Promised Land. That rock was Miriam's well, Rashi says, and Moses struck it in grief and anger at his sister's death, not really wanting to draw water for the clamoring Israelites.

Chancellor Ismar Schorsch of the Jewish Theological Seminary adds a modern midrash. Miriam had sustained Moses all his life—from his infancy to the crossing of the Red Sea and through the difficult desert years. Her death left him depleted, deprived of the sisterly support that had meant so much to him. Without her, he lost the compassion necessary to be an effective leader, and therefore lost his leadership.

The sages taught that despite the difficulties of Miriam's life, it ended, like that of her brothers Moses and Aaron, with a kiss of God. And although we may never know all of her story, we know that she left her mark on the history of Israel. For, said the prophet Micah in God's name, "I brought you up from the land of Egypt / I redeemed you from the house of bondage, / And I sent before you / Moses, Aaron, and Miriam" (6:4).

Shabbat HaGadol—the Great Sabbath

The Sabbath immediately before Passover is known as the Great Sabbath, *Shabbat HaGadol*, a prelude to this grand and pivotal festival on the Jewish calendar. On this Sabbath, rabbis in many lands preach long sermons that focus on the meaning and laws of the holiday and the details of its preparation. In many Orthodox synagogues, the congregation returns in the afternoon to study with the rabbi from the Haggadah, the basic Passover text. The name Great Sabbath may have come from the length of the rabbi's sermon and the intensity of the teachings on this day.

Tradition also connects the name with a Sabbath that fell on the tenth day of the month of Nisan in the year of the Exodus. Scripture says that God commanded every Israelite family to choose a lamb on that day, preparatory to sacrificing it on the fourteenth of the month, the eve of the last plague. According to the sages, the Egyptians worshipped the lamb as a god. By choosing a lamb as a paschal sacrifice, the Israelites took their first step toward defying the Egyptians and breaking the bonds of slavery. They also turned their backs on idolatry, for in slaughtering the lamb, they symbolically subdued the Egyptian gods. Therefore the Sabbath in which they selected their lamb for sacrifice became a Great Sabbath, and every Sabbath before Passover thereafter bears the same title.

But the most likely source for the term Great Sabbath is the prophet Malachi, whose words are read on this Sabbath before the festival: "Lo, I will send the prophet Elijah to you before the coming of the great and awesome day of the Lord" (3:23). In Jewish lore, Elijah will herald the arrival of the Messiah, and according to some reckonings, both will appear in the month of Nisan. This Sabbath is special because it introduces the theme of messianic redemption that will crop up time and again throughout the holiday of redemption now on the horizon.

The Thirteenth Day of Nisan

THE SEARCH FOR LEAVENED BREAD

A wooden spoon, a wax candle, and a chicken feather are the basic utensils needed for the first major ritual of Passover, the search for leavened bread, known in Hebrew as *bedikat hametz.*

Paradoxically, the search takes place in a Jewish home after it has been thoroughly cleansed of leavened goods—the *hametz*—and readied for Passover. To follow the reasoning behind this act, we have to begin with the prohibition against hametz during Passover.

The law comes from the Bible: "Seven days you shall eat unleavened bread . . . no leavened bread shall be found with you, and no leaven shall be found in all your territory." It continues, "And you shall explain to your child on that day, 'It is because of what the Lord did for me when I went free from Egypt' " (Exodus 13:6–8).

In the biblical narrative, unleavened bread, or *matzah*, represents the deliverance from Egyptian slavery because the Israelites fled that land so quickly there was not time for their bread to rise. The bread they ate was the flat, hard matzah.

In reality, the commandment to eat unleavened bread in celebrating Passover is given before the actual departure from Egypt and may originally have had other meanings. Some scholars believe it was connected to an ancient Israelite agricultural festival distinct from Passover, a Feast of Unleavened Bread that celebrated the start of the spring grain harvest. Unleavened bread was also used in sacrifices offered on the Temple altar, possibly to signify a break with pagan rituals that included leavened products. But at some point, matzah became the central historical symbol of Passover, a reminder of the triumphant and hurried Exodus from Egypt, and the holiday as a whole was given the name *Hag HaMatzot*, the Feast of Unleavened Bread. Because of the significance of matzah, not only did it have to be eaten during the holiday but its opposite, hametz, had to be discarded and shunned.

Accordingly, the rabbis set stringent rules for cleansing one's home of hametz. They defined hametz as bread or other products made from grains that ferment when they decompose, and specified five kinds of grain: wheat, barley, spelt, rye, and oats. Later, rabbis in Germanic lands added rice, beans, peas, corn, and peanuts to this list, foods from which forms of flour can be made that might be confused with the forbidden types. Spanish authorities did not outlaw these foods, so that it is still possible to have a Passover meal in a Sephardic Jewish home that includes items prohibited in an Ashkenazic one.

The rules against hametz extend to all utensils that have in any way come into contact with leavened foods, leading to the whirl of Passover housecleaning that may go on for weeks before the holiday. It involves using different dishes for the holiday from those used during the rest of the year, "kashering" pots and silverware to make them fit for Passover use, and systematically cleaning every room of a home in which hametz may have been eaten or used.

Furthermore, in order to keep quantities of packaged or canned leavened foodstuffs in the home that would be too wasteful to throw out, the owner must enter into a legal transaction with a non-Jew. Following a set formula, the Jew symbolically sells the family hametz to the non-Jew, who signs a bill of sale that officially transfers its ownership. After the holiday, the Jew officially buys back the hametz. In many communities, rabbis handle these transactions for groups of their congregants. All such leavened goods that remain in the home during the festival need to be separated and sealed off from Passover foods and utensils.

The search for leavened bread is the culmination of the entire painstaking process of cleaning, selling, changing dishes, and clearing out all hametz from the home.

The ceremony takes place in the evening, after sundown. A family member (often the mother) scatters bread crumbs on the windowsills of several rooms. The kabbalists introduced the practice some people still follow of using exactly ten pieces of bread, to represent the ten sefirot, the manifestations of God's holiness here on earth. By the light of a candle, parents and children hunt for the bread crumbs, sweeping them with a feather into a wooden spoon and then dropping them into a paper bag. When all the crumbs have been gathered, family members place the spoon and feather in the bag with the hametz and recite a formula that has come down to us in Aramaic:

"All leaven in my possession, which I have not seen or removed, or of which I am unaware, is hereby nullified and considered ownerless as the dust of the earth."

The next morning, usually between ten and eleven o'clock, they burn the bag of leaven and repeat a variation of the formula. No hametz may be brought into the home after this, and none eaten outside the home from noon on. That does not mean that everyone immediately begins to consume matzah instead. Matzah may not be eaten until the seder that evening so that it will seem a fresh and novel food for the holiday. Other foods may be eaten, however.

Throughout the Passover preparations, hametz and matzah are played off against each other in almost mystical fashion, the antithesis of one another yet strangely alike even in their differences. In the Bible, the negative ban on hametz is balanced by the positive commandment to eat matzah. Legally, matzah must be made only from the same five species of grain that form hametz (although in practice wheat is generally used). The matzah differs from the hametz in that it is not permitted to ferment. Therefore its dough—made of flour and water—must be kneaded and baked in less than eighteen minutes, the amount of time it takes fermentation to start according to rabbinic calculation.

Even the Hebrew words *hametz* and *matzah* are related. Their letters are identical, except for the *het* in *hametz* and the *he* in *matzah*. This shows us how quickly matzah dough can turn into hametz if its baking is delayed even a moment too long, the sages taught.

In rabbinic thought, the dichotomy between hametz and matzah extends beyond food to a deeper, more symbolic, more personal meaning. Hametz stands for instability and corruption—the corruption of Egypt, the corruption that may come from too easy a life. The sage Rabbi Alexandri equated the yeast in dough with the evil impulse, the leaven that interferes with purity of heart and mind. And the first-century Jewish philosopher Philo of Alexandria saw in the prohibition against leaven a warning against overweening pride, a "puffing up" with arrogance that gets in the way of goodwill and humanity. In that sense, the search for leaven that begins the many rituals of the Passover holiday involves more than a wooden spoon, a wax candle, and a chicken feather. It may call for some inner researching as well.

The Fourteenth Day of Nisan

PESAH EVE—THE FIRST SEDER

What is it about *Pesah*—Passover—that has made it the most widely celebrated of all Jewish holidays, even more than Rosh Hashanah or Yom Kippur? What is it that leads people who otherwise observe few rituals to stock their pantries with matzah and banish bread from their homes during the week of this festival? And what, as the eve of Passover draws near, makes seder invitations the hottest tickets in town—any town, anywhere that Jews live?

To be sure, this is the prime family festival of the Jewish calendar, gathering generations together around tables laden with symbolism and memories. Certainly the central holiday themes of freedom from bondage, of the victory of the downtrodden over their oppressors, make it compelling from one age to the next. But more than sentiment or history, more than family relationships or political assertiveness, there is in this holiday a pull of identity that draws in men and women from all parts of the religious spectrum and makes them feel at one with each other and their people.

A single sentence in the Haggadah, the seder manual, spurs that identification: "In every generation, let each individual feel as though he or she had actually gone forth from Egypt." The weeks of preparation, the special foods, the oft-repeated narrative of the Exodus from Egypt all converge on that one point of purpose—to see ourselves, each of us, as though we personally had been redeemed from slavery, headed toward freedom in our own land.

The text continues with a biblical verse: "And you shall tell your child on that day, 'It is because of what God did for me when I went out of Egypt' " (Exodus 13:8). The words are in the singular—"me," "I"—and as the seder progresses they move from metaphor to reality. We begin to understand in a very personal way the degradation of having been there, and to experience, if only for an evening, the wonder of having been rescued.

The word *Haggadah,* which literally means "telling," comes from that verse in Exodus, "And you shall tell . . ." The holiday is about telling the story and living its moments.

❖

The story, recounted in the Book of Exodus, begins in Egypt after the death of Joseph, when a new Pharaoh systematically enslaves and debases his descendants. In response to the slaves' cries, God sends Moses and his brother Aaron to the Pharaoh to seek their freedom. Ten plagues torment the Egyptians before Pharaoh bends to God's will. The tenth and most terrible strikes at midnight on the fifteenth of Nisan, wiping out the firstborn throughout Egypt but sparing all the Israelites. Totally defeated, not only does Pharaoh consent to free the Hebrew slaves, he and the Egyptians hurry them out for fear of further death and destruction.

In anticipation of that final plague, Moses commands the Israelites to prepare an offering to God on the fourteenth of Nisan of one lamb per family. After slaughtering the lamb, they are to sprinkle some of its blood on the lintel and doorposts of their homes to distinguish them from the homes of the Egyptians, where the deaths of the firstborn will occur.

The holiday name Pesah stems from the events of that evening. In its most commonly accepted translation, one that the Mishnah uses, its root means "skipped over," or "passed over," and refers to the passing over of the Israelite homes when Egypt's firstborn were struck down; hence the English name Passover. A lesser-known translation defines the term to mean "straddling," and refers to God as straddling across the Israelite homes to guard and protect them from the deadly plague.

In this explanation, the lamb slaughtered on the evening of the fourteenth was a "protective offering" to save the Israelite firstborn.

In honor of the salvation of Israel's firstborn, the firstborns in Jewish families are expected to fast on Passover eve. A lovely custom overrides the fast, however, for those who participate in it. A tractate of the Talmud is completed in the synagogue on that morning and celebrated, as such completions are, with a joyful meal. Fulfilling the obligation of eating that meal, called *se'udat mitzvah*, frees firstborns of the obligation to fast.

❖

In Temple times, thousands of people made pilgrimages to Jerusalem each year to offer a paschal sacrifice on the fourteenth of Nisan. A priest would burn parts of the lamb on the Temple altar and families would eat the remainder at a celebratory meal. Sometime after the destruction of the Second Temple in 70 C.E., when the sacrifice of animals had ceased, the seder meal on Passover eve became the centerpiece of the festival.

A seder follows in form the symposium of ancient Greece and Rome. That was a banquet at which guests reclined on couches or pillows, drank wine, and engaged in intellectual discourse. At an early time, perhaps even before the Temple fell, Jewish families knowledgeable about Hellenistic customs probably adapted some of them to their Passover meals, but they also imbued those customs with new, Jewishly significant meanings.

Thus participants recline on pillows as a sign of luxury and freedom, far removed from the humble manner in which the Hebrew slaves had to eat. The Mishnah underlines the importance of this symbolism by ruling that "even a poor person in Israel may not eat until he reclines." (In many homes, the leader reclines in token representation of others at the table.) Four glasses of wine are ritually prescribed and sanctified at the seder service, and discourse does not concern general philosophic ideas but focuses on the Haggadah and the details of the departure from Egypt.

The seder has its own internal order; the term, in fact, means "order." Before it even begins, a plate is set on the table displaying holiday symbols:

—A roasted shank bone represents the paschal sacrifice given at the Temple, and a roasted hard-boiled egg commemorates a holiday offering made at the same time. Some people regard the egg as a symbol of mourning for the destruction of the Temple. Some feminists add roasted fish and interpret all three cooked items as representing Moses, Aaron, and Miriam, the three leaders of the Exodus.

—Bitter herbs, known as *maror*, stand for the bitterness of the slaves' lives. Families usually use horseradish for this symbol.

—A sticky mixture of fruit, nuts, and wine, *haroset*, reminds participants of the mortar the Israelites used when making bricks for Pharaoh's buildings. Sephardic recipes often call for dates or figs, Ashkenazic ones nearly always for apples. Sweet and delicious, haroset is most people's favorite symbol and is eaten together with the maror to temper its bitterness.

—A vegetable such as celery or parsley, called *karpas,* will be dipped into salt water, symbolizing the salty tears the slaves shed.

—Salt water or vinegar for dipping is often placed alongside the other items.

—Three slices of matzah are set apart from the other symbols. They recall the two hallah breads used on the Sabbath and festivals, with the addition of the third matzah for Passover. At the seder, many traditional families use *matzah shemurah,* unleavened bread that may be hand-baked or machine-made but whose wheat has been meticulously watched from the time of harvest. (Some people praise its nutty texture and taste; some think it tastes like cardboard.)

Early in the ceremony, the leader breaks the middle matzah, wraps it in a napkin, and hides it to be used as the *afikoman,* the dessert, or final dish eaten. Traditionally, the children "steal" the afikoman and bargain with the adults for its return, for the seder may not be concluded without it— a technique designed to keep the young engaged.

A more serious form of engaging the young—and the older—is through questions and discussions revolving around the Haggadah. The obligation to question has its roots in the biblical verse "And when your children ask you, 'What do you mean by this rite?' you shall say . . ." (Exodus 12:26). A child symbolically fulfills that obligation for all present by reciting the four questions, the *Mah Nishtanah,* beginning with the famous words "How is this night different from all other nights?" A talmudic anecdote tells of the brilliant fourth-century Babylonian rabbi Abbaye, who as a child at his uncle Rabbah's seder asked why they had moved the table before dinner was served. Rabbah exclaimed, "Your question has exempted us from asking the Mah Nishtanah."

Rabbah was saying that curiosity about every aspect of the holiday is what counts, and Abbaye's simple question began the process of seeking answers.

In keeping with this theme, the Haggadah introduces four children, each with a different mode of inquiry: the wise, the wicked, the simple, and the child who does not know how to ask. The obligation of the parent is to speak to each according to his or her ability to understand, and to reprimand the wicked, the one who turns away and does not want to understand.

Ritually, the answers to the children's questions come from reading the Haggadah together. In reality, a child or grownup seeking direct responses to queries will never find them here. Instead the text meanders, from the story of Israel's slavery and its even-earlier worship of idols, to anecdotes about various sages, to the recitation of the ten plagues and a description of Egypt's defeat. The rabbis describe the pattern of salvation as beginning with the "shameful tale" (of bondage) and ending with the "praiseworthy narrative" (of freedom). Yet, by the time the reading ends, and even if they have not absorbed every word, all who are around the table know they have reexperienced an amazing epic in Jewish history.

❖

Toward the end of the evening, after the meal has been eaten, the grace recited, and a third cup of wine drunk, a participant opens the front door. All others stand and recite the words, "Pour out Your wrath upon the nations that know You not . . . for they have devoured Jacob" (Psalm 79:6–7). They are harsh words, probably composed after the destruction of the Second Temple and added to the Haggadah during the Crusades in the eleventh century to express the harshness of Israel's sufferings and its anger at those who would persecute and enslave it.

Throughout the seder proceedings, Elijah's cup, filled with wine, stands in the middle of the seder plate. The rabbis disagreed on whether four or five cups of wine should be drunk at the seder. They compromised by having four cups but including a fifth—Elijah's cup—filled but not drunk.

But the cup symbolizes more. Legend says that when the door is opened for the recitation of "Pour out Your wrath," the prophet Elijah comes through it to visit every Jewish home. In folklore, he will punish those enemies who have caused Israel pain. In rabbinic thought, he will announce the arrival of the Messiah. So while children watch his cup to see whether it is being invisibly drained of wine, adults view the filled cup as a beacon of possibilities, the promise of a future redemption that will complete the redemption of the past.

The Fifteenth Day of Nisan

PESAH, THE FIRST DAY

On the day Isaac was born, the sun shone in the sky as it never had before and never would again, the sages said, not until we experience the world to come. That day, the fifteenth of Nisan, later became the first day of Passover.

In Scripture, Isaac is the most enigmatic of the three patriarchs, a seemingly passive figure overshadowed by both his father, Abraham, and his son Jacob. The crucial event of his life is his near death at his father's hands. After that we read little about him until he reaches old age. Then, practically blind, he allows himself to be tricked into giving his blessing to his younger son, Jacob, instead of his elder and favorite, Esau.

Yet behind the sketchiness of his life story we can find glimmers of empathy and humanity in Isaac that we do not see in the other patriarchs.

The only child of Abraham and Sarah, he grew up fiercely protected by his mother and deeply attached to her. At her insistence Abraham cast his concubine, Hagar, and their son, Ishmael, out of his home, thus ensuring Isaac's position as his heir. The Bible records Sarah's death almost immediately after the story of Isaac's binding on the altar. The midrash ties the death to her shock and horror upon hearing of her son's trial, even though she knew he had been saved.

Isaac's grief at losing his mother is revealed in a passage poignant in its brevity. When he marries his cousin Rebekah he takes her into Sarah's tent, and, the text says, "Isaac loved her, and thus found comfort after his mother's death" (Genesis 24:67).

Perhaps it was that mother love which made Isaac particularly sensitive to his wife's longings for a child. Abraham's only response to Sarah's barrenness had been to accept her offer to take her maidservant Hagar as his concubine. Jacob grew impatient with his wife Rachel when she cried out, "Give me children, or I shall die" (Genesis 30:1). But when Rebekah was barren, Isaac "pleaded with the Lord on behalf of his wife," and his pleas were answered (Genesis 25:21). Unlike the other patriarchs, Isaac never took a second wife or a concubine.

The tradition criticizes Isaac for preferring Esau over Jacob, viewing his blindness in that sense as spiritual as well as physical, but its praise for him far outweighs any criticism. His courage and faith as a young boy ready to be sacrificed on the altar made him a model of religious devotion and piety. Indeed, the midrash connects his blindness to his dreadful trauma. As Abraham lifted his knife to his son, the angels wept for Isaac, it says, and their tears, falling into his eyes, dimmed them forever.

In Christian iconography, Isaac became the precursor of Jesus, who was actually sacrificed on the cross, but whose resurrection was prefigured by Isaac's rescue from death. Like Isaac, Jesus is also associated with the paschal lamb, in his case offered up to atone for the sins of the people. The crucifixion of Jesus, considered to have occurred during the Passover festival, reinforces that association.

Tragically, the connections between Jesus, Isaac, and the sacrifice of the paschal lamb became the source of terror and misery for Jews of many lands during the Passover festival. Throughout the Middle Ages, Christian communities accused Jews of slaughtering non-Jewish children and using their blood in various Passover rituals. These blood libels, as they came to be called, originated in the idea that, having been responsible for Jesus' death, the Jews now wished to crucify Christian children in cruel imitation of it. Eventually the accusations became less centered on the crucifixion than on the use of Christian blood in Jewish ceremonies, particularly in baking matzah.

For centuries, in one community after another, Christians tortured and massacred Jews during the first day of Passover or the days leading up to it. In Russia and other East European countries the blood libels continued into the twentieth century. Later, the Nazis incorporated them into their war against the Jews.

Time and again, as they suffered the blood libels, Jews identified with Abraham and Isaac in their test of faith. Often they saw their own misery as exceeding that of the ancient fathers, for their children *did* actually die on the altars of their beliefs. But they also sought comfort and succor in Isaac's ultimate salvation.

Despite the anguish that so often surrounded the Passover season, the holiday itself never became a time of bitterness or mourning. It always remained what it is today, a celebration of faith and freedom.

For Orthodox and Conservative families outside Israel, that celebration stretches into a second seder on the second night of the festival. The rituals are the same as those of the first seder, the blessings repeated, the songs sung again. But for some families, the second night becomes a time to focus on one or another aspect of the seder.

The Haggadah itself, for example, is the most popular of all Jewish books, with contents that reflect the strength and richness of Jewish life over time. It holds verses from the Bible, tales from the midrash, and poems from the Middle Ages. Recent editions often also include memorials to victims of the Holocaust. Many of the ceremonies in the Haggadah are described in the Mishnah, indicating that its basic form—and the order of the seder—must have been set by the time the Mishnah was redacted, about 200 C.E.

In every region in which Jews lived they produced Haggadahs, and they translated the work into every language they spoke. The oldest known Haggadah dates to the tenth century, when it was included in the prayer book of Saadia Gaon, leader of the Jewish community in Babylonia. Later Haggadahs were produced as separate manuscripts and often lavishly illustrated.

The first known printed Haggadah was published in Guadalajara, Spain, in 1482. Since then thousands of editions have appeared, and dozens of variations on it have been created. There have been Reform and Reconstructionist Haggadahs, Communist and Zionist ones, Haggadahs for soldiers fighting in the Second World War, and others in support of Jews in the former Soviet Union. More recently Haggadahs for gays, feminists, environmentalists, and other special-interest groups have become popular.

One intriguing feature of the traditional Haggadah is its delight in the number four. We read the four questions, ponder the four children, and drink four cups of wine.

Why the fours? The rabbis associated the four cups with God's four expressions of redemption in the Exodus narrative (Exodus 6:6–7): "I will free you," "I will deliver you," "I will redeem you," and "I will take you." (Some commentators connect a fifth expression, "I will bring you" [6:8] with Elijah's cup, and relate it to Israel's return to its land.)

The four children and four questions derive from four biblical passages that instruct the Israelites on how to teach their children about the Exodus. They are Exodus 12:26–27, 13:8, and 13:14, and Deuteronomy 6:20–21.

All the fours in the Haggadah allude to other fours in the tradition. Four generations of Israelites dwelt in Egypt, beginning with Jacob and his family and ending with Moses. After the Exodus the tribes grouped themselves in the wilderness into four camps under four different banners. Four empires enslaved Israel—Egypt, Babylonia, Persia, and Greece—and from all of them it was redeemed. And four matriarchs, Sarah, Rebekah, Rachel, and Leah, add merit to the Jewish people.

❖

Although the first and second seders are alike in almost every respect, one additional element in the Haggadah is included in the second seder. That is counting the *Omer,* which begins on the second night. The ritual opens with a benediction, and then participants recite, "Today is the first day of the Omer."

The Omer, which literally means "sheaf," was a barley offering brought to the Temple on the second day of Passover to mark the start of the grain harvest season. The Bible mandates counting forty-nine days from the beginning of this harvest to the time when the wheat crops would ripen. The fiftieth day would celebrate the wheat harvest with an offering of two loaves of bread. That day became the festival of Shavuot, the Feast of Weeks, and a time to celebrate not only the harvest, but—more important—the giving of the Torah.

Counting the Omer, known in Hebrew as *sefirat haOmer,* connects the two holidays, Passover and Shavuot, and links the Exodus to the revelation on Mount Sinai. Throughout the Omer weeks, observant Jews count aloud each day as they did the first.

❖

At the second seder's close, everyone sings the Passover favorite "Had Gadya," the song of one kid, for the last time. Written in Aramaic, it is based on German and French folk songs and was probably designed to keep children alert. But commentators have found deeper meaning in the little goat devoured by creatures that, in turn, devour each other. They have identified it with Israel, oppressed by one nation after another. In the end, God redeems the kid by conquering the most powerful destroyer, the Angel of Death. In this meaning, the kid is reminiscent of Isaac, the lamb taken out to slaughter but rescued by God. Isaac's children, the rabbis said, would pass from kingdom to kingdom and sorrow to sorrow, until they, too, would finally triumph over those who would destroy them.

The Sixteenth Day of Nisan

THE CITIES OF SODOM AND GOMORRAH ARE DESTROYED

It was a shining moment in the patriarch Abraham's life. With unwavering courage he stood before the all-powerful Deity and argued on behalf of the cities of Sodom and Gomorrah that had been designated for destruction. "Will You sweep away the innocent along with the guilty?" he pleaded. And: "Shall not the Judge of all the earth deal justly?" (Genesis 18:23, 25). Underlying his argument, the sages saw a daring reminder to God of the need to temper justice with mercy: "If You want to have a world," they interpreted Abraham's words to mean, "You cannot exact strict justice, and if You want strict justice, You cannot have a world. If You do not give in a little, the world will not endure."

Abraham didn't stop with rhetoric. In a memorable scene, he bargained hard to save the lives of all the inhabitants of the cities for the sake of the few among them who might be innocent. At first he asked pardon for the cities if fifty righteous people could be found in them, then forty-five, forty, thirty, twenty, and finally ten. Each time, God acceded to his request, moved, perhaps, by the passion of a man bent on rescuing others without a shred of self-interest at stake.

Although we never witness a search for the righteous, Scripture makes it abundantly clear that they don't exist. When God's messengers arrive in Sodom and are welcomed into the home of Abraham's nephew Lot, they find themselves beleaguered by the townspeople. "Where are the men who came to you tonight?" the crowd shouts. "Bring them out to us, that we may be intimate with them" (Genesis 19:5). Lot tries to appease the people by offering his daughters instead of his guests, but they go after him, almost crushing him against the door of his home before the messengers rescue him.

In every respect possible, the inhabitants of Sodom and Gomorrah prove themselves unworthy of Abraham's eloquent defense. In fact, his selfless behavior sets their brutal and self-serving actions in sharp relief.

The text offers few details about the Sodomite sins aside from the scene at Lot's home and the information that news of the outrage of these cities had reached the heavens. But the sages elaborated on their perfidy extensively. These people, they said, were blessed with an extremely rich and fertile land, yet they resented the arrival of any traveler, lest the visitor use their holdings. To make their point, when a traveler did stop by, they would make him lie on an ill-fitting bed. If he was too short for it, they would pull and stretch his legs to make him fit it. If he was too long, they would try to jam him in and then lop off the part of his legs that hung over. Moreover, every townsperson would steal something from the visitor until the person was stripped bare of all posessions. But when the visitor accused them, each would claim, "What is the fuss about? I took only a trifle."

So selfish and mean-spirited were these people that they made it illegal in their town to help a poor or hungry person. Once a young woman took pity on a starving man and brought him bread that she hid in her pitcher. When she was discovered, the townspeople smeared her naked body with honey and placed her on a rooftop, where swarms of bees came and stung her to death. It was her anguished cries that finally led God to avenge the "outrage" of these cities.

In tradition, the blatant cruelty of the Sodomites built on a more subtle and insidious evil: the evil of shutting oneself off completely from the needs of others. The prophet Ezekiel described the Sodomite transgression as "arrogance! She and her daughters had plenty of bread and untroubled tranquillity; yet she did not support the poor and the needy" (16:49). The rabbis labeled as a "Sodom type" the person who says, "What's mine is mine and what's yours is yours." Although that may be a commonplace attitude, it is also the attitude of persons unwilling to share what they have or to do a good turn for others even at no cost to themselves.

With the cries of their victims filling the air and Abraham unable to turn up at least ten good people, God destroyed the cities of Sodom and Gomorrah in a burst of brimstone and fire. The midrash places the destruction at dawn on the sixteenth day of Nisan, when both the sun and the moon were visible in the sky. It was a time carefully chosen, for had the devastation taken place during the day the moon worshippers among the Sodomites might say, "If the moon had been there, it would have protected us." Had it taken place at night, the sun worshippers might say, "If the sun had been there, it would have saved us." Both luminaries were present when the cities were annihilated, and God ruled over both.

Connections can be made between the great Flood that wiped out all the earth generations earlier and the desolation of the evil cities. In both cases the cause of the punishment was profound moral corruption. In both cases only one person and his family survived: Noah, the Flood; and Lot, the destruction of Sodom and Gomorrah. Unlike Noah, however, Lot was singled out not for his own deeds but because of the merit of his uncle, Abraham.

Lot's deeds themselves are somewhat questionable. He had chosen to live in Sodom although it was known as a degenerate city. He extended great hospitality to God's messengers when they came to investigate his city, but he treated his daughters barbarically by offering them to the mob as sexual substitutes for his guests. We don't know anything about his wife except that as the family fled from the cataclysm she looked back and was transformed into a pillar of salt. Some traditional sources suggest that she turned around out of motherly concern to see if her daughters were following behind. Some contemporary feminists have pointed out that in the text Lot never actually informed her that she was not to look back, an order he received from the messengers.

In the last we hear of Lot, the sexual immorality to which he was willing to expose his daughters finds its counterpart in the sexual immorality they impose on him. Living alone with him in a cave after the downfall of their city, they believe themselves to be the only persons left on earth. To perpetuate human life, they plot to make their father drunk and have sexual relations with him. Each

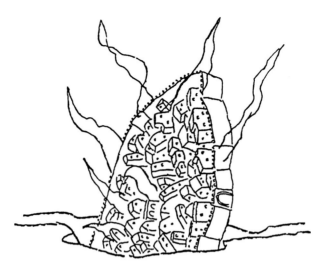

becomes pregnant from her incestuous union, and each gives birth to a son, one the progenitor of the people of Moab, the other of Ammon. Both peoples become Israel's enemies yet recognize a kinship with them.

It is a fitting ending to a story of sin and debasement, of chaos and destruction, of a people who insulated themselves from all human feelings and of a man whose humanity led him to plead the cause of the sinful along with the just. Centuries later, from the midst of the Moabite nation will come a woman who finds her way back to the children of Abraham and reties the kinship knot. She is Ruth, ancestor of the great King David, and her story is read during Shavuot, the next major holiday after Passover.

❖

The sixteenth of Nisan is the second day of Pesah, which Orthodox and Conservative Jews in the Diaspora observe as a holiday.

The Seventeenth through the Twentieth Days of Nisan

PESAH, THE DAYS BETWEEN

Like Sukkot, Pesah is a seven-day festival (eight days outside of Israel), with only the first and last appointed as holy days, when work is prohibited. Portions of the Hallel, the psalms of praise to God, are recited every day in the synagogue, along with special blessings that are also said on Sukkot and Shavuot. In these blessings, Pesah is referred to as *z'man heruteinu,* the "season of our liberation."

A custom of the intermediate days of Passover is for organizations to hold "third seders" that link a theme of the festival to the group's purpose. During the 1930s and '40s, Jews in the labor movement often conducted socialist seders in which participants sang labor songs and connected the struggles of working people to those of the Israelite slaves. Jews committed to the civil rights movement of the 1950s and '60s created "freedom seders," tying the cause of black liberation to the Exodus.

The most widespread of the thematic third seders have been feminist seders, which grew in popularity during the 1980s and '90s and are now held throughout the United States and in Israel (some of them during the week preceding Passover). Although they vary from place to place and year to year, these seders have in common the celebration of women of the Exodus, usually overlooked in traditional seders.

The stories of these women bear retelling, for while they appear only briefly in the first two chapters of the Book of Exodus, their influence underlies the entire freedom saga.

Foremost among them are two midwives, Shiphrah and Puah. The text describes them as "Hebrew midwives," leaving it unclear whether they were Hebrews themselves or Egyptian midwives to the Hebrew women. What is clear is that they disobeyed Pharaoh's orders to kill every male child born to the Hebrew women in his attempt to decimate the Israelite population. Instead, "they let the boys live" (Exodus 1:17), which commentators define as not only refraining from killing the children but helping to keep them alive by gathering food and water for those who were weak.

The defiance of these women may be the first recorded instance in history of civil disobedience in the name of a higher cause. Scripture attributes their resistance to their fear of God. They were also courageous women, and shrewd. To explain why they could not destroy the newborn males, they claimed that the Hebrew women were so "lively" (Exodus 1:19) they gave birth quickly before anyone could intervene. The Hebrew word used for "lively" is *hayot*, which can also mean animal-like. By implying that the Israelite women were like animals, or more earthy than the delicate Egyptian women, the midwives played to Pharaoh's own denigrating views of the slave people, making it easy for him to accept their excuse.

Two other main characters in the Exodus drama, Moses' mother, Jochebed, and his sister, Miriam, demonstrated their own form of cunning. After Pharaoh decreed that all Hebrew baby boys be thrown into the river, Jochebed did indeed place her son in the river, but in a wicker basket prepared to protect him. In that way she fulfilled Pharaoh's orders and at the same time mocked him. The river became a source of life, not death, for Moses.

Miriam joined her mother in foiling Pharaoh, compounding the joke on him by convincing his own daughter unknowingly to engage the baby's mother as a wet nurse. Miriam is recalled at feminist seders with a goblet of water placed on the table as a counterpoint to Elijah's cup. The water stands for Miriam's miraculous well, which nurtured the Israelites in the desert.

Pharaoh's daughter took pity on the babe she found in the basket, and in doing so, she rescued and then reared the child who would grow to defeat her father and free the people he enslaved. A midrash teaches that as a reward, the name Moshe, which she gave her adopted son, became the name by which he would always be called, even by God. She herself received the name Bithia, which means "daughter of God."

Besides these individual women, legend portrays the courage of the Israelite women as a group. Pharaoh forbade the Israelite men to return home at the end of the day, forcing them to sleep in the fields, lest they lose a moment's work time. What did the women do? They went into the fields and fed and washed their exhausted husbands and cohabited with them in order to bear children. Thus they thwarted Pharaoh's attempts to cut off the Hebrew people.

Because of these and other acts, the rabbis said: "Israel was redeemed from Egypt on account of the righteous women of that generation." Feminist seders pay tribute to the righteous women and explore the festival from a much-neglected female perspective.

❖

Women are featured again in a totally different context during the intermediate days: in the reading of the Song of Songs, particularly in Ashkenazic synagogues and usually on the Sabbath of Passover. (Some people also read it at the end of the first seder.)

One of the puzzles of the Hebrew Bible has always been why the Song of Songs was included in the holy canon. It is, after all, a collection of love songs—erotic love songs at that—between a woman and man. The woman, known as the Shulamite, is strong and direct about her love. She invites her lover to her "garden," goes after him when he has left her, celebrates her own sexuality and his. She and other women whose songs are heard appear to be on an equal footing with men, to glory in their femaleness and to be loved and praised for it. For his part, the male lover is both tender and powerful, enthralled by his female partner and transported by sensual love.

The book never mentions God or religion, the Exodus, Sinai, or the Temple. It sings of spring and brides, of vineyards and mandrakes, and of the sweet fragrance of myrrh and frankincense. In every way, it seems a series of secular poems, some of them wedding songs, some exuberant expressions of physical passion.

Yet the great Rabbi Akiva stated: "The whole world is not worth the day on which the Song of Songs was given to Israel; for all the writings are holy, but the Song of Songs is the holiest of the holy."

To Akiva and other sages, the Song was an allegory of the love between God and Israel, so deep and binding that it could be unashamedly expressed in sensuous terms. Because King Solomon's name appears in the poems, the rabbis attributed them to him, making it easier to accept them as sacred writing.

In a study of the Song of Songs, the scholar Gerson D. Cohen gave the most cogent explanation for their religious stature. He raised the question of why it would have occurred to anyone in the first place to treat these blatantly erotic poems as allegory. He answered by pointing out that unlike other peoples, Israel had no fertility rites and no love goddesses to worship. It was also the only nation that had a relationship to its God that centered on exclusivity, an absolute fidelity between the people and their one Deity. The prophets expressed that fidelity in marital terms, speaking of Israel as God's wife and admonishing the people to be ever faithful. But the rabbis longed for a way to convey the love that went along with marriage and apply it to their love of the Torah and their yearning for God's love. The Song of Songs filled that need, serving as a metaphor for an intimate, intense, and loving dialogue between humans and God that no magic fertility rite could equal.

Chanted in a distinctive melody, the Song of Songs enhances the sense of springtime and joy that mark the Passover season and the deeper sense of identity with a tradition and a history that the holiday as a whole evokes.

The Twenty-first and Twenty-second Days of Nisan

PESAH, THE LAST DAYS—THE MIRACLE AT THE SEA

"The ocean sounds, O Lord / the ocean sounds its thunder, / the ocean sounds its pounding. Above the thunder of the mighty waters, / more majestic than the breakers of the sea / is the Lord, majestic on high" (Psalm 93:3–4).

Thus sings the Psalmist of the miracle at the sea, when God parted the waters of the Red Sea for the Israelites to pass through, then closed them again over the pursuing Egyptian army. That miracle stands out in Jewish memory as the most potent symbol of God's dominance over nature and nations, of the vastness of the victory over Egypt, and of the everlasting hope for a future redemption.

Tradition places it on the evening of the seventh day of Passover. Hence the Torah section that describes it is chanted in synagogue on that day along with the Song at the Sea celebrating it.

As told in the Book of Exodus, after the tenth plague Pharaoh and his subjects sent the Israelite slave people away, happy to rid themselves of the troubles that had befallen them. No sooner had they left, however, then Pharaoh changed his mind and gave chase, leading a corps of hundreds of warriors with horses and chariots. In a replay of the past, Scripture informs us that "the Lord stiffened the heart of Pharaoh" (Exodus 14:8), further motivating him in his evil designs as he had been motivated through all the plague episodes. In a presaging of the future, the Israelites quickly forgot the suffering they had left behind and, frightened by the advancing Egyptian army, blamed Moses for having taken them out of Egypt. Their accusations and complaints would be repeated time and again during their wilderness years.

Responding to the people's cries, the angel of God who had guided them in their journey from Egypt moved behind them, as did the pillar of cloud that had hovered before them. As a result, a mysterious denseness separated them from the advancing enemy forces, smothering the Egyptians in darkness but illuminating the night for the Israelites. The midrash tenderly compares God's actions to that of a father walking on the road with his son in front of him. If robbers come from the front, the father places his son behind him. If a wolf comes from behind, he places his son before him. If robbers come from the front and a wolf from behind, he carries his son in his arms. If the boy suffers from the sun, the father places a cloak over him. If the child is hungry, the father feeds him; if thirsty, he provides water. Thus God protected and sheltered the Israelites from the Egyptians.

And now the miracle occurred. Commanded by God, Moses lifted up his rod and held out his arm. Within seconds a strong east wind arose and continued to blow through the night. It was a wind reminiscent of the one that swept across the waters as the world was being created. This time the wind split the sea, forming one wall of water on the right and one on the left, with a path of dry land between for the people to cross. In synagogue, when the reader chants the biblical description of the walls of water, the entire congregation joins in on the words "on their right and on their left" (Exodus 14:22, 29), as though giving added weight to those monumental walls.

Legend says that at the moment the sea split, all the waters in the universe—in wells and pitchers, lakes and glasses—divided, too, not to return until the Israelites had passed through the sea. Moreover, the people entered into the midst of the waters, but they walked on dry ground. Mothers held their children by the hand and found whatever they needed available to feed and care for them.

Behind the Israelites, the Egyptian forces followed fiercely. But as they entered the sea, their chariot wheels became bogged down and unable to move. Moses held out his arm one more time and the sea waters returned to their natural state, drowning Pharaoh's entire army, chariots, steeds, and all. From the shore, the Israelites could see the bodies of the Egyptians being washed up, confirmation that their former masters had not retreated to the other side but were indeed defeated and lifeless.

In legend, again, the earth opened up and swallowed the dead, for in spite of the Egyptians' cruelty they were humans, and God wished to pay them the respect of being buried in the ground. (Because of their humanness, and out of deference for their loss also, Jews recite only a truncated form of the celebratory Hallel during the last days of Passover.)

Scholars cannot locate the exact body of water the Israelites crossed; in Hebrew it is called *Yam Suf,* or the Sea of Reeds, although tradition equates it with the Red Sea. Nor can anyone explain in naturalistic terms just what happened there. But from a biblical standpoint the Israelite victory at sea is tinged with irony and ablaze with the triumph of Israel's God.

In an irony meant to be noted, Pharaoh's tactics toward the Hebrews backfired to hurt him. He had thought to drown their children in the waters of the Nile. Instead, he and his warriors were destroyed by water.

In contrast to Pharaoh's fate, the waters bend to God's will in this narrative. A midrash tells of the sea's revolt when Moses tried to divide the waters. Following God's command, Moses ordered the sea to split itself. It refused. He raised his rod as he had been instructed to do, and still it refused. Finally the glory of God manifested itself before the sea, and quickly the waters divided themselves. When Moses asked the sea why it had defied him all along but obeyed orders now, it replied that God's presence and nothing else, not even Moses and his staff, could make its waters recede.

In ancient mythologies, gods or sea monsters ruled the waters, just as supernatural beings controlled all parts of nature. The sea's resistance to Moses may hint at traces of those old myths in Jewish legend. But the sea's final obeisance to God reaffirms the most basic of Jewish tenets: God's transcendence over all dimensions of the universe. That is the theme behind the miraculous crossing. It is also the explanation of how a band of slaves could emerge from the depths of the sea, reborn as a nation of free people.

❖

Outside of Israel, Orthodox and Conservative Jews observe an eighth day to Passover, on the twenty-second of Nisan. When it ends, people pack away their Pesah dishes and utensils for another year, and leaven and ordinariness enter life again.

The Twenty-seventh Day of Nisan

YOM HASHOAH—HOLOCAUST REMEMBRANCE DAY

For almost twenty years after World War II, few people, including Jews, focused on the devastation of European Jewry the war had wrought. The term *Holocaust* itself didn't come into usage until some time after the war, and not until the 1980s—when Claude Lanzmann produced his epic film *Shoah*—did large numbers of Jews in America become familiar with the Hebrew word *shoah*, "catastrophe," for that devastation.

Why the silence? Historians say that it often takes a people two or three decades to absorb the shock of a catastrophic event. In the case of the Holocaust, the enormity of the horror overwhelmed—still overwhelms—the mind. The barbarity of Nazi Germany and the unimaginable suffering of the Jews seemed—still seems—incomprehensible. As late as 1993, at the dedication of the Holocaust Museum in Washington, D.C., Elie Wiesel said, "It is not because I cannot explain that you won't understand, it is because you won't understand that I cannot explain."

Aside from that, Jews in America wanted to put the war behind them and normalize their lives as part of American society. They preferred not to call attention to what was different about them or to harp on an image of their people as victims. In Israel, also, the thrust was toward strength, toward building a state whose very existence would erase centuries-old images of Diaspora Jews at the mercy of the nations among whom they dwelt.

Survivors themselves couldn't speak about what they experienced. Today, children of survivors tell of their parents' uncontrollable fears of strangers or of noises in the night. They recall hearing bits and pieces of the terrible truths about their parents' lives, but never enough details to make sense of what they heard. As much as they could, the survivors tried to push away the past and to concentrate on creating new lives.

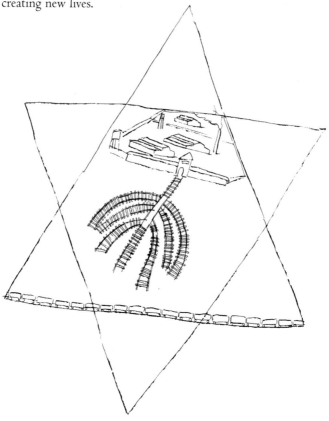

Only slowly, in the late 1950s and '60s, did survivors' stories begin to appear. Elie Wiesel's book *Night*, first published in France in 1958 and in the United States in 1960, made it possible for others to speak out. In Israel in 1961, the trial of Adolf Eichmann, the Nazi demon responsible for the death of millions of Jews, created awareness as never before of Nazi atrocities and the evil of their enterprise. For Jews, the trial opened discussion about the Holocaust that has continued to intensify with time.

Ten years earlier, on April 12, 1951, the Israeli Knesset had resolved to set aside a special day, the twenty-seventh of Nisan, as Holocaust and Ghetto Uprising Remembrance Day. For the most part, the resolution was ignored. In 1959, with interest in the Holocaust awakening, the government legislated public observance of the day. In 1961, the year of the Eichmann trial, it passed an amendment closing places of entertainment on this memorial day. After that, as the Holocaust rose closer to the surface of Jewish consciousness, the day became a fixed anniversary on the calendar.

How that specific anniversary date was chosen has a history of its own. Many people in Israel had wanted to memorialize the Warsaw Ghetto Uprising, which began on April 19, 1943, the first night of Passover. It had been the largest and longest-lasting of any Jewish uprising against the Nazis and the first wholly civilian resistance to them in all of occupied Europe. It held the Germans at bay for almost a month and cost them dearly in men and munitions. It also came to symbolize the isolation of the Jews, for the Warsaw rebels received few arms and little help even from Polish partisans who were themselves battling the Germans.

Certainly these ghetto fighters deserved tribute. But religious Jews bridled at the idea of a memorial on the first day of Passover, a season of joy when mourning is forbidden. Some rabbinic leaders urged that a general Holocaust commemoration be held on the tenth of Tevet, the fast day in memory of the ancient Babylonian siege of Jerusalem. That day had already been designated as the occasion to recite memorial prayers for Holocaust victims whose time of death was unknown. Others suggested incorporating Holocaust remembrances into Tisha B'Av, the day of mourning the destruction of the First and Second Temples.

The final, compromise date of the twenty-seventh of Nisan served several purposes. Falling as it does between the anniversary of the Warsaw Ghetto Uprising on the fifteenth of Nisan and Israel Independence Day on the fifth of Iyar, it commemorates the ghetto fighters, honors the memory of those who died in the camps, and points ahead to the rebirth that came with the founding of the State of Israel.

❖

Because the holiday is a relatively new one, no fixed rituals mark it. Many synagogues hold services in the evening at which congregants light yahrzeit (memorial) candles in memory of the six million. Often a survivor will read from a memoir or recount experiences that had been repressed for years. Often, also, the names of relatives of congregants who had been murdered in the camps are read aloud, the cadence of the names creating a poetry of mourning. In some communities, survivors' remembrances have been preserved on film or in writing, and are screened or read on this day.

The silence about the Holocaust has been broken for years now. Personal accounts and autobiographies stream into publishing houses, and aging survivors speak with urgency of the need to tell their histories before their lives end. Television programs and documentaries about the Holocaust appear regularly, and throughout the world, Holocaust memorials in the forms of museums, sculptures, bas-reliefs, or stone tablets have been created.

Yet, for many, the most moving form of remembrance is not a movie or television show, a monument or museum. It is the sound of a siren wailing. In Israel, sirens sound on Yom HaShoah; and when they do, all activity halts for a minute of silence. People look like figures in a wax museum forever caught in a moment of time as they stand immobilized, their thoughts riveted on the darkest period of Jewish history. Then the sirens sound again, the spell is broken, and the immobilized figures snap back to life. But the Holocaust has pierced their souls one more time.

IYAR
April–May

IYAR IS A MONTH OF COUNTING. First there is the counting of the Omer, which began on Passover and continues for forty-nine days until Shavuot. The entire month of Iyar falls within that counting period, starting with the sixteenth day of the Omer.

Then there is the first counting of the ancient Israelites in the desert after they left Egypt. The Book of Numbers opens with God commanding Moses to take a census of all males of twenty and up who are able to bear arms. Women and children are excluded, as are members of the tribe of Levi, whose role it is to care for the sanctuary, not to fight national battles. The census begins on the first day of the biblical second month and ends twenty days later, when more than 600,000 men have been counted.

The name Iyar itself bears no connection to numbers. It may stem from the Hebrew word *or,* meaning "light," and suggest the long days of light at this time of year. It is called *Ziv* in the Book of Kings, also signifying light. Legendary interpretations of its zodiac sign, however, tie it to darkness, not light.

The sign is Taurus, a black bull or ox, and in one somewhat convoluted interpretation it has a place in the Creation of the world. In this explanation, God began forming the world in the month of Nisan, not Tishrei. Satan, prince of darkness, demanded that darkness be the first element created. God refused, declaring that the world must first be illumined. So God created light and called it Day. Only then, as the second act of Creation, did God fashion darkness and call it Night. The white ram of Nisan, the first month, represents the light. The black ox, symbol of the dark, became the sign of the second month, Iyar.

The Fifth Day of Iyar
YOM HAATZMA'UT—ISRAEL INDEPENDENCE DAY

For anyone born after 1948 the State of Israel is a fact of life, an established nation among nations. Though it has lived under constant threats of war and been plagued by terrorist attacks, it is as much a reality as any of the world's nations, and more in the public eye than most.

It's difficult, therefore, for those who did not experience it to imagine what the world was like before the state was established. The image that comes to mind, far removed from politics yet somehow apt, is a scene from the movie *It's a Wonderful Life*, rerun on television every year during the winter holiday season. As the hero, played by Jimmy Stewart, contemplates suicide, his guardian angel shows him what his community would have been like had he not existed; what a bleak life friends and neighbors would have had were it not for him. For Jews of World War II and afterward (and for centuries earlier) the world was often a bleak place because it held no Jewish state. Had that state existed, the lives of millions of persons might have been different. Because it came into being, the lives of millions of others have been enhanced.

At the end of World War II, with European Jewry desolated by the Holocaust, world sympathy turned for the first time toward establishing a Jewish homeland in Palestine. Zionists, from Theodor Herzl in the 1890s to David Ben-Gurion in the 1940s, had been struggling for that homeland for decades. Much of the struggle came to be directed against Great Britain, which gained control of Palestine from the Ottoman Empire after World War I. Although the British had announced their support for a "national home for the Jewish people" in the Balfour Declaration of 1917, they reversed themselves in 1939. Responding to Arab demands, they issued a White Paper strictly limiting immigration into Palestine. Those limitations resulted in untold deaths of Jews trying to flee Nazi atrocities during World War II, yet barred from almost every country.

When the war ended, Zionists intensified their campaign to force Britain to open the doors of Palestine to Jews who had survived Hitler and the death camps and now found themselves homeless. The fate of the ship *Exodus 1947*, carrying 4,500 displaced persons, added to the pressure. When the ship tried to land in Palestine the British treated its passengers so cruelly, and returned them so callously first to France and then to Germany, that their plight attracted worldwide attention.

Finally, after the British took the question of Palestine to the United Nations General Assembly, a special committee recommended partitioning the country into independent Arab and

Jewish states. On November 29, 1947, the General Assembly, with a vote of 33 to 13, accepted the partition plan. Five months later, on Friday, May 14, 1948—the fifth of Iyar, 5708—at the Tel Aviv Museum, David Ben-Gurion read the Proclamation of Independence that created the State of Israel. Hours later, President Harry S. Truman recognized the new state on behalf of the United States, the first country to do so.

That is the background and those are the events that led to the creation of a Jewish homeland after almost two thousand years of exile and statelessness. The emotions, from the viewpoint of Diaspora Jews, are harder to set down on paper.

Controversy still rages about how much Jewish organizations in the United States and other free countries knew about the atrocities of the Holocaust and how much more they might have done to intervene. But however much they knew, throughout the war Jews as a whole felt devastated by the news from Europe yet helpless to stop the carnage. They pinned their hopes on an Allied victory, and increasingly came to believe that Jews must have a land of their own.

The war made Zionists of Jews who had barely identified themselves Jewishly along with those who had been deeply committed to the tradition. When the United Nations General Assembly began its roll call, Jews throughout the world collectively held their breaths and counted the votes. They responded with amazement and delight when the Soviet Union, no friend of the Jews or of Zionism, supported partition (motivated more by anti-British sentiments than pro-Israel ones). They shouted with joy when the motion for partition was passed, although the new state received tortuous and narrow borders.

The thrill of statehood turned almost instantly to anxiety when on the same day that the state was proclaimed five Arab nations invaded its territory. Numbers of young Jews from the United States and other lands rushed overseas to join the battle. Others worked to ship arms to the beleaguered country—illegal arms, because most nations had placed embargos on such shipments. A man who as a high school student had packed orange crates with guns recalled it as a "heady time." Finally, after the years of degradation, Jews had the ability to stand up to all the world.

Israel defeated the overwhelming Arab forces in a bitter war that cost countless lives before ending in 1949. As a result it was able to expand its borders beyond those originally allotted it. During the years that followed, and in spite of other wars and incessant terrorist attacks, it became what it set out to be: a homeland for Jews—from Yemen and Ethiopia, from Russia and the Arab lands, and for those born and raised in it.

In 1949, the Israeli Government declared *Yom HaAtzma'ut,* Independence Day, a legal holiday. Festivities begin on the evening before with a ceremony on Mount Herzl in Jerusalem in which torches are lit and a gun salute fired off. During the day, people celebrate with fireworks, parades, and song and dance festivals. An international Bible contest for young people is held; and at Hebrew University, government officials award prestigious cultural prizes. Jews in the United States generally mark the day with large parades, and in synagogues the Hallel is recited.

But there is another part to the event in Israel. The country observes the preceding day as *Yom HaZikkaron,* Remembrance Day, when it pays tribute to those who fell defending it. Memorial prayers are said, and, as it does on Yom HaShoah, a siren sounds signaling a stoppage of all activity. In this embattled land everyone has someone to remember. Every life has been touched by the struggle for independence and security in a country whose existence continues to prove its necessity.

The Eighteenth Day of Iyar

LAG BA'OMER — A DAY FOR CELEBRATIONS

Few of the many couples who marry on *Lag Ba'Omer* give much thought to why this is one of the very few days between Pesah and Shavuot when Jewish law permits weddings. If they were to investigate, they would find a conflicting array of explanations, all appealing, none definitive.

The explanations begin with the Omer period itself, those forty-nine days that are counted off one by one between the two festivals. This is a time of semi-mourning, when weddings and other celebrations are forbidden, and as a sign of grief, observant Jews do not cut their hair.

Anthropologists say that many peoples have similar periods of restraint in the early spring to symbolize their concerns about the growth of their crops. But the most often cited explanation for the Jewish practice comes from the Talmud, which tells us that during this season a plague killed thousands of Rabbi Akiva's students because they did not treat one another respectfully. The mourning behavior is presumably in memory of those students and their severe punishment.

According to a medieval tradition, the plague ceased on Lag Ba'Omer, the thirty-third day of the Omer. (The Hebrew letters *lamed* and *gimel*, which make up the acronym "Lag," have the combined numerical value of 33.) As a result, Lag Ba'Omer became a happy day, interrupting the sadness of the Omer period for twenty-four hours.

The talmudic explanation makes most sense when put into historical context. The outstanding sage Rabbi Akiva became an ardent supporter of Simeon bar Koseva, known as Bar Kokhba, who in 132 C.E. led a ferocious but unsuccessful revolt against Roman rule in Judea. Akiva not only pinned his hopes on a political victory over Rome but believed Bar Kokhba to be the long-awaited Messiah. Many of his students joined him in backing the revolt and were killed along with thousands of Judeans when it failed. The talmudic rabbis, still suffering under Roman rule and cautious about referring openly to past rebellions, may have been hinting at those deaths when they spoke of a plague among Akiva's students. Possibly, also, Lag Ba'Omer marked a respite from battle, or a momentary victory.

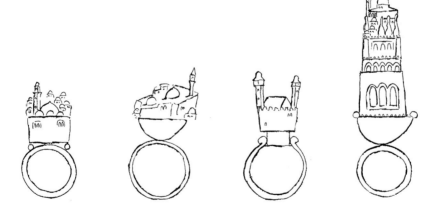

A completely different reason for the holiday concerns one of Rabbi Akiva's few disciples who survived the Bar Kokhba revolt, Rabbi Simeon bar Yohai. He is said to have died on Lag Ba'Omer.

Rabbi Simeon continued to defy the Roman rulers even after Bar Kokhba's defeat, and was forced to flee for his life and spend years in solitary hiding. Legend places him and his son Eleazar in a cave for twelve years, where a miraculous well and carob tree sustained them while they spent their days studying and praying. When they finally emerged, Simeon denigrated all practical occupations, insisting that people engage only in the study of Torah. For this God confined the two to their cave for another year, accusing Simeon of destroying the world with his rigid asceticism.

But Rabbi Simeon's otherworldliness resonated with mystics in his own time and later, so much so that tradition ascribes to him the Zohar, the key work of the Kabbalah (although critical scholars attribute it to the thirteenth-century Spanish kabbalist Moses de León). And in Israel, on Lag Ba'Omer, people flock to the site of his tomb in the village of Meron in the Galilee, near Safed, where they light bonfires and sing kabbalistic hymns. Hasidic Jews follow the custom of bringing their three-year-old sons to Meron to have their hair cut for the first time. (The custom of not cutting the child's hair until his third birthday is probably an extension of the law that forbids picking the fruits of a newly planted tree during its first three years.)

Unrelated to Rabbi Simeon, the kabbalists also give a mystical interpretation to the Omer period as a time of spiritual cleansing and preparation for receiving the Torah on Shavuot. The days and weeks of counting, they say, represent various combinations of the sefirot, the divine emanations, whose contemplation ultimately leads to purity of mind and soul. The somberness of this period reflects the seriousness of its spiritual pursuits.

Finally, on yet another tack, some authorities attribute the joy of Lag Ba'Omer to the belief that the manna that fed the Israelites in the desert first appeared on the eighteenth of Iyar.

Though its origins are uncertain, Lag Ba'Omer has become a minor holiday. (For Sephardim, the holiday is the day *after* Lag Ba'Omer.) Schoolchildren picnic and play outdoors with bows and arrows—a possible reminder of the war battles of Akiva's students—and in Israel plant trees. And every year numerous couples wed at this happy time, oblivious to Rabbi Akiva or Simeon bar Yohai, manna or mysticism.

The Twenty-third Day of Iyar

CRUSADERS MASSACRE THE JEWS OF WORMS, MAY 18, 1096

Life is so profoundly cherished in Judaism that the Talmud specifies only three conditions under which Jews are required to give up their lives to avoid violating the law: if forced to commit either idolatry, murder, or unchastity (meaning incest or adultery). All other laws may be broken to save a life. In times of religious persecution, however, or when Jews are ordered to desecrate a law publicly, they are expected to choose death rather than break the law. To die a martyr, in Jewish thought, is to die for *kiddush hashem*, for the sanctification of God's Name, and such a person is venerated as a *kadosh*, a holy one.

In vast numbers, the Jews of France and Germany who suffered during the Crusades chose to die as martyrs for the sanctification of God's Name rather than allow themselves to be converted and publicly humiliated by the mobs of people who joined the Christian holy war. Not only did they fall resisting their enemies but many gave themselves up willingly or actively committed suicide to demonstrate their loyalty to their faith. They viewed themselves as fulfilling the law on the highest level possible, and went to their deaths with a sense of having achieved a spiritual victory over those who would debase them and defile their religion.

❖

The original purpose of the Crusades had nothing to do with the Jews. When Pope Urban II called for the First Crusade on November 27, 1095, his goal was to drive the Muslims from Palestine—which they had ruled since the seventh century—and regain control of Christian holy places. But the thousands of Christians swept up in the expedition made the conversion of Jews they encountered along the way a top priority, with devastating results.

This is how a Jewish chronicler of the First Crusade, Solomon bar Simson, one of several who wrote about the catastrophe, portrayed the thought processes of the Crusaders: " 'Behold we journey a long way to . . . take vengeance upon the Muslims. But here are the Jews dwelling among us, whose ancestors killed him and crucified him groundlessly. Let us take vengeance first upon them.' "

The first city to experience that vengeance was Speyer, in the Rhine Palatinate, where Jews had lived in relative peace and security alongside the Christian population. The Crusaders arrived there on May 3, 1096, the eighth of Iyar, 4856. They managed to kill only eleven Jews, because the others had barricaded themselves in the synagogue. One "notable and pious woman," Solomon bar Simson wrote, "slaughtered herself for the sanctification of the Name. She was the first of those who slaughtered themselves . . ."

The slaughter was much more extensive in the next city, Worms, which became the site of the first large-scale massacre of the Jews. The violence there began on the twenty-third of Iyar, May 18, 1096. Some of the Jews tried to protect themselves in their own homes; others sought refuge in the bishop's castle. (For the most part, those Crusaders who attacked the Jews were peasants and townspeople, whereas churchmen and nobles tried to calm the masses. But there was a limit to how far they would extend themselves to help the Jews.) Both groups were doomed, and eight hundred people lost their lives.

"They stretched forth their necks, so that their heads might be cut off for the Name of their Creator," wrote Solomon bar Simson, depicting the voluntary martyrdom the people undertook when they saw they would be captured. Another chronicler described how a father blessed his son, and after "the lad replied 'Amen,' " the father slew him so that he would not be taken alive and forcibly converted. Then the man and his wife left the room and gave themselves over to be murdered.

The pattern of Worms was repeated at Mainz, Cologne, Regensburg—all along the Rhine Valley and beyond, where probably fewer than a hundred thousand Jews had achieved some degree of comfort and stability. In each case, the Jews fought back as best they could, but when given a choice between conversion or death either allowed themselves to be killed or killed themselves. In grisly detail and with great anguish, the Crusade chronicles describe the Jewish deaths. Sometimes they rage against God for having inflicted such pain on innocent followers. But more often, they present the deaths as sacrifices to God, reminiscent of the ancient Temple sacrifices. And more than any other theme, the writers call up the image of Abraham willingly and unquestioningly offering his son Isaac to God as a metaphor for the sacrifices of the Ashkenazic Jews of France and Germany.

It was an appropriate metaphor, for unlike pious co-religionists before them, these Jews did not regard themselves as being punished for sins they had committed. On the contrary, they believed that because of their deep faith, like Abraham and Isaac they were being put to the supreme test. They would meet that test unwaveringly, as did the patriarchs, by going to their deaths voluntarily and sanctifying God's Name in doing so.

The Crusade massacres in western Europe lasted through June of 1096, taking about five thousand Jewish lives. Eventually the Crusaders turned their attention elsewhere. (Three years later, when they reached Jerusalem, they set fire to the synagogues in which the Jews had taken refuge, killing hundreds, and sold many others into slavery.) Henry IV, the Holy Roman Emperor, permitted those small numbers of Jews who had been forcibly baptized to return to Judaism, and allowed the Jews of the Rhine region to rebuild their communities.

But Jewish life in Europe was never the same afterward. Though the Jews had experienced oppression before the Crusade era, they had not experienced the kind of mass murders that took place then, and they became more vulnerable than ever before. During the Second and Third Crusades, Jewish communities again fell under attack, although with less sweeping effects. Moreover, the barrage of anti-Jewish hatred the Crusades unleashed opened the way for other forms of persecution. Not least among them were the blood libels that plagued Europe's Jews for centuries (and in which, again, Abraham and Isaac served as archetypes).

The martyrdom of the Ashkenazic Jews became an inspiration for Jews in other dire circumstances, and many poems and penitential prayers relating to them were incorporated into the liturgies of European synagogues. Numbers of communities kept memorial books, called *Memorbücher*, listing the names of the martyrs, which were read aloud during services. The semi-mourning of the Omer period also acquired new meaning after the First Crusade because the slaughter had occurred during those weeks of counting.

Yet a generation after the First Crusade massacres, Maimonides raised a question about martyrdom that has not been resolved. He urged people to avoid martyrdom if they could, and in detailing the conditions under which a person should choose martyrdom over life, he stated that people who martyr themselves when they are allowed to break the law—that is, when martyrdom is not necessary—are no better than suicides. The statement caused a storm of protest from Ashkenazic rabbis, who argued that a person who chooses martyrdom even when it is not required deserves the highest praise.

It could be argued that those great numbers of Ashkenazic Jews who went so willingly to their deaths did not have to do so. They might have allowed themselves to be baptized and practiced their religion secretly while they awaited a time when they could return to it, as Spanish Jews were to do in later centuries. But the Jews who martyred themselves could not predict what the future would hold. In utmost faith and purity of belief they rejected any thought of apostasy. They regarded their sacrifice as a symbol for all time of the strength of Judaism. The best we can do now is revere their courage and religious devotion and grieve at the circumstances that led them to make the choices they did.

The Twenty-eighth Day of Iyar
YOM YERUSHALAYIM — JERUSALEM DAY

Jerusalem in the Torah is the "site where the Lord your God will choose to establish His name." It is the site that will hold a sanctuary, where the people of Israel will offer sacrifices and gather for worship. It is the site where they will "rejoice before the Lord" (Deuteronomy 12:11, 12).

Jerusalem, the prophet Zechariah predicts, will one day be called "the City of Faithfulness," whose squares will always be "crowded with boys and girls playing" (8:3, 5).

Jerusalem in the eyes of the Psalmist is a haven that draws the tribes of Israel together. Therefore, "Pray for the well-being of Jerusalem; / May those who love you be at peace" (Psalm 122:6).

Jerusalem, the rabbinic sages said, "is the joy of the whole earth." And, "There is no beauty like the beauty of Jerusalem."

Jerusalem, the mystics held, lies "exactly opposite the Heavenly Sanctuary, where the Divine Glory of the Holy One . . . dwells."

Jerusalem, the contemporary Israeli poet Yehuda Amichai writes, is "a port city on the shore of eternity."

Jerusalem has been central to Jewish feelings and memory from the earliest days of the nation's history. *Yom Yerushalayim*, Jerusalem Day, celebrates that centrality. More specifically, it marks the capture of the Old City of Jerusalem during the Six-Day War of 1967, leading to the reunification of the entire city under Israeli control. Jordan had taken the Old City during the war of 1948, and from then until 1967, Jews had been barred from it. When Israeli forces reached the Western Wall, the only remaining wall of the Second Temple precinct, they broke into exuberant rejoicing. The shofar was sounded, prayers of thanksgiving recited, and the determination expressed that Jerusalem never again be divided. Soon after, the annual holiday was declared.

Today, thirty years after reunification, the status of Jerusalem has become a topic of discussion in the overall peace negotiations between Israel and the Palestinians. There is a new consciousness among many Jews of the city's importance to Palestinians, yet there is also a powerful and widespread insistence that Jerusalem remain the unified capital of the Jewish nation.

The holiday itself has not been celebrated in a major way, but it does serve as a time of tribute to this city of cities in Jewish life.

❖

Jerusalem had been a fortified city and location of an ancient sanctuary when King David conquered it and made it his capital some three thousand years ago. Its inner fortress was called Zion, and soon Zion and Jerusalem became synonymous. Both names represented the city, the land, and, by extension, the Jewish people. When the prophets wanted to castigate the people, they spoke of the "filth of the daughters of Zion" and the "blood of Jerusalem" (Isaiah 4:4). When they wanted to console them, they proclaimed, "Awake, awake, O Zion! / . . . Put on your robes of majesty, / Jerusalem, holy city!" (Isaiah 52:1).

King Solomon built the First Temple in Jerusalem; and while it stood, pilgrims flocked there to offer sacrifices on the three great festivals of Pesah, Shavuot, and Sukkot. Jerusalem continued as the capital of Judah when the kingdom split into two, after Solomon's death. And when Judah fell to the Babylonians in 586 B.C.E., its exiles sang: "If I forget you, O Jerusalem, let my right hand forget her cunning" (Psalm 137:5).

From the Babylonian conquest until 1967, Jerusalem changed hands and rulers dozens of times. Like the characters in the Passover song "Had Gadya," one people after another came to devour, rebuild, conquer, or liberate the city:

The Persians, who defeated the Babylonians, permitted the exiles to return to Judah and build a new Temple in Jerusalem. In 70 C.E. the Romans burned down that Second Temple, sacked the city, and killed or enslaved many of its inhabitants. In 135, after the defeat of the Bar Kokhba rebellion, the Romans forbade Jews to enter Jerusalem, except to mourn the Temple on the Ninth of Av.

The Christians took over in 324, when Emperor Constantine gained control of Palestine. They made Jerusalem their holy city, with shrines and relics commemorating Jesus' life and death. Because they regarded their New Jerusalem as superseding the Old Jerusalem of the Jews, they renewed the Roman policy of excluding Jews from the city. The Muslims, who ousted the Christian rulers in the seventh century, eased those restrictions even while they turned Jerusalem into their own holy city, third after Mecca and Medina. The Christian Crusaders forced the Muslims from Jerusalem in 1099, but the Arabs regained the city in the twelfth century.

Jerusalem gradually deteriorated under the Ottoman Empire, with much of the Jewish community living in poverty, and it fell to Great Britain in 1917. When the British gave up their mandate over Palestine in 1947, the United Nations partition plan called for Jerusalem to be under international control. In the war that followed, however, Jordan won East Jerusalem and Israel held on to West Jerusalem, turning it, in 1950, into the capital of the new state. During the nineteen years of Jordanian rule—until Israel captured Old Jerusalem in 1967—Jewish cemeteries and holy places were neglected or desecrated.

❖

Throughout the vicissitudes of Jerusalem's history, it held its primary place in Jewish thought and emotion. "My heart is in the East, and I am at the edge of the West," wrote the medieval Spanish Jewish poet Judah Halevi, speaking to the collective longings of his people.

In memory of Jerusalem, Jews in all parts of the world learned to face toward that city when they prayed. Some hung cutouts or plaques embroidered with the word *Mizrah,* "East," on their walls to remind them of its direction. In honor of Jerusalem, Jews still affirm as they take the Torah scrolls from the ark that "instruction shall come forth from Zion, / The word of God from Jerusalem" (Isaiah 2:3). In reverence for Jerusalem, they recite the phrase "Next year in Jerusalem" at the close of Yom Kippur and Passover, expressing their enduring attachment to the holy city.

With the desolation of Jerusalem in their hearts after the loss of the Temple, the rabbis said, "The Holy One, blessed be He, weeps with Jerusalem. The ministering angels weep with her. Heaven and earth weep as well, as do the mountains and the valleys." But they never stopped loving the city or dreaming of its restoration.

"There are ten measures of beauty in the world," the sages taught, "nine in Jerusalem and one in the rest of the world. There are ten measures of wisdom in the world—nine in Jerusalem and one in the rest of the world. There are ten measures of Torah in the world—nine in Jerusalem and one in the rest of the world."

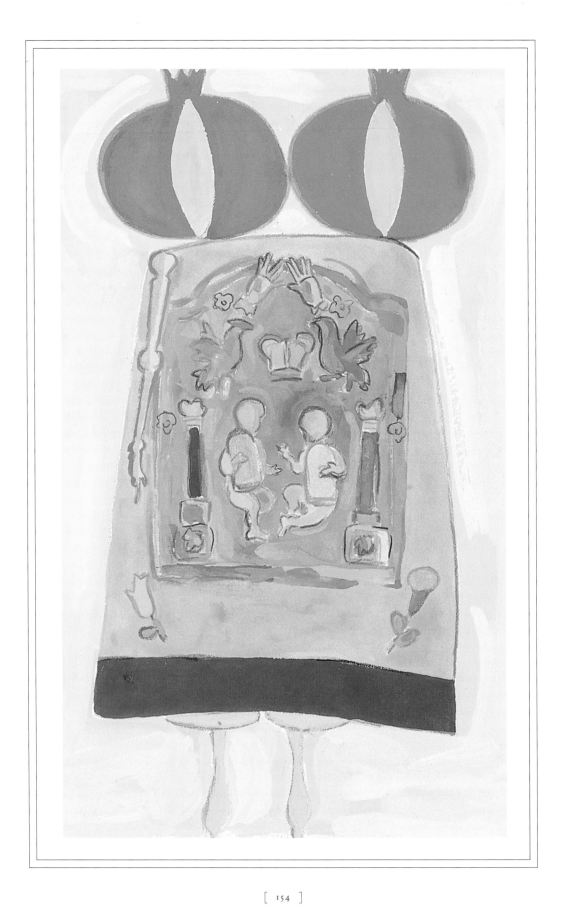

SIVAN

May - June

SIVAN IS THE ANNIVERSARY MONTH FOR THE GIVING OF THE TORAH TO THE CHILDREN OF ISRAEL AT MOUNT SINAI. Shavuot, the festival that celebrates that momentous event, falls on the sixth day of the month, and because of its importance, the three days before it also have a special status. Although the counting of the Omer continues until the holiday itself, the mourning customs resumed after Lag Ba'Omer end now and weddings and other celebrations may take place again.

This is a happy time before the holiday, recalling the gladness and excitement of the ancient Israelites as they prepared and purified themselves for receiving the Torah. The preparations culminated in that awesome day when not only were all the Israelite men, women, and children present at Sinai but, according to tradition, every Jew in every generation thereafter, forever more. It is that presence that this month honors.

For women, however, the biblical verse in which Moses instructs the Israelites about their preparations presents a sudden shock of exclusion. "Do not go near a woman," he says (Exodus 19:15), addressing only the men, as if women were not to be included at all. Although women have always regarded themselves as taking part in the revelation, the verse has created anger and pain. It has also posed a challenge. In an extraordinary turnaround of the sense of exclusion they have felt, contemporary women have made the Torah their own in ways no women before them ever had the opportunity to do. In groups and singly, women of all denominations study the Torah today, reclaiming the lives and stories of ancient women, seeking out lost meanings, and in many cases creating their own midrash. Their stories, poems, and interpretations have added new dimensions to the tradition. And that, too, is cause for celebration in this month of the Torah.

The zodiac sign for the month is Gemini, the twins, which some sources identify with the twin brothers Jacob and Esau. Others point out that unlike the animal symbols for Nisan and Iyar (the ram and the bull), two human figures represent Sivan. As such, they come to show us that humans have mouths to speak with, hands to clap together, and feet with which to dance. In other words, humans and only humans—both women and men—can say the words of the Torah and rejoice in them.

The Fifth Day of Sivan

SHAVUOT EVE — THE FEAST OF WEEKS

Staying up all night to study Torah is a kabbalistic custom, generally confined to members of some pious Hasidic sects. But it has become increasingly popular among all denominations of Jews as a once-a-year event to launch the festival of Shavuot. On the holiday eve, synagogues hold study sessions in which congregants read and discuss passages of the Bible, the Mishnah and Talmud, and mystical writings. Called *tikkun leil Shavuot,* these sessions set the mood for the next day's reenactment of the revelation and the giving of the Ten Commandments at Mount Sinai.

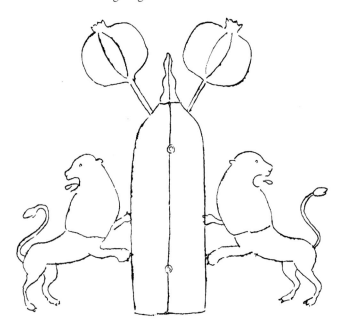

A traditional tikkun begins late in the evening and ends at dawn, when congregants attend early-morning services, but study groups do not always follow the same pattern. Some use other texts or concentrate on different parts of a single work each year, and in some communities the sessions last only until midnight. They end then with servings of coffee and cheesecake, a favorite Shavuot dessert.

The medieval mystics originated the late-night study sessions in symbolic anticipation of receiving the Torah, and the practice spread from them to the broader community.

The origins of Shavuot cheesecake are another matter. Indulging in it is part of the custom of eating dairy foods on this holiday, but the reasons for that diet are so buried in obscurity that the explanations offered seem ludicrous. One is that before the Israelites received the rules of the Torah they had not kept the dietary laws. Once given the laws, they realized that all their pots and pans were unkosher, so they ate uncooked dairy foods! Another points to an allegorical interpretation of a verse in the Song of Songs that compares the Torah to honey and milk (4:11). Never mind. Blintzes, borekas (Sephardic stuffed pastries), and cheesecake are this holiday's treats.

The association between Shavuot and the giving of the Torah has its own complexities:

The biblical name Shavuot, which literally means "Weeks," bears no relation to revelation. It refers to a farmers' festival in ancient times that concluded the seven weeks of counting begun on the second night of Passover. Also called *Hag HaKazir*, the "Feast of the Harvest," the festival marked the end of the barley and beginning of the wheat harvest in the land of Israel. In gratitude for their wheat crops, farmers would bring an offering of two loaves of bread to the Temple. Many would also bring thanksgiving offerings of the first fruits that had ripened on their trees, giving the festival yet another name, *Yom HaBikkurim*, "Day of the First Fruits."

The Mishnah describes a colorful procession in which farmers from small villages would gather in a large town to go together to Jerusalem. "Arise, let us go up to Zion, to the House of our God," the leader would announce as they set out on their pilgrimage. When they neared Jerusalem, flutists would greet them with music, and when they reached the Temple court, the priests would welcome them with hymns and psalms.

How, then, did these festivities of fruits and grains turn into a celebration of the Torah? Part of the genius of the talmudic sages was their ability to overlay old agricultural holidays with historical meaning. In the case of Shavuot, the rabbis calculated that the festival fell during the same three-month time period in which the Children of Israel had reached the wilderness of Sinai after leaving Egypt. They fixed the date for both events as the sixth of Sivan and made the Sinai experience the essence of the holiday. (Jews outside Israel observe the holiday on the seventh as well.)

Today, reminders of the agricultural basis for Shavuot appear in the plants and flowers that decorate many synagogues during the holiday. But even those acquired another meaning—to represent the green of the mountain from which the Torah was given. In Reform and some Conservative synagogues, the decorations add splendor to confirmation services, which celebrate the completion of the Hebrew school year and the graduation of its high-school students.

The mystics who instituted the tikkun for the eve of Shavuot pictured the holiday in part as preparation for a glorious wedding that would be reexperienced the next day, the marriage of God and Israel. The flowers that dress up the synagogue enhance the wedding atmosphere. Emphasizing it further, in many Sephardic synagogues on Shavuot day, a congregant reads aloud a specially created ketubbah (marriage contract) spelling out the bond between God, Israel, and the Torah. Even earlier, on the Sabbath preceding the holiday, most synagogues include a reading from the prophet Hosea, whose message of love and obligation prepares the way for the festival to come—a far cry now from the farmer's feast it once was:

> And I will espouse you forever:
> I will espouse you with righteousness and justice,
> And with goodness and mercy,
> And I will espouse you with faithfulness;
> Then you shall be devoted to the Lord. (2:21–22)

The Sixth Day of Sivan

SHAVUOT, THE FIRST DAY — STANDING AT SINAI

Thunder and lightning crashed through the skies, and the mountain quaked violently, smoke soaring up from within like the fumes of a gigantic furnace. The people quaked also as they stood at the foot of Mount Sinai to receive the word of God. In the midst of the noise and the terror, they could hear the wail of a shofar growing ever louder. The sound connected them to their origins, to the patriarch Abraham and his son Isaac, in whose stead a ram had been sacrificed to the God whose presence they awaited. The shofar, the commentator Rashi later said, was made of the horn of that very ram. Its sound, Nahmanides added, was the sound of Isaac's fear, mystically contained in the voice of God.

They had come out of Egypt, tribes of former slaves, barely remembering their past but willing to stake their future on a moment in a forbidding wilderness far from the sophisticated land they had left or the unknown one to which they were journeying. It was a moment that would transcend time and place, that would transform them and ultimately the world. It was a moment no historian can document, but one that has reverberated through history.

In the synagogue on Shavuot morning, Jews relive that moment as they read from the biblical scroll the portion that describes it: in some of the most poetic language in all of Scripture, Moses reminds the Israelites of how God had guided and protected them, bearing them "on eagles' wings" out of their slavery. He then lays out the terms of a covenant. If they faithfully obey and keep its laws, they will become God's "treasured possession among all the peoples" and "a kingdom of priests and a holy nation." Instantly, without hearing the details of the laws, the people accept the covenant with the words "All that the Lord has spoken we will do!" (Exodus 19:4–6, 8).

For that unqualified acceptance they and their descendants have accumulated great merit, tradition holds. A legend says that God offered the Torah to all the nations of the world. Each questioned its contents and, hearing some of its prohibitions, quickly rejected it. Finally God went to Israel, who accepted it immediately.

The legend comes to justify Israel's belief in its unique relationship with God, but it is modified by another, darker legend. In this, God turned Mount Sinai upside down and held it over the Israelites' heads. "If you accept the Torah," God said, "well and good. If not, this mountain will become your burial place." The implication here is that God forced Israel into its covenant, and therefore it should be forgiven when it breaks the rules. Also implied is a recognition that keeping the Torah's commandments was not always a simple act of love and acceptance. Persecuted and tortured over the years for their beliefs, Jews often felt burdened by the weight of the Torah, refusing to abandon it, but fearful they might be buried beneath it.

After preparing themselves for three days, the people stand in fear and wonder at the foot of the mountain. It is a mountain whose location nobody knows today. The Bible calls it Mount Sinai and, sometimes, "the mountain of God at Horeb," the name of the place where God appeared to Moses in a burning bush. Like the revelation itself, the mountain upon which it occurred remains outside and apart from the known and knowable.

In the synagogue, worshippers also stand as a reader chants the Ten Commandments.

"I the Lord am your God who brought you out of the land of Egypt . . ." (Exodus 20:2). Jews regard this statement as the first commandment, asserting God's existence. Christians generally view it as an introduction and combine it with what to Jews is the second commandment, "You shall have no other gods beside Me" (Exodus 20:3). Some Christian denominations divide what is the last commandment in Jewish tradition into two: "You shall not covet your neighbor's house: you shall not covet your neighbor's wife . . ." (Exodus 20:14).

The Israelites can see a thick cloud hovering over the mountain and hear the words of God emanating from it. (In Hebrew, the commandments are called *aseret ha'dibrot*, the Ten Words, or divine utterances; hence the English "Decalogue.") Everything in nature is still now, the midrash imagines. No bird sings, no ox lows, no waves break in the seas. Silence blankets the universe as all the dead who have been resurrected and all the souls of those not yet born listen to the voice that is like no other, a voice that has no echo.

Rabbi Johanan said that each and every word that came from God was transmuted into seventy languages corresponding to the seventy nations of the world. That is, all humanity, not only Israel, received them. Later, other peoples would build their own belief systems on those words from Sinai.

Rabbi Tanhuma said that God's voice came to each person according to his or her own strength—the old and the young, the women and the men all heard what they were able to absorb and understand.

The mystics said that the Ten Words at Sinai corresponded to ten words with which God created the universe. Hence Sinai was a new Creation.

But what do the people standing at Sinai actually hear themselves? How much of God's glory has been revealed to them? One tradition says they hear all the commandments directly from God as they are given; another, that they hear only the first two commandments themselves. Then, over-whelmed by what they have witnessed, they ask Moses to serve as their intermediary. Certainly, at some point—and the point is unclear in the biblical account—Moses does ascend the mountain toward which God had descended, and learns there dozens of laws.

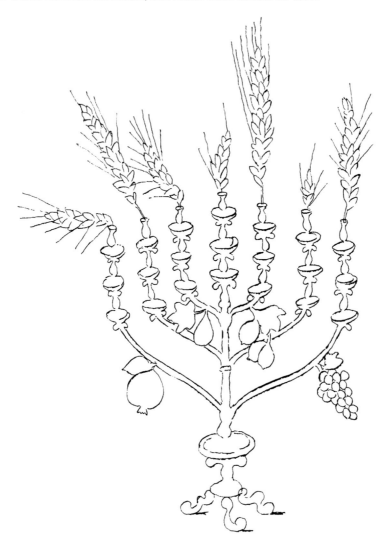

What Moses teaches the people becomes the bulk of the Torah, of which the Decalogue is only part. The word *Torah* means "teaching" and generally refers to the first five books of the Hebrew Bible, although it is also used for all of the Bible, and sometimes for all of rabbinic tra-dition as well. In fact, the sages tried to downplay the importance of the Ten Commandments for fear people would take them for the whole of Jewish belief. To that end they eliminated the cus-

tom, practiced when the Second Temple still stood, of having worshippers recite the commandments daily.

The rabbis made it a doctrine of Judaism that God revealed all the laws of the Torah to
Moses at Mount Sinai, and all, therefore, carry divine authority. To drive home that point, they pictured Moses having to fight with the angels to wrest the Torah away from them, so out of the human
realm was it. Further, they taught that along with the Written Law, the Oral Law—the interpretations and explications in the Mishnah, Talmud, and later writings—was also revealed at Sinai. The
way the tradition puts it is that what Moses received included "all that a mature disciple will in the
future expound before his teacher." In that sense the Oral Law is a process of seeking and uncover-
ing the depths of meanings in the Written Law.

Orthodox Judaism believes, therefore, that the Oral Law, like the Written Law, may not be
altered. Conservative Judaism holds that the Oral Law, though rooted in the sacred texts, evolved
over time and can be modified when necessary. Reform Judaism generally does not accept the Oral
Law as binding and regards the Written Law as open to interpretation.

❖

However much they saw or heard, whatever they actually experienced, for the ancient Israelites
the encounter at Sinai transformed them from a group of tribes into a people that defined itself by
a code of law and holiness. At the end of Moses' teachings, they restate their acceptance of the
covenant. "All that the Lord has spoken we will faithfully do," they say again (Exodus 24:7). Other
peoples of the ancient Near East had law codes and covenants drawn between kings and their
vassals. But only this people entered into a public ceremony of binding itself—marrying itself—to
its God. It would be a bond pulled at times almost to the breaking point, marked by deep disap-
pointments on both sides, often the cause of Jewish agony and suffering, yet reaffirmed by one
generation of Jews after another.

Shavuot is a holiday of affirmation, of standing again and again at Sinai. In many synagogues, before the reading of the Ten Commandments, a reader chants the *Akdamot,* an eleventh-
century hymn written in Aramaic that praises God and sings of Israel's love of the Torah. Together with the commandments, it helps re-create some of the magic and mystery of that moment
at the foot of a mountain in an isolated wilderness when the Children of Israel discovered
their destiny.

The Seventh Day of Sivan

SHAVUOT, THE SECOND DAY—READING THE BOOK OF RUTH

Aside from the chanting of the Ten Commandments, for many people the most moving part
of synagogue services on Shavuot is reading the Book of Ruth. Outside of Israel this is done on the
second day of the festival. The usual explanation for joining Ruth to Shavuot is that the book's

action fits the holiday's agricultural theme because it takes place during the barley harvest in the land of Israel. A lesser-known reason is that, as we learn at the book's conclusion, Ruth is the ancestor of King David, and in tradition he was born and died on Shavuot. Reading the book honors him along with Ruth.

The only biblical book besides Esther named for a woman, Ruth is a beautiful story about a young widow's devotion to her mother-in-law, a happy-ending tale in which each character finds pleasure and fulfillment as reward for caring about the other. But beneath the idyllic surface lies another narrative, unlike any in the Bible. It tells of two women struggling to make their way alone in a society geared toward men. They and not the men—at least not until the very end—are the main subject of the story, and they, and not the men, shape the Jewish future.

Within five short verses we learn that because of a famine a man named Elimelech, his wife, Naomi, and their two sons, Mahlon and Chilion, moved from Bethlehem in Judah to the country of Moab. The man died, the two sons married Moabite women—one named Orpah and the other Ruth—and about ten years later they also died, leaving their wives childless.

Now the women take center stage. Devastated by her losses, Naomi decides to return to her homeland. Although both her daughters-in-law offer to accompany her, she convinces Orpah to remain behind with her own family. But Ruth cannot be convinced. In the most famous words of the story, and among the best known in the Bible, she vows loyalty to Naomi: ". . . Wherever you go, I will go; wherever you lodge, I will lodge; your people shall be my people, and your God my God" (1:16).

Like Abraham, who leaves his land and family at God's command, by her own choosing Ruth leaves all that is familiar to her and sets out on a journey with Naomi to a land and people she has never known. It is a trying journey, originating in death and despair and fraught with adversity. Naomi is desolated by the losses she has suffered. "Do not call me Naomi. Call me Mara [bitterness]," she tells the women of Bethlehem when she and Ruth arrive there. "I went away full, and the Lord has brought me back empty" (1:20–21).

Ruth tries to fill Naomi's life by caring for her. She goes into the fields and gathers the grain that farmers, in accord with Jewish law, had left behind for the poor. In the course of her gleaning, she meets Boaz, who turns out to be her dead husband's kinsman. Also by law, he is expected to marry and protect her and perpetuate her husband's family name. Now it is Naomi's turn to care for Ruth. She does so by teaching Ruth how to alert Boaz to his duties as a kinsman—and to her own charms. In one act after another, the women treat each other with *hesed*, "loving-kindness," a word repeated like a heartbeat throughout the text.

The women's journey ends with Ruth marrying Boaz and giving birth to a son, Obed, who will become the father of Jesse, father of David. Naomi serves as the baby's nurse, her days full now with joy. Ruth, who left her own home to follow Naomi, builds up "the House of Israel" by becoming mother of a dynasty.

The book is named for Ruth, but both women are its heroes. Against all odds, they used courage and cleverness to turn bitterness into triumph. Of course, the text hints subtly that God was working in the background all along, making everything come out just the way it did so that in the end King David will descend from Ruth's son, Obed. What we see, however, is the women's deep love and friendship for each other. They are the only two women in the Bible whose relationship is described with the word *love*; the sisters Rachel and Leah may also have loved each other, but the text concentrates on their rivalry.

In the book's last paragraph, we suddenly lose the women and find ourselves in the more usual world of the fathers, with David's genealogy traced through his paternal line from Boaz and back to Perez, son of Judah. But the story has already been told, and the ties between David and Ruth are too clearly established to be minimized.

❖

As for those ties, worlds of differences, and not only generations, separate David and Ruth from each other. In contrast to the modest, rural young woman Ruth was, David gloried in being a powerful, charismatic monarch. He was a larger-than-life hero who fought valiantly in battle, wrote poems and songs (tradition labels him the "sweet singer of Zion" and attributes the Book of Psalms to him), and married many women. He became intimate with one of them, Bathsheba, while she was still wed to another man, had her husband killed to get him out of the way, and was punished for his sin by the death of the child they had together. Later in their marriage, Bathsheba gave birth to another son, Solomon, who would succeed David as king. David's life, told in the two Books of Samuel, was filled with intrigue, family conflict, and warfare.

Yet David did share some qualities with his great-grandmother. One was his loyalty to a friend. His love for Jonathan paralleled Ruth's love for Naomi. "I grieve for you, / My brother Jonathan," he cried after Jonathan fell in battle. ". . . Your love was wonderful to me / More than the love of women" (II Samuel 1:26).

And for all his wars and worldly success, David, like Ruth, often acted out of deep spiritual impulses. One incident stands out: After capturing Jerusalem, which would become his capital, he had the Ark of God containing the tablets of the Law brought to that city. As he led the procession, exulting in religious fervor, he "whirled with all his might before the Lord." When his first wife, Michal, criticized him for his public behavior, he snapped back that he would "dance before the Lord" as much as he pleased (II Samuel 6:14–21). His was a passionate faith, which guided him through his life.

Ruth's faith, as firm, was calmer, quieter. She had chosen it and clung to it just as she clung to her mother-in-law when Naomi felt herself abandoned. In the midrash, when Naomi tries to dissuade Ruth from joining her in leaving Moab, she spells out the difficult conditions of assuming Judaism. Ruth answers, "I am determined to be converted; better it should be by your hands than by another's."

One more reason we read Ruth on Shavuot is to publicly embrace others like her born outside the Jewish community who voluntarily assume the responsibilities of the Torah and fulfill them with love and kindness. For her devotion, Ruth the Moabite merited being the ancestor of David, Israel's greatest king, and from their line, it is said, will one day come the Messiah.

The Seventeenth Day of Sivan

SHABBETAI ZEVI PROCLAIMS HIMSELF THE MESSIAH, MAY 31, 1665

In today's terms, the bizarre man named Shabbetai Zevi who asserted that he was the Redeemer come to rescue the Jewish people would probably be diagnosed as suffering from manic-depressive disorder—an illness that creates in its victims extreme mood swings ranging from deep depressions to wild highs. Even in his own time, some people considered him mentally unbalanced, particularly in his youth, when he began to speak of himself as the Messiah, decree the abolition of traditional religious practices, and publicly pronounce God's ineffable Name, an act forbidden to Jews. Nevertheless, at the height of his popularity, Shabbetai Zevi had a following of thousands upon thousands of Jews from all parts of the world who did, indeed, believe he was the long-awaited Messiah who would redeem the Jewish people and restore the kingdom of David on earth.

How did so many people become caught up in a religious fervor so powerful that they were able to put reason aside and follow this strange man? One has only to look back in Jewish history or even at the recent past to recognize how profound that religious longing can be and how magnetic the pull of a charismatic leader. The brilliant Rabbi Akiva joined with scores of other Judeans in viewing Bar Kokhba as the Messiah in the second century, backing him in a disastrous revolt against Rome that led to a massive slaughter of Jews. Of a very different nature but a similar impulse, in our own day, a great many Lubavicher Hasidim believed their *rebbe* Rabbi Menachem Mendel Schneerson was the Messiah, and held on to that belief long after he became paralyzed by a stroke, and some even after his death.

In the case of Shabbetai Zevi, several factors came together to create the messianic excitement that won him widespread support. He appeared on the scene less than twenty years after the dreadful massacres of Jews in Poland instituted by the Cossack officer Bogdan Chmielnicki and at a period of repeated persecutions in Russia and Poland. The Jews in these and other European countries grasped on to the idea of a savior who would defeat their enemies and release them from their sufferings. Equally important, he presented his messianic visions at a moment in history when mystical influences had reached an all-time high among Jews. The expulsion of the Jews from Spain in 1492 led scholars to prolonged probings into the meaning of exile and the goals of Jewish life. The sixteenth-century kabbalists, centered in the city of Safed in Palestine, built on those probings to create a new spiritual awakening that touched Jews everywhere in the Diaspora. Even in lands in which Jews lived securely, rabbis and preachers became swept up in calculating the time of the Messiah's arrival and speculating on the new age he would institute.

In short, messianism was in the air. And though there had been messianic movements before his and would be others after it, nothing can compare to the frenzy caused by Shabbetai Zevi.

He was born in Smyrna in western Turkey in 1626, supposedly on the Ninth of Av, the anniversary of the destruction of both Temples—and the date, in tradition, when the Messiah would be born. He became learned in talmudic and kabbalistic teachings, but was ousted from his hometown because of his claims of being the Messiah and his strange behavior during his manic periods. He traveled to various cities after that, and might have been forgotten altogether were it not for a man half his age known as Nathan of Gaza, who was regarded as something of a prophet in Palestine because of his great learning and deep immersion in mysticism.

Nathan had an ecstatic vision in which he saw the image of Shabbetai Zevi engraved on the prophet Ezekiel's chariot (one of the key symbols of the Kabbalah) announcing him as the savior. From then on, he became Shabbetai's tireless promoter, spreading his gospel through numerous letters to Jewish leaders in many lands. Gershom Scholem, the great twentieth-century scholar of mysticism and author of a monumental biography of Shabbetai Zevi, describes Nathan as both "the John the Baptist and the Paul of the new messiah."

Urged on by Nathan, Shabbetai Zevi publicly proclaimed himself the Messiah in Gaza on the seventeenth of Sivan, 5425—May 31, 1665. With Nathan's backing, the Gazan community greeted his announcement with wild acclaim. Shabbetai took to riding regally around the town on horseback, and later circled Jerusalem on his horse seven times. Rumors of his miraculous powers began to spread, among them that he was leading the Ten Lost Tribes of Israel toward the Holy Land, or, in another version, that they were marching toward him.

Believers now characterized Shabbetai's wild, excited stages as "illuminations" and took seriously his predictions of the new utopian era about to begin. His charm and dignified manner during his quieter states added to his credibility, as did his ascetic practices and generous contributions to the poor. As Shabbetai gained more followers, rabbinic leaders and others who opposed him felt threatened by his massive support and either kept silent or outwardly joined the cause. During the year in which he was active, his fame spread from Palestine to Egypt, Turkey, and Persia as well as Italy, Holland, France, Germany, England, Poland, and Russia, and beyond Jewish circles to Christian ones.

Then it all came crashing down. In a euphoric state, Shabbetai announced that the day of redemption would be June 18, 1666—the fifteenth of Sivan, 5426. As a start, he would remove the crown of the Sultan of Turkey and reclaim the Holy Land as its king and Messiah. When he set sail for Constantinople in early 1666, excitement ran so high that many people sold all their possessions to acquire money to travel to Palestine. But news of his plans also reached the Turkish authorities. He was brought ashore in chains, put in prison, and later transferred to a fortress at Gallipoli.

At first his arrest reinforced his followers' fervor. Letters streamed into the prison from all parts of the world, and visitors arrived daily to see him. In a show of sympathy, Jews everywhere turned the usual Ninth of Av fast into a huge celebration of Shabbetai's birthday. Finally, concerned about the growing commotion, on September 16, 1666, the sultan had Shabbetai brought before him, and gave him the choice of death or conversion to Islam. To the horror of his followers, he chose conversion, taking the name Aziz Mehmed Effendi.

The news stunned the world Jewish community. Nathan, ever Shabbetai's prophet, offered an explanation for his leader's apostasy that grew out of, yet distorted, kabbalistic thinking. The mystics believed that sparks of holiness are buried deep in the impure and evil aspects of the universe. The process of redemption calls for releasing those sparks and thus restoring harmony in the world. Nathan explained that the Messiah has a special task. He must himself enter the domain of evil to personally rescue the sparks within it. Hence Shabbetai's conversion: he had to release the holy sparks that were buried in Islam, in essence exiling himself to the evil realm in order to redeem his people. Shabbetai was still a Jew, Nathan insisted, pretending to be a Muslim only to fulfill his mission.

Distraught though they were by Shabbetai's conversion, the majority of the community did not accept Nathan's rationalizations. Rabbis who had once been Shabbetai's followers themselves now worked—sometimes too zealously—to suppress the movement's messianic writings and forbid circulation of Shabbatean ideas. Yet several hundred people joined their leader in converting to Islam, viewing themselves also as secret Jews working to release the holy sparks.

Shabbetai died on Yom Kippur, September 17, 1676, just ten years after his conversion. Nathan declared that he was not really dead but had become part of the "supernal light" of the world. After his death, until the end of the eighteenth century, Shabbatean sects continued to uphold the mystical doctrines he and Nathan had preached. The mainstream community regarded the Shabbateans as heretics, and it was only with Gershom Scholem's extensive work on Jewish mysticism that their practices came to be studied.

Scholem believed that despite his behavior, Shabbetai Zevi unleashed a vitality in the Jewish community that energized it long after the messiah proved to be false. Yet his movement ended so tragically that in writing of him, Scholem raises a provocative question: "What price messianism?" he asks. Has the messianic idea been too destructive and difficult for the Jewish people to sustain?

The Twentieth Day of Sivan

FAST DAY—REMEMBERING THE CHMIELNICKI MASSACRES
IN POLAND, 1648

The scholar Yosef Hayim Yerushalmi points out in his book *Zakhor* that one way European Jews of the Middle Ages kept historical memory alive was by using existing calendar dates to commemorate new events. Rather than compiling detailed records and chronologies, they remembered the past by applying it to the present.

So it was that almost five hundred years after a leading French rabbi instituted a fast on the twentieth of Sivan to memorialize a blood libel in the town of Blois, Jewish leaders in Poland designated the same day as a fast in remembrance of the massacres of Jews in the Ukraine. The second fast replaced the first, but the new calamity called up memories of the older one and of the sufferings Jews endured from one century to the next.

The Blois tragedy on May 26, 1171, was the first of its kind in France. A Christian servant accused a Jew of murdering a child and throwing his body in the river. In response, authorities imprisoned all the Jews in the community, forcing them to choose conversion or death. Most chose martyrdom and were burned alive at the stake—thirty-three men, women, and children. Rabbi Jacob ben Meir Tam, known as Rabbenu Tam, the outstanding scholar of his time, declared the day of the atrocity, the twentieth of Sivan, a fast day for Jews in France, England, and the Rhineland. "This fast shall be greater than the Fast of Gedaliah ben Ahikam," he wrote, "for it is a day of atonement."

But the fast of the twentieth of Sivan and the mourning that accompanied it became much greater than Rabbenu Tam could have imagined when it was reinstituted in memory of the tens of thousands of Jews murdered in Poland and the Ukraine between 1648 and 1649.

Bogdan Chmielnicki, instigator of the terror, was a Cossack chief determined to free the Ukraine from Poland, which had ruled it from the fourteenth century. He won enthusiastic support from Ukrainian serfs, who hated their Polish overlords, and managed also to enlist the aid of the Tatar tribes of the Crimea. Historically, the Tatars had been enemies of the Cossacks, but they saw in Chmielnicki's venture an opportunity to take captives, whom they could sell as slaves in the Ottoman Empire.

Once the revolt got under way, both the peasants and the Tatars quickly directed their violence against Jews in every city they attacked. The serfs resented the Jews because they served as middlemen in Poland's economic system, administering the nobles' estates, collecting taxes for them, and often supervising the serfs' work. The Tatars had no particular animosity toward Jews, but, knowing that Jewish communities went to great lengths to ransom members who were taken captive, they perceived the uprising as an opportunity to extract significant amounts of Jewish money.

As they had during the Crusades, many Jews chose to martyr themselves rather than convert. But many others were not given that choice—the mobs wanted only to murder them, and the more savagely the better.

Like the Crusade chroniclers, contemporaries wrote of the events of 1648. Best known among them was Nathan Nata Hanover, who described the Cossack invasions of town after town. The first large-scale bloodbath, he wrote, began in Nemirov on the twentieth of Sivan. As word arrived that the Cossacks were approaching, the Jews locked themselves into a fortress, hoping to be rescued by Polish forces. Realizing that they could not take the town by force, the Cossacks pretended to be

Polish soldiers by carrying Polish banners. The Jews opened the fortress gates, and the mobs fell upon them, killing about six thousand people.

In another city, Tulchin, the Jews gave all their possessions to the Poles to be used as ransom for the entire town. But when the Cossacks also demanded Jewish lives, the Poles quickly acceded.

The carnage was repeated throughout the year. The chroniclers speak of more than one hundred thousand Jews killed and hundreds of communities destroyed. Deeply shaken, many Jews sought refuge in Germany and western Europe. Those remaining had to strain their resources to ransom the captives sold into slavery and find the energy to reestablish their lives. At the same time, they had to contend with new persecutions by Russians and Poles that followed on the heels of the Chmielnicki afflictions.

The Cossack rebellion also greatly weakened Poland itself. Some years later, in 1654, Chmielnicki swore allegiance to the Czar of Russia; and shortly after that, Russia annexed the Cossack region of the Ukraine. The Ukrainians hailed Chmielnicki as a hero, and erected a statue of him, which has remained standing in Kiev.

To Jews, the Cossack "hero" represents evil incarnate, or, in Nathan Hanover's words, "the Oppressor Chmiel, may his name be blotted out." In 1650, the Council of Four Lands, the Jewish governing body in Poland, declared the twentieth of Sivan a fast day in memory of his oppressions. It was a day Eastern European Jews observed until World War II, also remembering on that day the victims of the Blois blood libel five centuries before Chmielnicki.

Though Jews everywhere mourned the dreadful events of 1648, some saw in them a glimmer of hope for the future. Drawing on a passage in the Zohar, the mystics had predicted that redemption would take place in that very year, 1648. When, instead, disaster struck, they interpreted it as the "birth pangs" of the Messiah, a belief that a time of troubles would precede the savior's arrival.

A Polish rabbi, Israel ben Benjamin of Belzyce, preaching in the summer of 1648, began by describing those troubles. "Men, women, and children were killed, slaughtered, drowned . . ." But, he concluded, "Perhaps God will look and see from the heavens, and avenge the blood of His servants, spilled like water, permitting us to see wondrous acts . . ." That kind of thinking opened the way later for the widespread acceptance of Shabbetai Zevi as the longed-for Redeemer of Israel.

The Twenty-third Day of Sivan

JEROBOAM SON OF NEBAT, FIRST KING OF A DIVIDED ISRAEL,
BREAKS WITH TRADITION

King Jeroboam I, who reigned from about 928 to 907 B.C.E., has become known in Jewish tradition for a particularly venal kind of evil: he not only sinned himself, he caused others to sin as well. His actions set the stage for the eventual disappearance of the Ten Tribes of Israel.

Jeroboam didn't start out such a blatant transgressor. The Bible describes him as an "able man" and "capable worker" whom King Solomon had appointed to an administrative post (I Kings 11:28). But he later rebelled against Solomon and fled for his life to Egypt, where he remained until Solomon's death. When Solomon's son Rehoboam became king, Jeroboam led his countrymen in pleading with the new monarch to ease the forced labor and heavy tax burden Solomon had imposed to carry out his vast building projects, including the Temple in Jerusalem. Rehoboam arrogantly rejected the plea. Soon thereafter the people turned against him and anointed Jeroboam king of Israel. Only the tribes of Judah and Benjamin and the priestly Levite class remained loyal to Rehoboam, whom they accepted as the legitimate heir of David and Solomon. The nation was now split into two kingdoms, Israel in the north and Judah in the south, with its capital in Jerusalem.

But neither Jeroboam's rebellion nor his establishment of a new kingdom is completely responsible for his bad name. In fact, in the biblical view, God meant for the land to be divided as punishment for the worship of foreign gods and goddesses that Solomon had permitted.

Jeroboam's sin came from what he did with his kingship. Very quickly after gaining power he determined to strengthen his position by preventing his subjects from going to Jerusalem to worship at the Temple there. Instead, he had two golden calves built, one in Bethel, in the south of Israel, and the other in Dan, in the north. "This is your god, O Israel . . ." he proclaimed (I Kings 12:28), in the same words the earlier Israelites had used when they fashioned a golden calf to worship in the wilderness.

In tradition, the twenty-third of Sivan is the day Jeroboam stopped the pilgrimages to Jerusalem, an act once remembered with a fast day. On the fifteenth day of Heshvan, he instituted a new holiday meant to substitute for the Sukkot festival celebrated in Jerusalem a month earlier. The Bible recounts disapprovingly that it was a holiday "he had contrived of his own mind" (I Kings 12:33). A demonstration of that disapproval came the same day, as the king ascended the altar at Bethel to make a sacrifice. A "man of God," a prophet, denounced him and the altar he had built. Angered, the king stretched out his arm to have the man seized, but the arm froze in place and Jeroboam had to beg the man to pray for him before it was restored.

Jeroboam persisted in his ways, and though he lived to reign twenty-two years, his son Nadab, who succeeded him, was murdered along with his entire family. No heirs remained to continue the family line, the biblical penalty for Jeroboam's sins.

Some modern critics insist that the Bible exaggerated those sins, reflecting the viewpoint of the kingdom of Judah, which always regarded Jeroboam's monarchy as illegal. In this interpretation, Jeroboam did not actually encourage the people to worship the golden calves but was continuing a tradition begun in the wilderness that regarded the calves as a pedestal upon which God's spirit hovered. According to this view, also, moving the Sukkot festival to the month of Heshvan made sense for the northern tribes whose harvest season came somewhat later than that of the Judeans in the south.

Nevertheless, in mainstream Jewish thought, Jeroboam son of Nebat is said to have no share in the world to come because he sinned himself and caused others to sin as well.

From Jeroboam's time and continuing for almost two hundred years, the land of Israel remained divided into two states, with the capital of Judah in Jerusalem and of Israel in Samaria. At times the two kingdoms fought bitterly against each other. At other times they joined forces to resist outside invaders. Eventually both succumbed to those invaders, Israel to the Assyrians in 722 B.C.E. and Judah to the Babylonians in 586 B.C.E.

The Assyrians who exiled the Israelites settled them in various foreign provinces and, in turn, resettled the peoples of other conquered nations in Israel's territory. Some of the Israelite exiles probably kept their religious practices and national identities, and their descendants may have joined the Judeans in their exile in Babylon. However, most of the captives from Israel seem to have been assimilated completely into the lands they now inhabited. They disappeared from Jewish life, never to return.

That is the story of the Ten Tribes as historians know it. Folklore and legend are more exotic and more hopeful. How could a whole people have vanished, they ask. The answer is, they didn't; somewhere they exist, those Ten Lost Tribes of Israel. Time and again, different peoples have been identified as the ten, among them Ethiopian Jews and some American Indian groups whose practices seem to bear a vague semblance to Jewish ones.

The most romantic musings on the fate of the Lost Tribes describe them as having been carried away across the mythical river Sambatyon. It is a river whose waters run fierce and full for six days of the week, churning up rocks and preventing the Israelites from crossing and returning to their land. On the Sabbath, the river rests, not stirring at all—its name, according to Nahmanides, coming from the Arabic word *Sabbat*, for Sabbath. But because it is the Sabbath, laws forbid the exiles from traveling then. Someday, however, in the messianic era, the Ten Tribes will ford the powerful river during the week and rejoin their people in the land of Israel.

For now, the remnants of the state of Judah make up the ancestors of the Jewish people throughout the world. When Jeroboam son of Nebat became king of the Ten Tribes and broke with tradition, he took the first steps toward their oblivion.

TAMMUZ

June – July

WHEN THE PROPHET EZEKIEL RECOUNTED THE ABOMINATIONS HE HAD WITNESSED IN A VISION OF THE TEMPLE COURTYARD, HE INCLUDED THE WOMEN WHO SAT TOGETHER NEAR ITS NORTH GATE BEWAILING TAMMUZ (8:14). The reference is to a goddess-worshipping cult that survived into First Temple times in spite of the prophets' many exhortations against paganism. The cult's source was Babylonian mythology, itself rooted in earlier Sumerian beliefs.

It was a folk cult, particularly popular among women, who may have been more enticed by it than men because they were excluded from Temple ritual. It was built around the goddess Ishtar, lover of the beautiful fertility god Tammuz. Every year in the month of *Tammuz,* which bore the god's name, he descended into the netherworld, and all vegetation withered and died (as it does during this hot summer month in the Near East). But Ishtar would go after him and despite many difficulties manage to resurrect him so that by the following spring the earth would blossom again. The women, and some men, bewailed the god's disappearance with formal dirges and mournful poems. When Ishtar returned and Tammuz after her, they paid tribute to her with incense and libations.

In Greek mythology the story of Venus and Adonis, who also dies but from whose blood the anemone flower grows, is related to that of Ishtar and Tammuz. Some scholars say that the fast of the seventeenth of Tammuz on the Jewish calendar carries traces of the old mourning period for the god Tammuz. If so, those traces, like fragments of ancient myths in other aspects of the calendar, are buried beneath layers of historical meanings. In this instance, the day of mourning in the middle of Tammuz memorializes the breaching of Jerusalem's walls first by the Babylonians and then by the Romans.

But the name Tammuz surely comes from the Babylonian month of the same name. Religiously, the month carries little joy, with the fashioning of the golden calf assigned to it. In the midrash, God's punishment for that event was to deprive Israel of any happy festivals in Tammuz or the two months that follow it.

Nor is the zodiac sign for Tammuz appealing: Cancer, the Crab. Legend interprets it to symbolize humans, who, like crabs, must crawl around scratching a living from nooks and crannies. But others offer a more cheerful explanation: the crab, whose life depends on water, represents Moses, whose life was saved by being hidden in and then drawn from the waters of the Nile.

The Sixth Day of Tammuz

THE TALMUD IS BURNED IN PARIS, JUNE 1242

It may have been the first time in history, certainly in Jewish history, when a trial was held not of a person or group but of a written work, the Talmud. The trial was a formal one, with a prosecutor attacking the Talmud and defenders pleading its case. Unfortunately, the verdict had been determined long before it began: the Talmud was found guilty and condemned to the stake.

Historians disagree about the day and year of the great bonfire that consumed thousands of handwritten volumes of the Talmud on the orders of Pope Gregory IX and King Louis IX of France. Some place it on June 6, 1242—the sixth of Tammuz, 5002—the date given here; some, on June 17. Others assign it to June of the year 1244.

In any case, the event was calamitous. To a far greater extent than in modern times, the Talmud was the foundation of Jewish culture during the Middle Ages. Its teachings and the laws that evolved from them—the *halakha*—governed every aspect of the people's lives. Attacking them was a way of controlling the Jewish population by destroying the source of its sustenance.

The chief prosecutor in the trial, Nicholas Donin of La Rochelle, knew that well. He had himself converted from Judaism to Christianity after a falling out with his teachers because of his own rejection of the Talmud. Bent, it seems, on revenge, in 1236 he sent Pope Gregory IX a list of thirty-five accusations against the Talmud and other rabbinic writings. Key among them was that in their reliance on the Talmud the Jews had forsaken the Bible and its prophetic teachings.

It was a charge that reached a receptive audience. Medieval Christianity eagerly sought the conversion of the Jews. In the Christian view, the Hebrew Bible forecast the coming of Jesus and the end of Judaism as it had been practiced. If Jews so valued the Talmud, the reasoning went, they must be neglecting the Bible and therefore blinding themselves to its truths. The Talmud, then, was a barrier to their conversion.

On June 9, 1239, Pope Gregory responded to Donin by ordering the archbishops and kings of France, England, Spain, and Portugal to confiscate Jewish books on the first Saturday of Lent in the following year—March 3, 1240—and to hand them over to Dominican and Franciscan friars for examination. Greatly influenced by the friars, Louis IX was the only ruler to obey the Pope's orders. Although the Pope also directed that books discovered to have doctrinal "errors" be burned immediately, Louis decided to hold a trial first, a disputation in which the Jews could publicly defend their works. He may have done this simply for his own enjoyment.

Louis's mother, Blanche of Castile, presided over the debate, which took place in the king's court on June 25–27, 1240. On one side was Donin; on the other, Rabbi Yehiel ben Joseph of Paris, the leading scholar in France, who may have been the teacher Donin opposed before his conversion and who excommunicated Donin for his views. Three other rabbis were called in for separate questioning by a panel of judges, but only Yehiel and Rabbi Judah ben David of Melun had a chance to speak.

Donin's main complaints were that the Talmud was heretical because it led Jews to disregard biblical law, that it contained anti-Christian teachings, and that it blasphemed Jesus. Yehiel answered all the charges, showing, among other things, that not the Talmud but the most basic principles of Judaism prevented Jews from converting. In a moment of high drama he warned the court, "And even if you punish *us*, we and this our law are dispersed throughout the whole world; in Babylonia, Persia, Greece, the lands of Islam, and the seventy nations beyond the rivers of Ethiopia—there this law of ours will still be found."

Predictably, the clerical court found the Talmud guilty as charged. In June 1242, some twenty-four cartloads of manuscripts of the Talmud were publicly burned in Paris. That number of manuscripts represented years of painstaking writing in these centuries before the invention of the printing press and were the intellectual bedrock of the community. The German Rabbi Meir ben Baruch of Rothenburg, visiting the city at the time, wrote an elegy, *Sha'ali Serufah Ba'esh* ("Ask, O you who have been burned in fire"), that is still included among the *kinot*, the dirges, chanted on the Ninth of Av in Ashkenazic synagogues.

The book burning marked a radical departure in relations between Christians and Jews. Though Christian leaders had long criticized the Talmud, they had never before physically assaulted it. Tragically, the French Jewish community's own conduct in regard to Maimonides' works a few years earlier may have influenced this event. When rabbis opposed to Maimonides' thinking allowed their grievances to reach the Dominicans, they opened the door to Christian intervention into internal Jewish matters.

But apart from Jewish behavior, the Dominican and Franciscan orders themselves had a major role in devising this new approach to Jewish texts. Established earlier in the thirteenth century, they had become increasingly aggressive in their wish to convert the Jews. The accusations against the Talmud by Donin—who may himself have been a Franciscan friar—gave them a perfect opportunity to take a public stance against this most important source of Jewish strength.

The burning had a devastating effect. Without manuscripts from which rabbis could study and teach, French scholarship declined, although Yehiel continued to conduct classes from memory. Even more significant, in burning the Talmud, the Church had reached into the very essence of Jewish belief, leaving Jews throughout Europe stunned and uncertain of what they would have to face next. Indeed, in later centuries not only books but Jews themselves would be burned at the stake of Christian zealotry.

The Sixteenth Day of Tammuz

AARON FASHIONS THE GOLDEN CALF

Just three months after escaping from Egypt to begin a new life as a people set apart from others and devoted to one God, the ancient Israelites made themselves a calf to worship much like the bulls people worshipped in the land they had left.

Just forty days after the overwhelming experience of revelation in which they heard the divine commandment "I the Lord am your God who brought you out of the land of Egypt . . . You shall have no other gods beside Me" (Exodus 20:2), they created an image out of gold and declared, "This is your god, O Israel, who brought you out of the land of Egypt!" (Exodus 32:4).

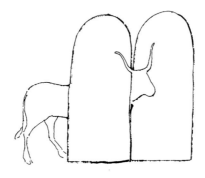

The Book of Exodus tells of how Moses ascended Mount Sinai to receive the Ten Commandments on stone tablets "inscribed with the finger of God" (31:18). He remained there forty days and nights. Distraught because he had not returned, the Israelites prevailed on his brother Aaron to make a god to lead them, as Moses had led them under God's directions. Aaron collected and melted the people's earrings to fashion a golden calf. He then built an altar before it and announced that the next day would be a great festival. The people joyfully brought sacrifices to the altar, and soon began dancing and reveling around the animal statue.

How could they? After all they had experienced, after entering into a public covenant with their God, what led them so quickly to commit what would later be regarded as Israel's gravest sin?

Fear, for one thing. Moses had served as their intermediary with the God they could not see. Now that he seemed to have disappeared, a basic, existential fear gripped them. Without him, what would happen to them? A midrash pictures Satan initiating their anxiety by showing them an image of Moses, dead, being carried on a bier. Rashi suggests that they miscalculated the time when Moses would return. He had told them he would be gone forty days. They thought that included the day he went up the mountain, but in fact his counting began the next day. Therefore they expected him on the sixteenth of Tammuz instead of the seventeenth, which he had intended, and became terrified by his absence.

Some biblical scholars claim that the Israelites did not regard the calf they built as a god in itself but merely as the pedestal upon which the invisible God would stand, much as the cherubim in the Tabernacle served as the pedestal for God's throne. The Israelite purpose, then, was not to worship the calf but to draw God's presence into their midst by means of it. The same has been said about two golden calves King Jeroboam of Israel set up at a much later time, using the same words as those pronounced here, "This is your god, O Israel . . ." (I Kings 12:28).

But those very words suggest that the early Israelites, like Jeroboam's subjects, did treat the calf as a god, or, at the very least, confuse the pedestal of the divine throne with the divinity itself. Certainly, when the Israelites brought burnt offerings to the altar and danced around the golden figure, they had, in the words of the Psalmist, "bowed down to a molten image/. . . exchanged their glory/ for the image of a bull that feeds on grass" (Psalm 106:19–20).

Inexperience in the worship of a single, invisible God is also partly responsible for the Israelites' quick slide into idol worship. The fourth-century Palestinian sage Rabbi Huna said it well. Looking to defend the people, he imagined Moses reprimanding God with these words: "Sovereign of the Universe, you ignored all the countries in the world and had your children enslaved in Egypt, where everyone around them worshipped lambs. How can you be angry at them when they worship a calf?" The Israelites had spent almost all their lives in a land in which cults deified cows, bulls, and rams as symbols of strength and fertility. How could they resist the pull of these cultic gods when the one person able to connect them to the God of their ancestors seemed to have forsaken them?

But, most important, the Israelites sinned because, with Moses away, they had no leader strong enough to prevent them from doing so. The tradition treats Aaron kindly, largely because he was the first high priest and the priestly line descended from him. According to some Bible critics, sections of the texts gloss over his guilt because they were edited by priestly redactors out to enhance his reputation. Be that as it may, in the biblical account, when Aaron and his sister Miriam gossip about Moses, she is stricken with leprosy; he is not. Here, in the golden calf incident, he escapes punishment, although three thousand worshippers will be killed for their sin.

The talmudic rabbis also looked for ways to justify Aaron's behavior, as if to explain why, in spite of it, he became high priest. He was afraid he would lead the Israelites into even greater sin if he refused to make the calf, they said, for then the people might kill him. He tried to stall for time before forming the calf by promising a feast the next day. He was a man who loved peace and tried only to bring peace to the despairing tribes.

But the biblical narrative itself reveals his weakness. He does nothing to calm the people's fears about Moses' absence. He personally collects the gold earrings, fashions the calf, and builds the altar for worship. Worst of all, when Moses returns and demands to know what has happened, Aaron shifts the blame entirely to the people, who, he says, were "bent on evil." He tells of gathering their gold and hurling it into the fire, as if he had no other choice, and, he says, "out came this calf," as if he had nothing to do with creating it (Exodus 32:22, 24). He assumed no responsibility in leading the people, allowing them to give in to their lowest impulses. What a contrast to his younger brother Moses, who assumed total responsibility for his people, even to assuaging God's wrath.

Atop Sinai, God informs Moses of the golden calf below, referring to the worshippers as "your people, whom you brought out of the land of Egypt" (Exodus 32:7). It is the only time in the Bible that Moses, not God, is credited with the Exodus, and it is done in anger. God then threatens to destroy the Israelites and offers to make Moses himself the progenitor of a new nation. Like Abraham before him, who had pleaded for the people of Sodom, Moses pleads for the Israelites. He argues that to destroy them now after they had been rescued from Egypt would appear as if God had cruelly taken them from Egypt only to annihilate them later, in that sense handing the Egyptians a victory. Renouncing any wish to form his own nation, he states that if God will not forgive Israel, he does not want to go on living. Moses' words convince God to reconsider.

The contrast between Moses and Aaron leaps out at us in this incident. Without Moses the people felt frightened and lost. They were easily seduced into turning toward the old gods they knew and understood far better than the magisterial, invisible one Moses served. And Aaron, who should have stopped them, did not have the strength or self-confidence to do so. He would later become an exemplary high priest and die beloved of the people of Israel. But it has to be said that in their moment of crisis he failed them.

The Seventeenth Day of Tammuz

FAST DAY—THE ROMANS BREACH THE WALLS OF JERUSALEM,
AND OTHER CATASTROPHES

Five dreadful things happened on the seventeenth of Tammuz, the Mishnah informs us: Moses broke the tablets of the Law; the daily sacrifice in the First Temple ceased; the Romans breached the walls of Jerusalem; and someone named Apostomos burned the Torah scroll and also placed an idol in the Second Temple.

Whether all these events actually happened on that day—and just what they were—is less important in Jewish thought than the concentration of emotion around the destructions of the First and Second Temples, both represented in this list. The sacrificial services in the First Temple may actually have ceased earlier, for the prophet Jeremiah gives the ninth of Tammuz as the date the Babylonians broke through Jerusalem's walls. As for Apostomos, his identity is obscure, but he may have been an official who desecrated the Second Temple. The point is that the two tragedies are forever linked in Jewish memory, and days of mourning for one encompass the other.

Of a different order is Moses' act of breaking the tablets he had received at Sinai. The rabbis arrived at this date by calculating that the Israelites made the golden calf on the sixteenth of Tammuz and Moses descended from Sinai the next day to the spectacle of his people cavorting around their idol.

Though unlike the other incidents, the breaking of the tablets forms a backdrop for them. For, the sages said, every misfortune Israel suffered can be traced in part to the sin of the golden calf.

Because of that sin, Moses smashed the tablets to the ground. It was a deed that represented more than unbridled temper. In ancient Near Eastern law, breaking tablets that held the terms of a treaty meant abrogating the treaty. In shattering the tablets, Moses also shattered the covenant the Israelites had concluded with their God.

After punishing the people (a dreadful punishment in which the Levites, Moses' tribesmen, killed three thousand idol worshippers), Moses ascended Sinai again, pleaded with God to forgive the Israelites, and received a second set of tablets.

Those tablets were placed in the Ark, the holiest part of the Tabernacle the Israelites built in the wilderness. When King Solomon erected the First Temple in Jerusalem, he had the Ark with its contents installed in it. The Bible doesn't mention the broken tablets, but the fourth-century Babylonian sage Rabbi Joseph taught that they rested in the Ark alongside the whole ones. Even shattered, they retained their sanctity.

According to some sages, when the Babylonians destroyed the First Temple, they took the Ark and its contents with them. Others taught that the Ark was mysteriously hidden in a woodshed and remained there undiscovered all the time the Second Temple stood. It disappeared with that Temple's demise.

❖

While they stood, the Temples each served as the hub of religious life wherever Jews had settled. Nevertheless, in the rabbinic view the First Temple was destroyed primarily because the people practiced idolatry—as if the desires that led to the golden calf had never actually been rooted out. (The cult that bewailed the god Tammuz at the Temple gates gives proof that idolatry did continue through the First Temple period.) The Second Temple was another matter. That was destroyed, in rabbinic thought, because of the "hatred without cause" that turned Jew against Jew.

The hatred existed among quarreling sects vying for influence and power. The Sadducees, the priests and aristocrats, closely adhered to Temple rites and rejected the Oral Law, the unwritten traditions and interpretations that essentially governed Jewish life. Politically, they tended to ally themselves with the Roman rulers, who had won control of Judea in the first century B.C.E. The Pharisees, the sages and scholars who interpreted the law, hated the Romans, but were generally pacifists. There were more extremist Zealots among them, however, who openly opposed Rome.

As Roman rule became increasingly corrupt and oppressive, the Zealots grew more militant both in their attitude toward Rome and in pressing other Judeans to join their cause. In 66 C.E., they began a full-scale insurrection that pitted them against overwhelming forces. When Roman legions led by their general, Titus, breached the walls of Jerusalem on the seventeenth of Tammuz, 70 C.E., the end was near. Three weeks later the Romans marched into Jerusalem, burned down the Temple, and carried off its treasures. They killed thousands of Judeans and sold thousands of others into slavery.

After the fall of Jerusalem, the Sadducees disappeared as a sect, as did the Zealots some years later. The Pharisees remained the teachers of Judaism and transmitters of the tradition.

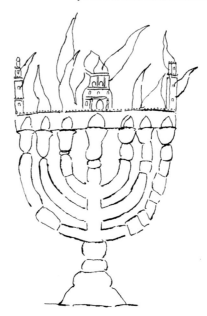

In remembrance of the breached walls before the two destructions of Jerusalem and its Temples, the most pious Jews fast on the seventeenth of Tammuz from sunup to sundown. The three weeks between then and the fast of the Ninth of Av form a period of semi-mourning, when weddings and other celebrations are forbidden and the observant do not buy new clothes or cut their hair, as a sign of mourning.

The tradition of mourning Jerusalem and the Temple began after the Jews were exiled to Babylonia. When they returned from exile and began rebuilding the Temple, they asked the priests and prophets whether they should continue to observe fasts now that they had been restored to their land. The prophet Zechariah, who recorded the question, did not give a direct answer. Instead, he urged the people to treat one another with justice, and promised that a time would come when their fasts would be turned into occasions for gladness.

Much later, Maimonides envisioned that future time as the messianic era, when all fasts would be abolished. Until then, the fasts in memory of the two destructions remain part of the Jewish calendar. Like the tablets that Moses broke, they continue to have their own sanctity, even today when Jews once again possess a homeland in Israel.

The Twenty-ninth Day of Tammuz

RASHI DIES, JULY 13, 1105

Here is a translation from Hebrew of a seemingly ordinary passage from the Book of Exodus. It concerns a basin and stand in which the priests ritually washed their hands and feet upon entering the Tabernacle, sometimes called the Tent of Meeting, the wilderness sanctuary the Israelites built: "He made the laver of copper and its stand of copper, from the mirrors of the women who performed tasks at the entrance of the Tent of Meeting" (Exodus 38:8).

And here is a translation from Hebrew of Rashi explicating the passage:

> The daughters of Israel possessed mirrors they gazed into when they adorned themselves. They did not refrain from bringing even these as a contribution to the Tabernacle. But Moses rejected them because they were made to satisfy the evil inclination. Whereupon the Holy One blessed be He said to him: Accept! For these are more beloved to me than everything else, for by means of them the women raised up many hosts in Egypt. When their husbands were weary from their hard labor, the women would give them food and drink, and they would take the mirrors and each would look in the mirror together with her husband. She would entice him by saying, "I'm more beautiful than you," and in that way the women would arouse their husbands so that they would make love and the women would become pregnant and give birth there . . . That is the significance of the text, "mirrors that raised up hosts" . . .
>
> Onkelos translates "of the mirrors . . ."
>
> *Mirours* in Old French.

Why this long explanation? Because Rashi sees a number of problems in this "ordinary" passage, and wants to resolve them.

First, who are the "women who performed tasks"? The Hebrew word used in the passage is *zove'ot*, and it appears in this text but no place else in the Pentateuch. Modern scholars generally believe the word describes women who did menial work in the sanctuary, but Rashi takes a totally different approach. Based on its Hebrew root, he defines the word *zove'ot* not as women at all but as "hosts," large numbers of people. Therefore, instead of "mirrors of the women," he reads "mirrors that raised up hosts." How can mirrors raise up hosts? The charming legend, adapted from an early midrash, tells of how the Israelite slave women used their mirrors to seduce their husbands into having sex and thereby increasing the numbers of Hebrew children in Egypt even as Pharaoh was trying to curtail them.

Next, why would such objects of vanity as mirrors be used to make utensils in which priests ritually cleansed themselves? Rashi's answer comes from God's response to Moses in the midrash. Moses regarded the mirrors as instruments of the evil impulse and therefore rejected them as contributions from the women. But God informed him that they were more important than anything else because they symbolized the devotion of the Israelite women to sustaining life despite the dreadful conditions of slavery under which they lived.

Finally, were the basin and stand actually fashioned from the mirrors? Earlier passages about the construction of the Tabernacle and its vessels speak of many Israelite donations of gold, silver, and copper, but do not mention mirrors. (Ancient mirrors were made of a polished disk of copper or brass, which would have been melted down to make utensils.) Rashi confirms that the Hebrew word *mar'ot* in the text does literally mean "mirrors" by citing the highly regarded Aramaic translation of Onkelos, who lived in the second century C.E. In case any doubt still remains, he translates the word into Old French, his own language, by writing *mirours* in Hebrew transliteration.

Thus, through legend and language, Rashi, the beloved commentator on the Bible and Talmud, managed to turn a somewhat dull verse into a rich and colorful passage. The techniques he used here appear throughout his commentaries.

❖

The name Rashi is an acronym for Rabbi Solomon ben Isaac, who was born in Troyes, France, in 1040. Legend says that the prophet Elijah himself announced the boy's birth to his father, Rabbi Isaac, because of Isaac's own piety. Isaac had a precious stone the emperor wished to buy for a great deal of money to use in one of his idols. Rather than further idolatry by selling the stone, Isaac dropped it into the sea, pretending he had lost it accidentally. For that act, Elijah promised him that in a year his wife would bear a son who would be a precious jewel, beyond compare in the entire world.

Rashi did quickly gain a reputation as a brilliant and unique scholar. As a young man he studied under outstanding rabbis in the German academies of Mainz and Worms. After returning to Troyes, he opened his own school, which attracted students from France and Germany, but earned his living cultivating vineyards and making wine, a common occupation among French Jews of the time.

He had three daughters, who—unlike most medieval Jewish women—were Jewishly educated, and, according to some historians, put on phylacteries. At least one daughter, whose name may have been Rachel, was known to be learned enough in the Talmud to be able to write down her father's response to a rabbinic question when he was too ill to record it himself.

All the daughters married prominent scholars and had children who won fame in their own right. Three of Rashi's grandsons, Samuel ben Meir (called Rashbam), Isaac ben Meir, and Jacob ben Meir Tam (Rabbenu Tam) became leaders of a school of scholars known as *tosafists.* They wrote extensive commentaries on the Talmud that used Rashi as their point of departure. Sometimes they opposed their grandfather's interpretations; in many other cases they expanded and elaborated on them. With time, their method of study extended beyond France, to Germany and eventually Spain.

It's not surprising that Rashi's commentary on the Talmud should become the base for generations of scholarly study. With lucid language and lively detail, he explained complex ideas in a way that opened worlds of knowledge to his students. At first those students copied his commentaries and circulated them in booklet form; later the commentaries were added to the talmudic text. Today all standard editions of the Talmud include Rashi's commentary next to the text on the inner side of the page.

Rashi's commentary on the Five Books of Moses was the first known Hebrew book printed, in 1475. It remains the most popular of all biblical commentaries, the one schoolchildren study almost as soon as they begin to learn Scripture itself. Critics have attributed its popularity to the many midrashim Rashi includes, like the legend about the Israelite women in our passage above, and have accused him of relying too heavily on legendary material. In reality, Rashi intended only to clarify the text, to seek out and explain its literal meaning, called the *peshat*. He may have accepted legendary explanations too readily at times, but even when he used complicated exegesis, or *derash*, his purpose, he said, was to solve a problem as he saw it.

"I . . . am concerned exclusively with the straightforward meaning of the verse," he wrote in one comment, and revised his work often to try to achieve it. That same quality of seeking the direct meaning set his commentary to the Talmud apart from those of the tosafists and later interpreters.

He wrote in clear, concise Hebrew. When he felt it necessary, as in our example, he referred to an Aramaic translation or added a word or phrase in French to make sure his readers—who spoke French in their everyday life—grasped his point. More than one thousand of these French references, known as *le'azim*, appear in his Bible commentary and about thirty-five hundred in the Talmud commentary. They are among the earliest existing examples of that language, a gold mine of source material for scholars of Old French.

Under Rashi's influence, the talmudic academies of northern France came to overshadow the German ones where he himself had studied. Sadly, after the Talmud was burned in Paris in 1242, those schools declined and Jews left France for other lands. But they carried their scholarship with them, and spread Rashi's fame wherever they went.

With fame came the many legends that surround his life. A popular one tells that on a visit to Worms during her pregnancy with him, his mother pressed against the wall of a narrow street to avoid danger. The wall opened up to receive her, forming a niche that supposedly remained standing for years. Folklore also connected the "Rashi Chapel," a house of study attached to the Worms synagogue, to Rashi's stay in that city, although it was actually built in the seventeenth century. The Nazis destroyed the synagogue and the chapel on Kristallnacht in 1938, and the German government reconstructed them in 1961.

Perhaps the most meaningful legend, because it comes closest to truly characterizing Rashi, is one that says that he died while writing the word *pure* in his commentary on a talmudic passage.

July - August

THE LION HOVERS AS A SYMBOL OVER *AV*, THE MOST MOURNFUL MONTH ON THE HEBREW CALENDAR, THE MONTH IN WHICH THE JEWISH PEOPLE TWICE SUFFERED THE DESTRUCTION OF THEIR TEMPLE AND WERE TWICE EXILED FROM THEIR LAND. Its zodiac sign is the lion, Leo, which the midrash sees as appropriate in many ways: Israel suffered punishments because it did not heed the words of God, of whom it is said, "A lion has roared, / Who can but fear?" (Amos 3:8). The prophet Jeremiah described Nebuchadnezzar, the Babylonian destroyer of the First Temple, as a lion in the verse "The lion has come up from his thicket: / The destroyer of nations has set out" (Jeremiah 4:7). And the Temple itself, like Jerusalem, is called *Ariel*, the lion of God, as in "Ah, Ariel, Ariel" (Isaiah 29:1).

In an eerie coincidence, which mystics might see as no coincidence at all, the zodiac sign is also appropriate because the great kabbalist Isaac Luria died in this month. He was known as *HaAri*, "the lion."

The rabbis contrasted Av to the month of Adar with its Purim festival. "When Adar comes, gladness increases," they said. "When Av comes, joy is diminished." Like heavy draperies that shut out all sunshine, the gloom of destruction and exile darkens the first weeks of the month for traditional Jews. The three-week state of semi-mourning that begins on the seventeenth of Tammuz intensifies as the fast of the Ninth of Av—*Tisha B'Av*—approaches. Most serious are the days before that fast—in the Ashkenazic tradition, the nine days from the beginning of the month; in the Sephardic, the week immediately preceding Tisha B'Av. During this time the observant refrain from eating meat or drinking wine, except on the Sabbath or such special occasions as a circumcision. They do not shave or cut their hair, and the most Orthodox do not swim, bathe, or launder their clothes.

The nine days reach a climax in the twenty-four-hour fast of Tisha B'Av, and when it is over, the angst and despair that have filled the liturgy for weeks begin to ebb. Now Av becomes known as *Menahem Av,* "Av the comforter," a time of healing when the words of the prophets read in the synagogue offer consolation. It is a term meant also to project hope for the future, for in the midrash "Menahem" is another name for the Messiah, who it is believed will be born on the day the Temple was destroyed.

The Fifth Day of Av

RABBI ISAAC LURIA, THE GREAT KABBALIST, DIES, JULY 15, 1572

It could be said that Isaac Luria was to the Kabbalah what the talmudic sages were to the Bible. They interpreted and expounded on the biblical texts without openly revising any of them, yet their teachings shaped all later Jewish practice. Similarly, Luria built his mystical doctrines on kabbalistic systems that developed long before his time. Yet his thoughts had such a profound effect on all kabbalistic doctrines that came after him that they are crucial to any understanding of Jewish mysticism.

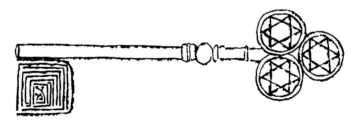

It's not easy to penetrate Luria's thoughts, or any kabbalistic ideas for that matter, and intentionally so. Kabbalists kept their theories hidden, available only to those initiated into their secrets. But for those on the inside, the world of the Kabbalah is rich in symbolism and spiritual exploration. It's a world obsessed with the mysteries of God's existence, the nature of Creation, and the human role in the workings of the universe. The word *Kabbalah* means a "receiving," in this case a mystical receiving or mystical tradition.

That tradition originates in the Bible. The prophet Ezekiel's vision of God's throne on a chariot, for example, became a major reference point for kabbalistic study. Some of the outstanding talmudic sages, including Rabbi Akiva, also engaged in mystical speculation, but the rabbis regarded such activity as dangerous for anyone under forty and not deeply versed in traditional knowledge. Still, mystical study went on for centuries, reaching its high point in Spain with the *Zohar*, the classical text of the Kabbalah.

Luria's Kabbalah came to fruition in the heated mystical atmosphere of sixteenth-century Safed in the Galilean region of Palestine. Many refugees from the Spanish expulsion of 1492 had settled there, and it later attracted Jewish intellectuals from other lands. By Luria's time the town had become the spiritual axis of the Jewish world.

Born in Jerusalem in 1534, Luria had spent his youth in Egypt, where he was reared by a wealthy uncle after the death of his father. He took up kabbalistic studies early in life and devoted himself so fully that for several years he lived as a hermit on the banks of the Nile. He visited his wife and family only on the Sabbath, and even then rarely spoke, except about religious matters. In his mid-thirties he moved to Safed, where he became known as a visionary. His students said of him that he received revelations from the prophet Elijah and that at night, during sleep, his soul ascended to heaven and communed with the great sages of the past.

To those admiring disciples he was *HaAri*, "the lion," from the initials of the Hebrew phrase *HaElohi Rabbi Yitzhak*, "the divine Rabbi Isaac." The disciples themselves became known as "lion whelps." Some saw him—and he may have seen himself—as the Messiah, son of Joseph, who, in tradition, will prepare the way for the ultimate Messiah, son of David.

Although rooted in earlier kabbalistic thinking, Luria's ideas were original and exciting. Crucial to all kabbalistic thought was speculation on the process of Creation. How could the hidden and immaterial God, known as *Ein-Sof*, "Without End" or "Infinite," the mystics asked, both create a material universe and remain in relationship with it without losing the essence of Godhood? The answer centered on the sefirot, the divine emanations or stages through which God is revealed in the material world. There are ten sefirot in kabbalistic thought. The tenth, Shekhinah, or *Malkhut*, is regarded as the feminine aspect of God and the divine stage closest to our world.

Into this basic system (which actually varied among kabbalists), Luria introduced his new concepts, developed, surprisingly, around the notion of a tragic flaw at the time of Creation.

One of his fundamental ideas was that of *zimzum*, or limitation. It held that for Creation to take place, God had to withdraw somewhat, to pull inward and limit the divine space in order to make room for that which is not divine to exist. A void resulted from this divine retreat, and into the void God directed beams of light—divine energy—through which our world was built.

But here—in a second major part of Luria's scheme—the flaw occurred. God created vessels to hold the light. (The vessels of light correspond to the sefirot of earlier systems.) But several of the vessels could not contain the intensity of energy in them, and shattered into bits. Though much of the divine light returned to its source, some sparks fell downward and were scattered. As a result, our universe remains "broken," imperfect, with nothing as it was meant to be. Moreover, from the shards of the broken vessels forces of evil, called *kellipot*, or shells, took form. Many of the divine sparks, particularly those of the Shekhinah, fell into them and became trapped there.

A third, most revolutionary, element in Luria's doctrine is the concept of *tikkun*, repair or perfection. The broken vessels must be mended so that all things can be returned to their proper places. Much of that repair had been set in motion before the creation of humans, but Adam's sin turned everything back to its broken state. Now the task of restoration is a complex process calling, among other things, for a partnership between God and humans. By studying Torah, fulfilling the commandments, and practicing good deeds, the people of Israel, in particular, have the ability to raise the sparks, free the Shekhinah from the evil shells, and put the world in order again.

When that goal is achieved and the universe is healed, the Messiah will arrive and redemption will take place. For Luria, redemption is not the beginning of the process of perfection, as it is in some traditional thought, but the end result. The work of bringing it about rests with the Jewish people.

The twentieth-century scholar Gershom Scholem, who unraveled the mysteries of the Kabbalah, points out that Luria's theories satisfied deep-felt Jewish needs. They placed Jewish suffering, intensified after the Spanish expulsion, into a broader, cosmic context in which Israel's exile reflected the larger exile of the Shekhinah, and in that sense of God.

Luria died during an epidemic on the fifth of Av, 1572, at the untimely age of thirty-eight. His closest disciple, Hayyim Vital, wrote down many of his mystical theories—which he had never systematized himself—but in true kabbalistic fashion kept them quietly hidden. Others, however, popularized Luria's ideas, so that within a generation after he died his Kabbalah had replaced most earlier systems.

Lurianic Kabbalah waxed and waned in popularity over the centuries, but many ideas were simply absorbed into Jewish culture and their origins forgotten. Today the concept of *tikkun olam*, repairing the world, is so popular again in various Jewish circles that it runs the risk of becoming a cliché. People have shown new interest in the tikkun, the late-night study session held on the eve of Shavuot, a form of repairing through learning. And many Jews with little religious background have applied the concept of mending the world to social action, such as protesting bigotry or caring for the poor and homeless. Few know that the major source of the doctrine of repair was the "Ari," whose visionary claims most would find strange but whose vision of a perfect world still beckons as an ideal.

The Seventh Day of Av

THE EXPULSION—THE LAST JEWS LEAVE SPAIN, JULY 31, 1492

"Oh, hear and see: has ever the like been seen or heard of in the whole world?"

It is hard to imagine in our post-Holocaust age that any other period in Jewish history could have seemed as catastrophic as the Nazi era was to those who endured it. Yet without the foresight of afflictions to come, and even with knowledge of past miseries, the more than one hundred thousand Jews expelled from Spain in 1492 could not conceive of another calamity as overwhelming as theirs. The words above, written by their chronicler Solomon Ibn Verga, expressed the shock they felt as outcasts from a land Jews had inhabited for centuries.

Unfortunately, the experience of expulsion was not unique to Spanish Jewry. England had expelled all its Jews in 1290, France in 1306, and various German cities during the fourteenth and fifteenth centuries. Yet none of those tragedies had the impact on Jewish history of the expulsion from Spain. There are reasons for this. In no other country had there been as many Jews. In no other had they become as proud and powerful. Moreover, when Jews were forced from other lands, they knew they could find shelter in Spain. The Spanish Jews saw about them only "enemies on one side and the sea on the other," in the words of one exile.

Because it was the last major expulsion, the end of the Spanish Jewish community marked the end of a significant Jewish presence in Western Europe. In years to come, new centers of Jewish life would rise in the East, particularly in Poland and Russia. But the finest and most cultured Jewish center of its time was gone forever.

Religious moralists of the period attributed the tragedy to God's wrath at the sinful, assimilated Spanish Jews. The less pietistic, like Ibn Verga, blamed it on the envy and enmity Jews had aroused because of their wealth and success. But the reality is more complex, an unsavory mix of Christian religious zeal and royal greed.

❖

The origins of the expulsion go back to the eighth century, when Arab Muslims out of North Africa began wresting control of Spanish lands from Christian rulers. Although these conquerors did not treat Jews as equals with Muslims, they did allow them religious freedom. For three centuries under Muslim rule, from about 900 to 1200, Jews enjoyed a Golden Age in Spain in which science, philosophy, and literature flourished. Jews became leaders in medicine and commerce and held high positions in the courts of the Muslim caliphs.

The situation changed when fanatic fundamentalist Muslims known as Almohads invaded Spain in 1146. They persecuted both Jews and Christians, often forcing them to choose between death and conversion to Islam. Oppressed by the Muslims, Jews supported Christian princes who had set out to reconquer Spain. As these rulers gained power, they employed Jews as financiers and tax collectors, relying on Jewish skills in commerce and welcoming Jewish money in their treasuries. For their part, the Jews looked to the kings for protection against both the Church and the masses of people, many of whom resented their growing influence.

In 1391, that protection failed them when mob riots, instigated by the monk Ferrant Martínez, swept across the Spanish kingdoms of Castile and Aragon. Now it was Church leaders who gave Jews a choice between conversion and death. Thousands of Jews died for their faith, but thousands of others accepted baptism as their ticket to life. Many of these *conversos*, or New Christians, continued to live secretly as Jews. The Spanish contemptuously labeled them Marranos, literally "swine."

During the next hundred years, conversions continued under Church pressure. The Church regarded any person who had converted, whether by force or not, as a Christian, entitled to the rights of Christians but also forbidden ever to return to Judaism. On the one hand, this allowed conversos to rise to heights of wealth and prestige in Spanish society, moving into the ranks of the nobility and the Church itself. On the other, those conversos who remained hidden Jews lived in constant danger of being discovered and put to death.

The Inquisition realized their worst fears. The Church had created the Inquisition in the thirteenth century to ferret out heresies. One of its major instruments was the *auto-da-fé*—Portuguese for "act of faith"—in which a person accused of heresy was publicly tortured to force confession and then, in many cases, burned alive at the stake. The Spanish conversos, always suspected of being secret Jews, were a perfect target for the Inquisition.

In 1480, at the urging of Tomás de Torquemada, the queen's confessor, the Catholic monarchs Ferdinand and Isabella invited the Inquisition to Spain, and in 1483 named Torquemada inquisitor general. Trapped by his single-minded fervor, thousands of conversos were tortured and murdered. So great was his zeal that he even had the bones of conversos discovered to have been faithful Jews in their lifetime dug up and publicly burned.

The Israeli historian Benzion Netanyahu regards Torquemada's behavior as a sign of his anti-Jewish racism. In a revisionist view that differs from that of other historians, Netanyahu contends that most conversos actually became loyal Christians. Still the Inquisition pursued them, because of deep hatred of the Jews. The Old Christians did not want these newcomers in their midst and determined to destroy them by accusing them of privately practicing Judaism.

Netanyahu also argues that King Ferdinand did not share this hatred of the Jews but felt compelled to go along with the sentiments of the masses. That may be, but, again urged by Torquemada, Ferdinand and Isabella decided to rid the country of its Jews. In that way, the practicing Jews could no longer influence the conversos and the royal couple could unify their land under one Catholic religion. At the same time they could swell their coffers by confiscating Jewish money and property.

On March 31, 1492, the Catholic monarchs signed an edict of expulsion, to be promulgated at the end of April, giving the Jews three months in which to leave. Christopher Columbus noted in his diary that he set sail in the same month in which the edict had been issued. Money for his voyage, incidentally, had been raised by financiers of Jewish descent, and among the crew was one Luis de Torres, a Jew who was baptized shortly before boarding.

The last Jews left Spain on July 31, 1492, the seventh day of Av, and two days before the fast of Tisha B'Av. The majority of the exiles crossed the border into Portugal, whose king, John II, had agreed to accept them temporarily upon payment of large sums of money. Five years later, his successor, Manuel I, had the entire Portuguese Jewish population forcibly converted to Christianity. It was an act almost as traumatic as the expulsion from Spain itself and in a real sense finally emptied the Iberian Peninsula of all openly practicing Jews.

Other refugees from Spain went to North Africa and Turkey, and some to Italy and the Netherlands. The Sephardic culture they carried with them became a major part of the Jewish heritage. But never again would it reach the heights it had achieved on Spanish soil.

Solomon Ibn Verga was among the Jews expelled from Spain and forcibly baptized in Portugal. In his book *Shevet Yehudah* (*The Scepter of Judah*), published posthumously in 1553, he described the anguish of the Spanish Jewish refugees, sometimes using imaginary dialogue or settings to capture their inner spirit. One scene stands out. It is of a man whose wife and two sons had died from starvation and fatigue. In agony, the man cried:

"Master of the Universe! You go to great lengths to force me to desert my faith. Know for a certainty that in the face of the dwellers of heaven, a Jew I am and a Jew I shall remain; all that You have brought upon me or will bring upon me shall be of no avail."

It was a fitting summary of the feelings of the Spanish Jews who chose expulsion over conversion to Christianity. And it was a summary of the determination of thousands of conversos who remained Jews in their hearts and were burned alive because of that.

Shabbat Hazon—the Sabbath of Isaiah's Vision

The vision with which the Book of Isaiah begins is less seen than heard. It is the sound and spirit of God reproaching the people of Judah with words of disappointment and despair. " 'I reared children and brought them up— / And they have rebelled against Me!' " (1:2). That theme of rebuke and sadness, of the people's transgressions and God's disillusionment, forms the prelude to the Tisha B'Av fast that will take place in a few days. Isaiah's opening prophecy makes up the prophetic portion read in synagogue on the Sabbath before Tisha B'Av. The Sabbath takes its name, *Shabbat Hazon,* from the chapter's first words, *Hazon Yeshayahu,* "the vision of Isaiah."

The choice of reading may seem odd because Isaiah did not live during the period of the First Temple's destruction, which is commemorated on Tisha B'Av. Jeremiah did, and, in fact, portions from his prophecies of destruction are read on the two Sabbaths preceding this one. Isaiah prophesied more than a hundred years earlier, from about 740 to 700 B.C.E. Oddly also, the words of exhortation in this prophecy came at a time when the people he addressed—the kingdom of Judah—were enjoying peace and prosperity under the reign of King Uzziah. On the surface his gloom seems inappropriate, out of sync with real life around him.

Yet the reading suits this day. If the final destruction of Judah was a century away, Isaiah was to witness in just a few years the end of its sister kingdom of Israel, overcome by the Assyrians. Nor would he be able to prevent Judah itself from becoming a vassal to Assyria after Uzziah's death, the beginning of its own downfall.

More to the point, Isaiah's message to the Judeans, and specifically to the wealthy aristocrats of Jerusalem, pierced beyond their success to the corruption of their lives. He spoke with disgust of the rituals they practiced mindlessly. "What need have I of all your sacrifices?" he cried in God's name. "Devote yourselves to justice; / Aid the wronged," he challenged them (1:11, 17).

It was a universal message that reached beyond its own time. It could have special meaning before the Tisha B'Av fast because it emphasizes the uselessness of religious practices that are not backed by deeds. Like a similar prophetic reading on Yom Kippur, it insists that all the prayers and fasts in the world cannot compensate for the evil of ignoring justice.

Isaiah's prophecy opens with "Hear, O heavens, and give ear, O earth" (1:2), reminiscent of Moses' words to Israel before his death, "Give ear, O heavens . . . / Let the earth hear" (Deuteronomy 32:1). In starting that way, it evokes the sense of exile and loneliness Moses suffered, shut out as he was from the Promised Land. Isaiah also foresees a tragedy to come, although he cannot know that in the future his people will twice be exiled from that Promised Land.

On Shabbat Hazon, the reader chants the prophetic portion in the mournful melody of Lamentations, the book read on Tisha B'Av. The reading concludes with words of encouragement: "Zion shall be saved in the judgment; / Her repentant ones, in the retribution" (Isaiah 1:27).

The Eighth Day of Av

TISHA B'AV EVE—LAMENTING THE DESTRUCTION OF THE TEMPLES

It is sundown on the eighth of Av. The synagogue lights are dimmed and the curtain to the ark has been removed, leaving it bare and unadorned. Members of the congregation sit on low chairs or stools, some on the floor. Many hold candles whose tiny flames provide the only real illumination in the room.

Like visitors to a house of mourning, people do not greet each other as they enter the synagogue. Earlier in the evening, those who have undertaken the obligatory twenty-four-hour fast ate a final meal that avoided meat and wine but included a hard-boiled egg and bread dipped in ashes. In that they resembled mourners who eat an egg after returning from the cemetery to symbolize the cycle of life.

On this evening the entire congregation is in mourning, performing the rituals prescribed for grieving the loss of a close family member. These mourners have gathered to lament events that happened more than two thousand years ago, but for this evening and the next day the grief will seem as poignant as any in contemporary life. For this is the beginning of the Ninth of Av, the day that marks the Babylonian destruction of the First Temple in 586 B.C.E. and the Roman destruction of the Second in 70 C.E. It is immaterial that the First Temple was probably burned down on the tenth of the month and that the exact day of the second destruction is unclear. The Ninth of Av is branded in Jewish memory as the anniversary of national disasters.

This is so much the case that through the years numbers of catastrophes have been connected to it, as if the date holds some dire magnetic force that draws misfortune to it. Thus the Betar fortress, the last stronghold of the Bar Kokhba war, was said to have fallen to the Romans on the Ninth of Av, 135 C.E. King Edward I issued an edict for the expulsion of the Jews from England in July 1290, believed to be on Tisha B'Av, and the expulsion from Spain in 1492 is linked to this fast day, although the last Jews actually left that country on the seventh of Av.

Looking back to the early history of Israel, the rabbis taught that the calamities of the Ninth of Av began when God decreed on that date that the generation that had left Egypt would die in the wilderness without entering the Promised Land. The punishment itself resulted, according to Scripture, from the report of ten of the twelve spies Moses had sent to scout out the land of Canaan. Two, Joshua and Caleb, spoke with confidence of the Israelites' ability under God to conquer the territory. The other ten spoke too much. Going beyond their assignment to describe what they saw, they dwelt on their own fears. "We looked like grasshoppers to ourselves, and so we must have looked to them," they said (Numbers 13:33), portraying the inhabitants as invincible giants.

The Israelite multitudes responded to the spies' words with loud cries to return to Egypt. For their lack of faith, God condemned them to roam in the desert until they all died off. The sages imagined God saying, "These people have cried for no reason. I shall give them reason to cry on this day for all time." Thus, in rabbinic thought, was born the tragedy-filled Ninth of Av, its recurring exiles foreshadowed by the wanderings of the ancient Israelites.

❖

In the darkened synagogue, after the evening service, congregants read all five chapters of the Book of Lamentations, *Eikhah* in Hebrew, literally meaning "how." The "how" is not a question but the first word of an opening statement that reflects the trauma of the Babylonian destruction: "How lonely sits the city / Once great with people!" (1:1). For years a powerful city, Jerusalem has been reduced to rubble, its women raped, its children dead from lack of food and water, its leaders exiled, its prophets and priests executed. Verse after verse, the book builds a picture of grim desolation. Its main image is of the "daughter of Zion," the spirit of Jerusalem and Israel, mourned by her people but also mourning for them.

The people rage at God in this book: "See, O Lord, and behold, / To whom You have done this!" (2:20). They wonder in confusion about the catastrophe's cause: "Our fathers sinned and are no more; / And we must bear their guilt" (5:7). And they try in their agony to find some glimmer of hope: "The kindness of the Lord has not ended, / His mercies are not spent" (3:22).

Each chapter of Lamentations is an alphabetical acrostic, except for the last. In tradition, the prophet Jeremiah recited the entire book and the scribe Baruch ben Neriah wrote it down. But most modern scholars believe that several authors who lived through the devastation wrote its various sections.

Like the keening of the daughter of Zion over her people, the melody for Lamentations has the quality of unrelieved sorrow. In many synagogues, individual congregants sing portions aloud while others follow softly. At the end, the entire congregation, wrung out from the relentless sadness, joins with growing strength in the words, "Turn us to You, O Lord, and we shall return. Renew our days as of old" (5:21).

Before the evening closes, the congregation usually sings several kinot, or dirges, together. The best known in Ashkenazic synagogues is *Eli Ziyyon v'Areha*, "Wail, Zion and Its Cities," written in the Middle Ages but reliving in detail the horrors of the second destruction. Here again, the image of a woman's suffering serves as a symbol for the anguish of the nation: "Wail, Zion, and its cities," the refrain goes, "like a woman in labor pains, and like a maiden dressed in sackcloth to mourn the betrothed of her youth." In many Sephardic congregations, the main dirge follows the form of the four questions of the Passover seder, connecting the bitter herbs of Passover to the bitterness of the Jewish experience.

When services end on Tisha B'Av eve, congregants file out of the synagogue in silence, as they came in. The events recalled during the evening may have been ancient ones, but the pain they generated has been reawakened enough times in Jewish history to feel raw and real.

The Ninth Day of Av

TISHA B'AV—MOURNING AND CONSOLATION

Rabban Gamaliel, Rabbi Eleazar ben Azariah, Rabbi Joshua, and Rabbi Akiva (all first-to-second-century sages) came up to Jerusalem. When they reached the Temple Mount, they saw a fox running out of the ruins where the Holy of Holies had once stood. The other sages began to weep, but Rabbi Akiva laughed.

"Akiva, you always surprise us," they said. "We weep, and you're merry."

"Why are you weeping?" he asked.

They answered, "Should we not weep when our holiest place has become the haunt of foxes?"

"That is why I am merry," he said. "For Scripture says, 'And call reliable witnesses, the priest Uriah and Zechariah son of Jeberechiah' [Isaiah 8:2]. Now what connection has Uriah with Zechariah? Uriah lived at the time of the First Temple and Zechariah in the time of the Second Temple. But what did each of them say?

"Uriah said, 'Zion shall be plowed as a field, / Jerusalem shall become heaps of ruins' [Jeremiah 26:18; Akiva is identifying Uriah with the prophet Micah].

"Zechariah said, 'There shall yet be old men and women in the squares of Jerusalem' [Zechariah 8:4].

"So long as Uriah's prophecy of doom had not been fulfilled, I was concerned that Zechariah's words would not be fulfilled. Now that Uriah's prophecy has come true, I am certain that Zechariah's prophecy will come true."

"Akiva, you have comforted us," they said. "Akiva, you have comforted us."

Although the gloom of Tisha B'Av hangs heavy over this day of tragic remembrances, hints of hopefulness poke through, much like Akiva's faith in the future. The most uplifting aspects of the commemoration come from the part of the story not told in the course of the day, but without which there might be no telling at all.

It is the part that concerns Rabban Johanan ben Zakkai, the leading sage at the time of the Second Temple's destruction. Johanan was a Pharisee and a moderate who had hoped for a peaceful settlement of the war with Rome. When he saw that would not happen, he devised a bold plan. He arranged for some of his students to pretend he had died and then carry him out of Jerusalem in a coffin. In that way he avoided the extremist Jewish Zealots who prevented any Jews from leaving the embattled city, and also eluded Roman detection. According to the Talmud, in making his escape he had the secret help of his nephew, a Zealot himself.

Johanan went to the Roman general Vespasian—who would soon become emperor—and asked for the safety of the coastal town of Jabneh and its small group of scholars. In the rabbinic story, Vespasian granted the request because of Johanan's stature. Historians suggest that, actually, after leaving Jerusalem, Johanan was probably thrown into a Roman internment camp in Jabneh, where he informally began teaching other scholars. In either case, after some time Johanan managed to build an academy near Jabneh that revived Jewish spiritual life in this period of despair. Under his influence, Jabneh became the religious and governmental center of the Jewish world. Its court of law (bet din) replaced the now dead Sanhedrin, the supreme court in Jerusalem, and its scholars regulated the calendar and gave the canon of the Bible its final form.

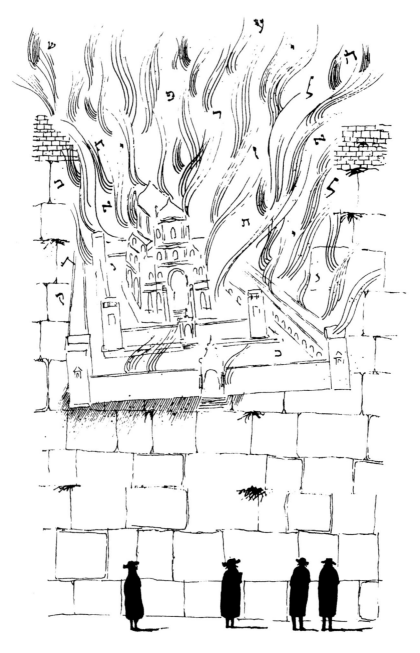

When the Temple was destroyed, Johanan saw the fires from a distance and, shaken with sorrow, tore his clothes and wept. Still, he could assure his students that the sacrifices once brought to the Temple were not the only means of atoning for sins. Prayer and acts of loving-kindness, which could be performed anywhere, were as effective. And even while he and his disciples lamented the loss of the Temple, he showed the way to transferring Temple rituals—such as carrying the lulav and etrog on Sukkot—to the synagogue and home, thus assuring the continuity of Judaism.

One of Johanan's most learned disciples, Rabbi Joshua ben Hananiah, followed in his teacher's footsteps. When ascetics went to extremes in mourning Jerusalem and the Temple, Joshua restrained them, saying, "Not to mourn is impossible, because the blow has fallen. To mourn excessively is also impossible, because we do not impose such a hardship on the community." Therefore, he told them, the nation should mourn symbolically. "A person may stucco his house, but he should leave a little bare . . . A person may prepare a full-course dinner, but he should omit an item or two . . ." (Today, Rabbi Joshua's advice is continued in the custom of breaking a glass at a wedding in commemoration of the destruction.)

Rabban Johanan, Rabbi Joshua, and others at Jabneh kept alive the memory of the Temple and the longing for its restoration, but they—like Rabbi Akiva—did not allow grief to paralyze the community. Their spirit permeates the observance of Tisha B'Av.

❖

In the religious community, the day begins with morning services at which people do not don tallit or *tefillin* (prayer shawls or phylacteries) because these are regarded as religious ornaments, unsuitable for the day's grieving. A harsh Torah portion is read, in which Moses warns of the punishment that will strike the nation if it strays from the commandments. The prophetic portion from Jeremiah, chanted in the doleful tune of Lamentations, includes the verse "Oh, that my head were water, / My eyes a fount of tears! / Then would I weep day and night / For the slain of my poor people" (8:23). The artist Ben Shahn illustrated that verse in Hebrew in a famous drawing of a woman's head bowed in dejection. Before services end, worshippers again recite dirges, often from a separate book of kinot.

Work is permitted during the day, but the fast continues. The observant refrain even from studying the Torah, because this is regarded as an act of joy. Only the Books of Lamentations and Job—which has its own sadnesses—are permitted, along with parts of the prophets and the Talmud that deal with the desolation of Jerusalem.

But then come the afternoon and evening services, and the air of gloom begins to lift. Now worshippers wear the tallit and tefillin omitted in the morning—the only time during the year when tefillin are worn in the afternoon. The Torah reading includes Moses' prayer to God to forgive the Israelites for the sin of the golden calf, and God's promise: "I hereby make a covenant. Before all your people I will work such wonders as have not been wrought on all the earth or in any nation . . ." (Exodus 34:10).

The somberness of the long hours gives way to feelings of relief and reconciliation. The ordeal has ended. People eat with restraint after the fast because the Temple is said to have continued burning through the next day, but, like Rabbi Johanan, the community looks to the future. Immediately after Tisha B'Av a spate of weddings takes place, forbidden for all those weeks beforehand.

The question has often been raised of why we continue to observe Tisha B'Av with the State of Israel a reality in our lives. The answer lies in the continuity of Jewish tradition. We may live as individuals in the present, but we also live as a people in history. Tisha B'Av embodies so much of the angst and suffering of Jewish history that to put it aside would be to deny part of our peoplehood. That's not to say, however, that we need to behave as if nothing has changed since the fall of Jerusalem in the year 70. In recognition of the change, some contemporary rabbis advocate ending the Tisha B'Av fast and its mourning rituals early in the afternoon instead of in the evening, as a conscious celebration of Israel's existence.

Another thought would be to conclude the fast by reading aloud the words of the prophet Zechariah with which Rabbi Akiva comforted his companions, and rejoice openly in them. Uriah's prophecy of doom came true more than two thousand years ago. Zechariah's prophecy of return was fulfilled in our lifetime. So many old men and women and young boys and girls walk and play now in the squares of Jerusalem.

Shabbat Nahamu—the Sabbath of Comfort

There is something comforting in the very fact that only three Sabbaths are devoted to prophecies of rebuke and doom during the period before Tisha B'Av but seven Sabbaths after Tisha B'Av hold prophecies of consolation and gladness. Those priorities seem right. From a religious standpoint, the prophets' warnings and reproaches read in the synagogue set the mood for the three dark weeks of mourning the tragedies of Tisha B'Av. But from a human standpoint, what is needed after dwelling on those tragedies is an abundance of comfort and hope, encouragement and love.

The seven readings of consolation, called *sheva d'nehamata*, provide all of those. They offer a vision of a joyful future in which Israel, reunited with God, will be honored and gloried by the nations of the world. The first of the seven Sabbaths takes its name from the opening words of the reading, *Nahamu, nahamu Ami*, "Comfort, oh comfort My people" (Isaiah 40:1).

This prophecy and the others that follow were written by a prophet known only as Second Isaiah. Although in tradition one person wrote the entire Book of Isaiah, modern critics agree that the prophet of the second half of the book, chapters 40 to 66, lived about two hundred years after the first Isaiah. Some speculate that a third, anonymous, prophet wrote the last ten chapters.

Second Isaiah prophesied during the Babylonian exile, at a time when Persia was forcing the great Babylonia to its knees. Soon the Persian king, Cyrus, would permit the exiles to return to their land. This Isaiah spoke—sang, because his words are so lyrical—of the imminent return and the glorious redemption to follow.

The prophet understood the soul of his people. He felt their despair after being exiled and sympathized with their belief that God had abandoned them. In this first comforting prophecy, he reassured them that God had forgiven their sins and watched over them as a shepherd watches over his flock. "He gathers the lambs in His arms," he told them, "And carries them in His bosom; / Gently He drives the mother sheep" (40:11).

No other prophet spoke as tenderly as this Isaiah, or as poetically. He could portray God as a mighty king, but also a loving mother. "Can a woman forget her baby, / Or disown the child of her womb?" he asked. "Though she might forget, / I never could forget you" (49:15). And exuberantly he urged the people out of despondency: "Arise, shine, for your light has dawned" (60:1), he exclaimed. Later kabbalists would adapt this verse to their moving Sabbath hymn "Lekhah Dodi."

The seven Sabbaths of consolation cover the seven weeks between Tisha B'Av and Rosh Hashanah, a time when Jews turn their attention from national tragedy to personal scrutiny and from death and destruction to the beginnings of a new year. The prophet's words of love and inspiration ease those transitions.

The Fifteenth Day of Av
TU B'AV—THE FESTIVAL OF THE VINEYARDS

A charming pageant gave final closure to the gloom of the Ninth of Av during Second Temple times. On the fifteenth of the month, the day of the full moon, the young, unmarried women of Jerusalem would dance and sing in the vineyards to celebrate the grape harvest. These carefree "daughters of Jerusalem," as the Mishnah calls them, form a counterpoint to the "daughter of Zion" who weeps over her destroyed city in the Book of Lamentations.

The vineyard dancing also took place on Yom Kippur afternoon, possibly to designate the end of the grape harvest, but also as a balance to the solemnity of that fast day. The Mishnah states that no days in ancient Israel were as happy as these. The women would dress in white clothes they had borrowed for the occasion so that those who were poor might not feel shamed by what they wore. As a kind of precursor to the modern Sadie Hawkins Day, they would beckon to the single men of the town as they danced:

"Young man, lift up your eyes and see who you would choose for yourself. Do not look for beauty, but look rather for family . . ."

The sages suggested playfully that the most beautiful maidens would urge the men to consider their appearance; the aristocratic would point to their lineage; and the least attractive would ask to be selected "for the sake of heaven."

We'll never know how many marriages actually resulted from this mating game in the vineyards, but it must have been a happy ritual, especially for the women, who usually led sheltered lives.

In one unhappy instance in early Jewish history, a group of men did literally snatch their brides from the midst of women dancing in the vineyards. It happened in Shiloh, the religious center of Israel at the time of the judges, long before Solomon's Temple was built. The tribe of Benjamin had been ostracized by the others because its members had brutally raped the concubine of a man visiting Gibeah in their territory. Learning of the Benjaminites' behavior, the other tribes had waged war against them and killed off large numbers, including many women. They then vowed never to allow Benjaminite men to marry their daughters.

After a while, the tribes regretted the loss of Benjamin, and the vow they had made. They devised a complicated plan to allow Benjaminite men to wed women from their midst without breaking the vow. Part of it called for the Benjaminite men to come to the vineyards at Shiloh when the women were dancing and carry them off to be their wives. This the men did—an act only a degree or so less barbaric than their original brutality, but one that reunited them through marriage with the other tribes.

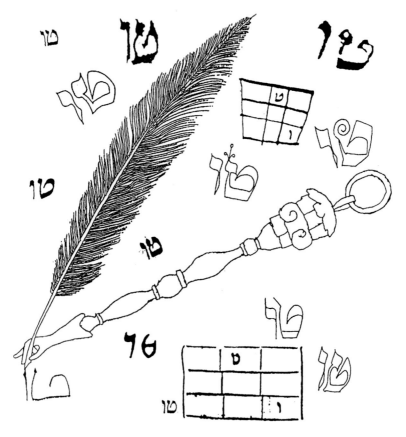

Whether the kidnapping of the dancing girls occurred on the fifteenth of Av or another vineyard festival is unclear. The Talmud does tell us that at some point on the fifteenth of Av the tribes lifted their ban against marriage with the Benjaminites, a cause for great celebration.

In reality, the fifteenth of Av was probably an old midsummer folk festival that had no basis in Jewish history. Called *Tu B'Av* (the Hebrew letters for *tu* equal the number 15), it parallels the minor midwinter festival of Tu B'Shevat, a holiday of trees.

As they were wont to do, however, the sages offered a string of unconnected reasons for this festive day. Among them:

An old law forbidding members of the various tribes from intermarrying with one another was abrogated then.

The last person doomed to die in the desert died, and with that the Israelites' punishment for heeding the evil report of the ten spies to Canaan ended.

The Romans permitted the Jews to bury the dead who had fallen at Betar, the last stronghold of the Bar Kokhba war, a burial previously forbidden.

This was one of nine days when families brought offerings of wood to the Temple to be used in burning sacrifices on the altar. The priests, the Levites, and families who were not sure of their tribal descent brought their wood offerings at this time.

Finally, on Tu B'Av people stopped felling trees for those wood offerings because from then until the next summer the sun would no longer be strong enough to dry out the wood. The celebration heralded the approach of autumn. Now the days would begin to grow shorter and the nights longer—more time to study Torah, the rabbis said.

All those talmudic reasons notwithstanding, Tu B'Av has generally slipped into oblivion as a holiday. What we are left with only is a diaphanous image of young women dressed in white dancing gaily in the vineyards while they flirt sweetly with the young men watching them.

ELUL

August–September

TOWARD THE END OF THE BOOK OF ESTHER A VERSE READS IN HEBREW *ISH LE'REIEIHU U'MATANOT LA'EVYONIM*, WHICH MEANS SENDING GIFTS "TO ONE ANOTHER AND PRESENTS TO THE POOR" (9:22), AND REFERS TO THE PRACTICE OF CELEBRATING THE JEWISH VICTORY OVER THE WICKED HAMAN BY EXCHANGING GIFTS AND GIVING CHARITY.

A verse in the Song of Songs, often recited during weddings, reads *Ani l'dodi v'dodi li*, which means "I am my beloved's / And my beloved is mine" (6:3). In rabbinic thought, it refers to the great mutual love between God and Israel.

The initial letters of each of these passages in Hebrew spell the name *Elul*, the last month before the Jewish New Year. The verse about sending gifts is said to allude to material aspects of the month's activities—giving charity to the poor, buying clothes for the holiday, preparing festive foods, and such. The love verse speaks to the spiritual side of the month, with its emphasis on repentance and the renewal of closeness to God.

That spiritual side gets recognized on the very first day of Elul, the day of the new moon when, in tradition, Moses went up to Mount Sinai to receive the second tablets of the Law after he had smashed the first. He stayed there forty days and returned on the tenth of Tishrei, Yom Kippur, and his return with the new tablets signaled God's forgiveness of Israel for the sin of the golden calf.

Beginning on that first day, the shofar is sounded in the synagogue every morning after services, except on the Sabbath. Legend says that Moses had the shofar blown as he left the Israelite camp to ascend Mount Sinai so that the people would not think he had deserted them, and sin again. The blowing stops on the morning before Rosh Hashanah to separate the shofar sounding on Rosh Hashanah, which is commanded in Scripture, from the daily sounding, which grew from custom. Another view: The blowing stops on the morning of Rosh Hashanah to confuse Satan into thinking that the holiday has passed and that he can no longer present his complaints against people.

In preparation for the days to come, during Elul the observant have their tefillin and *mezuzot*, the parchment scrolls affixed to their doorposts, examined to make sure they are in perfect condition. Many people visit the gravesides of parents and friends during this time. And on a happier note, people exchange New Year's cards or add messages at the end of their letters extending each other wishes to be inscribed and sealed in the book of life.

Considering the seriousness of the month's activities, it is somewhat surprising that the rabbis did not find an interpretation for the zodiac sign in keeping with its spirit. The sign is Virgo, the virgin, and the best they could do was state that Israel can be compared to a virgin, presumably because of its purity. But we can go further and say that the symbol of the virgin fits a month in which Jews strive to wipe the slate clean from the past year and rediscover the innocence they once knew. Elul is a busy month of preparing to be reborn.

The Eighteenth Day of Elul

ISRAEL BA'AL SHEM TOV, FOUNDER OF HASIDISM,

IS BORN, C. 1698

From a letter of the Ba'al Shem Tov to his brother-in-law, Rabbi Gershon of Kitov, about 1752: "On Rosh Hashanah of the year 5507 [1746] I performed, by means of an oath, an elevation of soul, and saw wondrous things I had never seen before . . . I ascended from level to level until I entered the chamber of the Messiah . . . I asked Messiah: 'When will you come, Master?' And he answered: 'By this you shall know: When your teachings will become public and revealed in the world, and your wellsprings burst forth to the farthest extremes . . .' "

At face value, such a description might seem, at best, the retelling of a dream, or, more likely, the hallucinations of a person under the influence of mind-altering drugs. But we are speaking here of the Ba'al Shem Tov, the founder of the Hasidic movement, whose followers knew, and know, that many things were possible for him that ordinary people can barely fathom. His soul *could* ascend to the upper reaches of heaven and be graciously received there by the Messiah. Indeed, when the wellsprings of his teachings have spread out to all parts of the world . . .

Well, who knows? He wrought miracles in his time, healing the sick, comforting the poor— and cutting through the often grim dailiness of Jewish life in Eastern Europe to infuse it with love and song. If his own life is a mystery to us, his followers might say it is because he lived it on so many levels, in this world and the world above, and left behind what is far more important than biographical facts: a way of looking at God and the universe that uncovered deeper joys and meanings than had been understood before.

The facts are few, gleaned mostly from collections of legendary tales about him published by his pupils after his death. It is known that he was born in Okop, in the Ukrainian province of Podolia. Hasidic calendars list the date as the eighteenth of Elul, 1698. Eighteen is equivalent to the Hebrew word *chai*, or "life," and that association may account for the assigned birth date. Historians disagree about whether he was born in 1698 or 1700.

Legend has it that he was born to poor and old parents as a reward for his father, Rabbi Eliezer. The father was so pious that even the heavens praised him. Urged by Satan that he be tested, Elijah the prophet came to Eliezer one Sabbath afternoon disguised as a beggar carrying a knapsack. Although the stranger was profaning the Sabbath, Eliezer greeted him warmly, fed him the third Sabbath meal, and next morning gave him food and money. The prophet then revealed himself and announced that Eliezer would be blessed with a son who would brighten all Israel.

The parents may have died when he was very young. Israel worked as a teacher's assistant, a beadle at the local house of study, and a ritual slaughterer. He married, his wife died, and he married again. His second wife, Hannah, was promised to Israel by her father, but after his death her brother thought Israel a simpleton and urged her to divorce him. Instead the couple moved to the Carpathian Mountains, where Israel spent much time in solitude and contemplation. For a living, he quarried clay, which she sold in the nearby villages. They had a son named Zevi and a daughter, Adel, who became known for her piety and whose grandson would be one of the most famous of all Hasidic masters, Rabbi Nahman of Bratslav.

We learn from tales that at the age of thirty-six Israel revealed himself as a leader and teacher. A preacher visiting his home awoke in the middle of the night and saw a blinding light beside the stove. Thinking the stove was on fire, he rushed toward it with water. But when he approached he saw Israel sitting and studying, and a beautiful light shone from him, like the light of a rainbow. The preacher fainted. When he awoke he questioned Israel, who at first denied anything unusual had occurred. Pressed further, he showed his true self, and then began to travel and teach his ways.

He became known as the Ba'al Shem Tov, "Master of the Good Name," often shortened to the acronym *Besht.* He was not the first Ba'al Shem. The title had been applied for hundreds of years to wonder-workers who used secret, mystical names for God in healing the sick and exorcising evil spirits. But to his believers, the Ba'al Shem Tov rose far above those predecessors. His powerful personality and the message he carried drew both ordinary folk and learned men to his side wherever he went.

It was a simple message: God is everywhere and in everything. We have only to seek the divine in all our activities and we will give meaning and holiness to our lives. Achieving holiness, he taught, was not a matter of endless study or ascetic practices but of *devekut,* "adhesion" to or communion with God.

The concept of devekut stemmed from the teachings of Isaac Luria and the sixteenth-century kabbalists, but with a twist. For those mystics, close communion with God was an ideal to be reached only by a few profoundly spiritual persons and with much effort. In the Besht's vision, every Jew can attain intimacy with God through sincere faith and heartfelt worship. One path toward that goal is to contemplate the words and letters of the Torah, for they are vessels that hold the divine light. Concentrating on them in study and prayer releases that light and the God spirit within it.

Most appealing in the Besht's teachings was his emphasis on the joyful love of God. "It is the aim and essence of my pilgrimage on earth," he said, "to show my brethren by living demonstration how one may serve God with merriment and rejoicing." So he taught his followers to express their strongest spiritual emotions by singing and dancing during worship. And he insisted that the prayers of the humblest villager, or the whistling of an illiterate boy, could reach heaven as easily as the words of the most elite scholar.

Needless to say, his innovative approach did not sit well with the established scholars and rabbis who governed Jewish community life. As masses of people flocked to the Ba'al Shem Tov, opposition to him also grew. His opponents, later known as *Mitnaggedim,* bitterly opposed his teachings and those of his followers. They saw in his great popular appeal echoes of the disastrous mass acceptance of the false messiah Shabbetai Zevi some hundred years earlier. Though the Besht never made messianic claims for himself, his reputation as a miracle worker aroused suspicion. Moreover, his role as a man of the people flew in the face of the serious talmudic scholarship traditionally required of Jewish leaders.

But to those he touched, the Besht's words and practices were a breath of fresh air in the often dry, legalistic world of the scholars. Other spiritual leaders seeking change joined him as disciples, becoming known as *zaddikim*, "righteous men," or rebbes, "teachers." The movement that developed around them was called Hasidism, and its followers Hasidim. Those were also terms with a past. There had been pietists known as hasidim during the talmudic period, and another hasidic movement in twelfth-century Germany that emphasized ethics and saintliness. But Hasidism as we know it today grew from the vision and teachings of the Ba'al Shem Tov.

❖

The Hasidism we know today, however, is no longer the revolutionary force the Besht inspired but the most conservative of Jewish movements. Television cameras love to dwell on the figures of Hasidic men with their beards and sidecurls, and their black robes and hats fashioned after the eighteenth-century dress of the Eastern European lands from which their ancestors came. There are many Hasidic sects in Israel and the United States, reestablished after the Holocaust and still bearing names based on regions where they originated, such as the Satmar Hasidim from Hungary. Some are anti-Zionist. Many have closed themselves off to contact with any but extreme Orthodox groups, viewing others as heretical, just as their movement itself was once seen as heretical. The most intellectual and worldly are the Lubavicher, who emphasize the study of Jewish texts and do widescale outreach programs to gain followers.

The Hasidim split into their different groups after the death of the Besht, when the movement spread so broadly that it could no longer be led by one person. By the third generation, these groups had become like royal dynasties, with a son or close disciple inheriting a zaddik's mantle, a system that continues today. The early zaddikim were regarded as holy men in close association with God. Many had large courts to which their followers came to seek advice about every aspect of their lives. Although some of these leaders became corrupt with the power and wealth showered on them, many served as true spiritual guides for their followers. In that, they continued the pattern of leadership begun by the Besht.

❖

The Ba'al Shem Tov died in 1760, supposedly on Shavuot. Ill and in bed, legend says, he had predicted that he would pass away when two clocks in his room stopped. As his life left him, his disciples noticed that the clocks had stopped. It is said that one of them also saw his soul departing from his body in the form of a blue flame.

During the Besht's lifetime, that flame ignited a movement that would become firmly entrenched in Jewish life and imagination. However much the movement changed, it stayed true to his ideal of putting song and gladness at the center of religious experience, and from that ideal there grew melodies and tunes that have had a lasting influence on Jewish liturgy and music. Around that man about whom we have few facts and those who came after him there also grew a lustrous literature of legends and tales that is a source of wisdom and strength for all Jews.

Selihot—a Night of Supplication

In a mysterious and beautiful encounter, beyond the ken of human reason, Scripture tells us that God passed before Moses and proclaimed to him the aspects of divine mercy. Earlier, Moses had pleaded, "Oh, let me behold Your Presence!" (Exodus 33:18). In response, God had placed him in the cleft of a rock and shielded his vision so that the divine light would not consume him.

Hidden in his cave, Moses was permitted to see the Deity only from the back, but he could hear the sound of God's words. Those words have become known as the "Thirteen Attributes of Divine Mercy." They form the heart of the prayer services for forgiveness, the selihot, said before the Rosh Hashanah holiday.

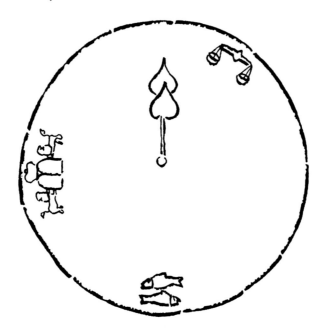

In Ashkenazic communities those services are held for at least four days before the holiday, in many synagogues beginning at dawn. The first service, which may be the only one most people attend, usually takes place at midnight on the Saturday night before Rosh Hashanah, or, if the holiday falls early in the week, on the previous Saturday night. The timing connects the prayers to the traditional date for the beginning of Creation, the twenty-fifth of Elul, as a reminder of God's power and grace in forming the vast universe.

In the Sephardic tradition, selihot begin on the first day of Elul and continue until Yom Kippur—the forty-day time span during which Moses remained on Mount Sinai receiving the second set of tablets.

The selihot service includes various piyyutim, or liturgical poems, and groups of penitential prayers, and introduces the special melodies that will dominate the Rosh Hashanah liturgy, setting the mood for the days ahead. Climaxing each section of prayers and poems, the congregation recites aloud the words Moses heard in the cleft of the rock, the Thirteen Attributes of God:

The Lord,

The Lord,

God

Compassionate and

Gracious,

Slow to anger,

Abounding in kindness and

Faithfulness,

Extending kindness to the thousandth generation,

Forgiving iniquity,

transgression,

and sin, and

Granting pardon (Exodus 34:6–7).

There are other ways of dividing the passage to arrive at the number 13, but this is the most generally accepted. The terms "the Lord, the Lord" are counted twice because in rabbinic thought the first expression refers to God as showing mercy even before a person sins, knowing that sin will occur at some time. The second signifies God's willingness to forgive the sinner after a transgression and to accept repentance.

The rabbis also treated the name God, in Hebrew *El*, as a separate attribute, because they regarded it as a name that denotes particular compassion. As Rashi explains it, the Psalmist's cry, *Eli, Eli*, "My God, my God, why have You abandoned me?" (Psalm 22:1), is a call of pain to a God of mercy rather than to one of strict justice, and from there we learn that *El* refers to the consoling aspect of God.

The last phrase in the listing of attributes, "granting pardon," actually appears in Scripture as "He will not grant pardon to the guilty," but the rabbis used only part of the Hebrew phrase to change its meaning and hold out the hope of forgiveness for all who seek it.

The sages picture God as wrapped in a prayer shawl in that mystical moment with Moses, like the reader in a synagogue. "Whenever Israel sins," they imagined God saying, "let them perform this rite before Me, and I will forgive them." Hence the prominence of this listing in the selihot services before Rosh Hashanah, and later throughout the holiday and the Day of Atonement.

Another dialogue between Moses and God gives emotional power to the selihot services. In it Moses pleads for God's forgiveness after the ten spies have drained the people of their faith in the Promised Land. "Pardon, I pray, the iniquity of this people according to Your great kindness, as You have forgiven this people ever since Egypt," he says humbly, and the reader and congregation repeat the request during their prayers. God answers, "I pardon, as you have asked" (Numbers 14:19–20), and the reader and congregation chant—sometimes shout—the words with enthusiasm.

Further along in the services, worshippers recite a short group of communal sins, the *vidui*, or confession. "We have sinned, we have betrayed, we have stolen . . ." it goes, in Hebrew alphabetic order, and with it the community assumes responsibility for the deeds of every member. Later, this and a longer confession will become the staples of Yom Kippur prayers.

One other part of the selihot liturgy stands out. It is one of the oldest, dating back to the Mishnah, compiled about eighteen hundred years ago. It calls up a slew of ancient heroes to act as witnesses to the possibility of salvation. "Who answered our father Abraham on Mount Moriah, May He answer us," it requests. "Who answered his son Isaac when he was bound on the altar, May He answer us," and on through Moses and Aaron and Jonah and Esther, and finally, "all the righteous and devout" through all the generations.

For the purposes of this night of penitence, nothing of Jewish history matters but the deeds of God and the ancestors. Recovering those deeds in one's own life, repenting transgressions, and resolving to change become the tasks ahead.

The Twenty-fifth Day of Elul

THE CREATION OF THE WORLD BEGINS

When God set out to create the world, legend tells us, the twenty-two letters of the Hebrew alphabet, which had been engraved on the holy crown, began to compete with one another. Each wanted to be the letter from which the world would be formed. After hearing all sides, God selected *bet*, the second letter of the alphabet, and began Creation with the word *bereshit*, as we read, "*Bereshit* God created the heaven and the earth" (Genesis 1:1). Why the letter *bet*? Because it is also the first letter of the word *berakha*, blessing. And because this letter is closed on three sides and open only in front to show that we are not permitted to investigate what is above or below, or what came before the world as we know it. We are charged to look forward only, toward the path of righteousness.

Certainly the word *bereshit*, formed with the chosen letter *bet*, holds many of the mysteries of Creation. The first word of the Hebrew Bible, it opens the concise, compressed, exquisitely majestic account of the Creation of the world.

But what does it mean? The text says: *Bereshit bara Elohim et hashamayim v'et ha'arez*, which traditionally has been translated as "In the beginning God created the heaven and the earth." That translation and the interpretation most Jewish commentators gave those words implies that nothing at all existed until God created heaven and earth—a world formed out of nothingness. Grammatically, however, the translation doesn't quite fit the Hebrew words. To avoid the grammatical difficulties, many modern translations link the first verse with the second and read, "When God began to create heaven and earth—the earth being unformed and void . . ." And that translation seems to imply that instead of creating from nothing, God put order into a universe that may have already existed in some unformed and chaotic state. Such an interpretation is anathema to Jewish thought, which regards everything in existence as coming from God.

Recognizing the grammatical difficulties, Rashi rationalizes them by stating that this passage does not give us the sequential order of Creation. He points out that the passage also refers to a "wind from God sweeping over the water" (Genesis 1:2), although there had been no previous mention of the creation of water. From this we learn, he claims, that God created water and other elements before creating the earth, but Scripture does not reveal to us the chronology of each event as it occurred. It simply gives us an overview of Creation.

In a more philosophic vein, the commentator Nahmanides holds that in fact God did not create everything in the universe out of nothing. Rather, God first created a thin substance—what the Greeks called primal matter—out of which God then constructed all other things. Nahmanides follows the mystics in redefining the Hebrew words *tohu va'bohu*—usually translated as "unformed and void." "Tohu," he says, is what is created from nothingness, and "bohu" is the form it assumes, the substance it becomes.

Another mystical interpretation solves the grammatical problem of the text by splitting the first word, *bereshit*, into two: *be*, meaning "with" and *reshit*, defined as "Wisdom," one of the ten manifestations of the divine on earth. God created the world with Wisdom, the mystics said, citing a verse in the Book of Proverbs in which Wisdom speaks (8:22): "The Lord created me at the beginning of His course." (In Proverbs, Wisdom appears as a character, urging people toward piety and morality.) From a different angle, the midrash identifies Wisdom with Torah. Before creating the world, God created the Torah, and with the heavenly Torah as a blueprint—*be reshit*—God fashioned the universe.

Many other philosophers, theologians, and grammarians have pondered the meaning of the first words of Genesis and the question of whether anything existed before God began creating. Despite their conjectures, Jewish tradition has consistently viewed God as the prime Being who formed everything else in the cosmos. Or, in the words of the midrash, "Before the world was created, the Holy One, blessed be He, with His Name alone existed." So insistent is the tradition on God's aloneness in Creation that the rabbis taught that no angels were created on the first day lest people mistakenly believe they assisted God in forming heaven and earth.

❖

If Scripture is somewhat ambiguous about how Creation began, it leaves no doubt about God's absolute control over the created world. In some respects the biblical account parallels the creation stories of other ancient Near Eastern peoples. *Tehom*, the Hebrew word for the watery deep, for example, resembles Tiamat, the name of the Babylonian goddess of the deep. But no gods or goddesses appear in the biblical story. No cosmic battles take place between primal forces vying for power, as they do in the mythologies of neighboring lands. This God is omnipotent and superior to all things in nature.

The rhythm of the text drives home that point. "God said . . . ," we read time and again. "God saw . . . ," "God separated . . . ," "God called . . . ," "God made . . ." And as if to emphasize it further, Scripture tells us that on the fifth day God created the great sea monsters—the very monsters who fight against the gods of fertility and creation in ancient myths. The monsters that early peoples feared and worshipped as gods are here created by the One God.

That creation appears effortless for God, quickly effected with words: "Let there be light . . . Let there be an expanse in the midst of the water . . . Let the water below the sky be gathered . . ." (Genesis 1:3, 6, 9). Ten utterances in all, the sages taught, brought the entire universe into being. Nine of them were, "And God said," and the tenth was the word *bereshit,* itself a divine utterance.

The process through which Creation takes place is one of separation and a balancing of opposites. God separates heaven and earth, light and darkness, upper waters and lower waters, land and sea, sun and moon, day and night, and eventually man and woman. But one thing remains whole: God's own nature. The rabbis speculated on the different names for God in the Creation narrative and ascribed them to different divine attributes. (Modern critics ascribe them to different biblical authors.) They connected "Elohim," in the first chapter, with God in the attribute of justice. They regarded "Adonai" (as the Tetragrammaton is traditionally pronounced), which appears in the second chapter, as God in the attribute of mercy. God began to create the world in the attribute of justice only, they said, but soon recognized that it could not exist on justice alone. Therefore God combined mercy with justice, as we see from the term "Adonai Elohim." The unity of the two allows the world to subsist.

❖

At the apex of all of creation stands humanity. Volumes have been written about the disparity between the two versions of human creation presented in Genesis. In the first chapter, God creates man and woman together as one being, as equals. In the second chapter, God creates man from the dust of the earth and woman from man's rib, a creation some have used to justify placing women in a subordinate position to men. In reality, the role of woman as seen through the Creation narratives is not subordinate. The overriding theme of both stories is the closeness of men and women. Created as flesh and bone of each other, on the same day and equally in the image of God, the first woman and man are true companions. Together they are given reign over their universe.

But that reign itself has raised objections. Environmentalists and others have argued that too often it has led us to an anthropocentric view of the world that allows the humans at its center to exploit—and abuse—its resources. It is true that God tells Adam and Eve to "master" the earth (Genesis 1:28). Still, the message the rabbis gleaned from the text as a whole was one of responsibility for the world we inhabit. They pictured God leading Adam around the Garden of Eden and saying, "Do not corrupt or destroy My world, for if you corrupt it, there will be no one to set it right after you."

There is another, still-deeper message in humanity's position at the pinnacle of the created world. A theme that repeats throughout the narrative is the goodness of what has been created. As each stage of Creation is completed, we read, "And God saw that this was good," until we reach the end of Creation on the sixth day, when "God saw all that He had made, and found it very good" (Genesis 1:31). We live in a world filled with poverty, suffering, crime, and illness. Is it too naïve to suggest that the ultimate lesson behind the biblical story of Creation is the need for humans to reclaim the goodness with which it all began?

The Twenty-ninth Day of Elul

ROSH HASHANAH EVE—MAY YOU BE INSCRIBED

FOR A GOOD YEAR

New Year's Eve, December 31, of the secular year is a night for partying and merrymaking. Highway police are alert to drunken drivers and rowdies that night, but even the most subdued will toast one another at midnight to welcome the new year. The holiday ends a month of festivities that begins after Thanksgiving, peaks with the Christmas season, and stretches to a final, all-out New Year's Eve celebration.

New Year's Eve in the Jewish religious year is observed with prayers and contemplation of the days ahead. The only drinking called for is wine for the kiddush, which sanctifies the holiday. The new year arrives at sundown, and long before midnight everyone has gone to bed—a good night's sleep is needed for the next day's synagogue services, the longest of the year with the exception of Yom Kippur. The eve of the religious new year ends a month of spiritual preparation. It begins ten days of reflection, repentance, and prayer.

Clearly, Jews do not take their new year lightly.

In the synagogue, the day before Rosh Hashanah's arrival begins with early-morning selihot services, these more extensive than those of any other day. Immediately after services, some traditional congregations include a ceremony, called *hatarat nedarim*, that allows individuals to annul the vows they have made during the year, much like the communal abolition of vows on Kol Nidrei night. Like that one, this annulment releases people only from vows that affect them personally, and not from commitments to others. The ceremony takes place before three people, who constitute a religious law court that may formally declare the vows void.

By evening, the holiday atmosphere can be felt everywhere. Students have arrived home from college to be with their families, and young couples with their children join parents and grandparents for the festive first meal of the new year. Many people set the dinner table in white to echo at

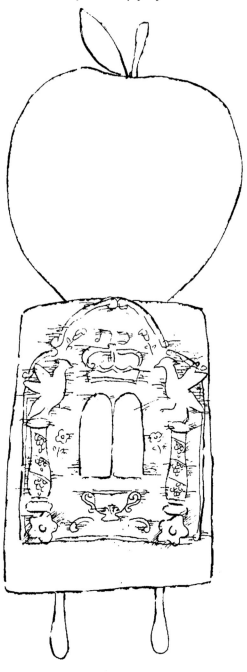

home the white coverings of the ark and reading table that now appear in the synagogue. Apples and honey, symbols of sweetness, stand ready for the evening dinner.

Holiday candles are lit at sundown, and the *sheheheyanu* blessing is added to the traditional benediction in gratitude for having reached this season. In earlier days, only male family members went to synagogue for evening services, while mothers and daughters fussed at home over last-minute dinner preparations. Today many women attend services, participating in all holiday rituals.

The special holiday prayer book, the *mahzor,* is used for the first time during the evening service. The name means "cycle," for originally the mahzor included prayers and poems for the entire year's cycle of festivals. Only later, over the course of time, did the New Year and Day of Atonement liturgies come to make up their own mahzor.

Two verses in the service prepare us for the themes that will dominate Rosh Hashanah: "Sound the shofar on the new moon, announcing our solemn festival. It is Israel's eternal ritual; the God of Jacob calls us to judgment" (Psalm 81:4–5). The shofar will sound the next day, a call to the people of Israel to wake up to the judgment that is soon to be upon them. On the Sabbath before Rosh Hashanah the usual prayer for the new month—in this case Tishrei—is omitted because the holiday itself begins the new month. Unlike Passover, the other "new year" on the Jewish calendar, which comes in the middle of the month on the full moon, Rosh Hashanah falls on the new moon. These verses hail its arrival.

At the end of evening services, everybody greets everybody else with the wish *l'shanah tova tikatevu,* "may you be inscribed for a good year," and returns home for a festive dinner.

In my parents' home, as far back as I can remember, and deep into their old age, my father would kiss my mother lightly on the lips upon returning from synagogue and wish her a happy new year. "Happy New Year," she would reply, returning his kiss. And invariably she would add, "and next year again." I imagine that at some time those words will become part of my greeting as well. They are a shorthand wish for all that we pray for in the coming year: health and well-being and the ability to begin the cycle of Jewish days again and again and to appreciate its every moment.

EPILOGUE
The End of Days

JEWISH IMAGININGS OF THE MESSIANIC ERA

And it shall come to pass in the end of days,
That the Mount of the Lord's house
shall stand firm above the mountains,
And shall tower above the hills;
And all the nations shall gaze
on it with joy (Isaiah 2:2).

THE END OF DAYS, A TIME BEYOND THE DAYS AND MONTHS AND YEARS AS WE KNOW THEM, EXISTS IN JEWISH IMAGINATION AS AN ERA OF PEACE AND TRANQUILLITY, WHEN HUMANKIND WILL BE DRAWN TOGETHER IN FRIENDSHIP AND DEVOTION TO ONE GOD. In the prophet Isaiah's visions, the end of days will be like their beginnings, like the Garden of Eden, an age in which all the world's creatures will dwell side by side in goodness and harmony. At that time, too, as the prophet foresees it, a leader from the stock of Jesse, a descendant of King David, will govern Israel and the entire world in righteousness under God's dominion.

The future ruler the prophet foretold came to be seen in Jewish thought as the Messiah, the "anointed one," who will usher in the days to come, the messianic era. Tradition usually views the Messiah as a man, but how and when he will arrive and exactly what that era will be like have been the subjects of endless, often contradictory, speculations. Some of them have already appeared in various places in this book. But, taken together, the imaginings of the Messiah make up a great patchwork of dreams and hopes that has added depth and texture to Jewish life, and sometimes danger.

He will come riding in on a donkey, in some versions. He will come flying in on a great cloud, in others. He sits among the poor, bandaging the sores of the sick, and will come today—if Jews would but heed God's voice. He will come after a Sabbath that every Jew has observed properly, or perhaps two such. He will be preceded by another Messiah, the son of Joseph, who will herald his coming and then be killed battling the enemies of God. He will be preceded by the prophet Elijah, who will prepare people for redemption.

He will come, in one persistent belief, only after that period of dreadful destruction and desolation known as the "birth pangs of the Messiah." In the imagery of the prophet Ezekiel—elaborated on by the rabbis—it will be a period of intense wars between God and the powers of evil, the mythical empires of Gog and Magog. Earthquakes will shake the land, mountains will be overthrown, and torrential rains and hailstorms will cause misery on earth. In a subtler mode, the Mishnah pictures the messianic birth pangs as a period of moral deterioration when insolence will increase and drunkenness abound, when the young will shame the old and children will turn against parents.

So terrible will be that period before the advent of the Messiah, according to some, that the third-century sage Rabbi Johanan could say, half-seriously, "Let the Messiah come, but let me not see him!" Better to give up the joys of the messianic age than suffer the agonies that will precede it.

But oh, those joys! Here the most fanciful of Jewish fantasies come into full play. In the messianic era, the earth will be so fertile that trees will bear fruit every day and loaves of delicious bread will grow from the ground. It will be so fertile that one grape will be large enough to serve as a huge keg of wine. In that new age, the sun will give forty-nine times as much light as it does now, and God will order it to heal anyone who is sick. All the cities of the world will be rebuilt then, even the wicked Sodom and Gomorrah, so that no place on earth will be desolate. But Jerusalem will be rebuilt with precious stones to make known the glory of Israel.

More: in the days to come, there will be a wondrous banquet at which the pious will eat the delicious meat of primeval creatures—the sea monster Leviathan, the beast Behemoth, and the huge bird Ziz. The diners will sit under a magnificent tent, a sukkah, made of the skin of Leviathan. God will stretch the remainder of the skin over Jerusalem, and the light streaming from it will shine from one end of the earth to the next.

And more: in the end of days, there will be no more weeping or wailing or anguish in the world, only rejoicing. And there will be no more death in the world.

But if those alive when the Messiah comes will bask in these splendors and live forever, what of those already dead? A belief that the dead will come back to life is a basic doctrine of Judaism. Maimonides includes it as one of the thirteen fundamental principles of faith for Jews, and it is still affirmed in the traditional daily liturgy. Nevertheless—and to the credit of this tradition—nothing about this doctrine is fixed or rigid. It, too, remains amorphous.

Will the resurrection take place before the messianic age? During it? And what will happen after it occurs?

The theories have varied over time. Generally, the tradition has come to regard the messianic era as ending at some point and the resurrection as occurring then. At that time the dead will arise from their graves with bodies and souls reunited (and some say, dressed in the clothes they wore during their lifetime). They will be judged in the heavenly court and sent to their final reward or punishment in the world to come.

The messianic era seems to exist, then, in Jewish thought, between this world as we know it and the next, a golden age that may not last forever but will bring with it serene happiness and an end to suffering.

That goal has given Jews incentive enough over the centuries to long for a Messiah who will restore them to their own land and save them from the suffering they knew only too well. The longings grew most intense in periods and places of most persecution.

Sometimes in the past—and the present—the wishes have led to intricate calculations of the exact date of the Messiah's arrival. "Blast those who calculate the end," the third-century Palestinian sage Rabbi Jonathan ben Eleazar once said, "for when their computed end arrives but the Messiah does not, they say, 'He'll never come.'"

Better to wait patiently, the rabbis said, to dream but not to dwell on expectations. When Rabbi Akiva declared Bar Kokhba the Messiah in his war against Rome during the second century, Rabbi Johanan ben Torta retorted, "Akiva, grass will grow in your cheeks and he will still not have come!"

Better to dream. When the dreams turned into actions, they invariably ended in disaster or disillusionment. Bar Kokhba's war led to the death of thousands of Jews. Shabbetai Zevi's false messianic claims led to chaos and a myriad of broken hearts.

It is the dream of a Messiah and a better age to come that has fueled the Jewish spirit. On a historical level, one might say that the dream has been partially fulfilled with the establishment of the State of Israel and the ingathering of Jews from all parts of the world. But on a spiritual level, and at its noblest, the dream builds on the visions of Isaiah and other prophets of a day outside the reach of time and history. It is a day at the end of days when the people of Israel, restored to their land, will be delivered from all evil. But it is also a day of universal deliverance, when wars will cease and nations will live with one another in unity and understanding. The one preoccupation of the whole world then, Maimonides taught, will be to know God. For "in that day," said the prophet Zechariah, "there shall be one God with one name" (14:9) for all of humanity.

SELECTED SOURCES

The notes that follow give the classic Jewish sources used in *Jewish Days*. Most important is the Talmud, made up of the Mishnah, the code of law edited by Judah HaNasi about 200 C.E., and the Gemara, the laws, legends, and interpretations of the Mishnah. Most of the references here are to the Babylonian Talmud, redacted around the year 500. They are presented in the notes in their standard form, by tractate name and page number, as in "*Yoma* 84b." The Jerusalem Talmud, compiled about a hundred years earlier, is indicated with a "J." References to the Mishnah, such as "Mishnah *Hagigah* 1:8," indicate the tractate, chapter, and paragraph.

Along with the Talmud, the major source of midrash used is the *Midrash Rabbah*, a collection of legendary materials on each of the five books of Moses and the Five Scrolls—Song of Songs, Ruth, Lamentations, Ecclesiastes, and Esther—edited from the fifth to tenth century. Citations are to the five-volume work translated by H. Freedman and Maurice Simon (London: Soncino Press, 1977). Book, chapter, and section are given, as in "*Genesis Rabbah* 10:9." The *Mekhilta*, another key reference, is a collection of interpretations on the Book of Exodus, from the first and second centuries. The accepted reference form, used here, gives the tractate and chapter. The edition used is *Mekilta de-Rabbi Ishmael*, 3 vols., translated by Z. Lauterbach (Philadelphia: Jewish Publication Society, 1933–35). The *Pesikta Rabbati*, a ninth-century work that contains sermons and midrashim for festivals and special Sabbaths, was translated in 2 vols. by William G. Braude (New Haven: Yale University Press, 1968). References are to *piskas*, or sections.

A midrashic work cited from the Hebrew is the *Midrash Tanhuma*, a compilation of rabbinic homilies on the Pentateuch. Citations, as in "*Tanhuma*, Yitro, 11," are to Torah portions and paragraphs. The *Pirkei de-Rabbi Eliezer* contains early narratives built around biblical stories, referred to by chapter numbers.

Among medieval works noted is *The Zohar*, the prime text of Jewish mysticism, translated by Harry Sperling and Maurice Simon (London: Soncino Press, 1984), cited by volume and page. References to Maimonides' *Code* (*Mishneh Torah*), published in 1180, are based on volumes in the Yale Judaica series (New Haven: Yale University Press, 1949–1972) and Isadore Twersky's *A Maimonides Reader* (New York: Behrman House, 1972). The most frequently cited Bible and Talmud commentaries are those of Rashi (Rabbi Solomon ben Isaac) in the eleventh century and Nahmanides (Rabbi Moshe ben Nahman) in the thirteenth. Contemporary Bible commentaries include *The JPS Torah Commentary*, 5 vols. (Philadelphia: Jewish Publication Society, 1989–96); *The Torah: A Modern Commentary* (New York: Union of American Hebrew Congregations, 1981); and *The Five Books of Moses*, translated with commentary by Everett Fox (New York: Schocken Books, 1995).

The classic contemporary source for rabbinic legends is Louis Ginzberg, *The Legends of the Jews*, 7 vols., translated by Henrietta Szold (Philadelphia: Jewish Publication Society, 1968). Judah Nadich, *Jewish Legends of the Second Commonwealth* (Philadelphia: Jewish Publication Society, 1983), picks up in chronology where Ginzberg leaves off. One more important source for legendary materials is Hayim Nahman Bialik and Yehoshua Hana Ravnitzky, *The Book of Legends, Sefer Ha-Aggadah*, translated by William G. Braude (New York: Schocken Books, 1992).

Helpful books about the holidays include Abraham P. Bloch, *The Biblical and Historical Background of Jewish Customs and Ceremonies* (New York: Ktav, 1980); Theodor H. Gaster, *Festivals of the Jewish Year* (New York: William Morrow, 1978); Irving Greenberg, *The Jewish Way* (New York: Simon & Schuster, 1988); Eliyahu Kitov, *The Book of Our Heritage*, 3 vols. (Jerusalem and New York: Feldheim Publishers, 1978); Hayyim Schauss, *The Jewish Festivals*, translated by Samuel Jaffe (New York: Schocken Books, 1975); Michael Strassfeld, *The Jewish Holidays* (New York: Harper & Row, 1985); and Arthur Waskow, *Seasons of Our Joy* (Boston: Beacon Press, 1982).

Important general works are Salo Baron, *A Social and Religious History of the Jews*, 16 vols. (New York: Columbia University Press, 1952–76); Heinrich Graetz, *History of the Jews*, 16 vols. (Philadelphia: Jewish Publication Society, 1893–98); Max Margolis and Alexander Marx, *A History of the Jewish People* (Philadelphia: Jewish Publication Society, 1944); Leo W. Schwarz, ed., *Great Ages and Ideas of the Jewish People* (New York: Modern Library, 1956); and Encyclopedia Judaica, 16 vols. (Jerusalem: Keter Publishing House, 1971).

Most biblical translations are from the TANAKH, the new Jewish Publication Society translation (1985). Occasionally I have changed that translation according to my understanding of a text or to fit with a rabbinic interpretation.

NOTES

Preface: The Times of Our Lives

[3] "holiness in time": Abraham Joshua Heschel, *The Sabbath*, softcover (New York: Farrar, Straus and Giroux, 1951), 8. More than anyone, Heschel emphasized the centrality of time in Jewish thought.

[7] Mondays and Wednesdays: Louis Ginzberg, *The Legends of the Jews*, 7 vols. (Philadelphia: Jewish Publication Society, 1968), 5:39.

Shabbat: The Sabbath Rest

[10] observe and remember: *Mekhilta*, Bahodesh, 7.
[10] God created Sabbath: *Genesis Rabbah* 10:9.
[10] "mountains hanging by a hair": Mishnah *Hagigah* 1:8.
[10] "They sowed . . .": *Shabbat* 49b.
[11] foretaste of world to come: *Berakhot* 57b.
[11] tailor with needle: Mishnah *Shabbat* 1:3.
[11] eve of first Shabbat: *Ethics of the Fathers* 5:8.
[11] additional souls: *Zohar*, 3:136a.
[11] Rabbi Hanina, Rabbi Yannai: *Shabbat* 119a.
[13] two angels: Ibid., 119b.
[13] sanctity to heavenly hosts: *Zohar*, 3:135b.
[14] King David to die on Sabbath: *Shabbat* 130a.
[14] nightmare: Ibid., 11a.
[14] infant alone: *Yoma* 84b.
[15] Sabbath given to *you*: *Mekhilta*, Shabbata, 1.

Rosh Hodesh: Celebrating the New Moon

[17] why the moon was created: *Genesis Rabbah* 6:1.
[18] moon encroached on sun: Ibid., 6:3.
[18] moon complained: *Hullin* 60b.
[18] Israel restored; Israel has portion in world to come: *Genesis Rabbah* 6:3.
[19] "It is hallowed!": Mishnah *Rosh Hashanah* 2:7.
[19] evil omen: *Sukkah* 29a.
[19] man in the moon: Ginzberg, *Legends*, 5:275; *Baba Batra* 75a.
[19] warriors born in Adar II: Ginzberg, *Legends*, 6:465.
[20] since the 1970s: the first and still most important source on women's Rosh Hodesh celebrations is Arlene Agus, "This Month Is for You: Observing Rosh Hodesh as a Woman's Holiday," in *The Jewish Woman: New Perspectives*, ed. Elizabeth Koltun (New York: Schocken Books, 1976), 84–93.

Tishrei: September–October

[23] first day of seventh month: Leviticus 23:23–25; Numbers 29:1–6.
[24] Nisan, ancestors redeemed: *Rosh Hashanah* 11a.
[24] even one good deed: Maimonides, *Code*, "Repentance," 3:4.
[24] world created in Tishrei: *Rosh Hashanah* 10b.
[25] confusing Satan: *Rosh Hashanah* 16b.
[25] wake-up call: Maimonides, *Code*, "Repentance," 3:4.
[25] each note has meaning: Nahmanides on Leviticus 23:24.
[26] God "remembered" Sarah: *Rosh Hashanah* 11a.
[27] purpose of Abraham's test: *Pesikta Rabbati*, piska 40.
[28] shofar reminiscent of ram: Rashi on Leviticus 23:24.
[28] Sarah's cries: *Leviticus Rabbah* 20:2.
[29] three books: *Rosh Hashanah* 16b.
[30] "Everything is foreseen": *Ethics of the Fathers* 3:19.
[32] "death of the righteous": *Rosh Hashanah* 18b.
[32] parable of prince: *Pesikta Rabbati*, piska 44.

[32] Ezekiel Landau: in *Jewish Preaching, 1200–1800*, ed. Marc Saperstein (New Haven: Yale University Press, 1989), 61.

[33] galbanum: Rashi on Exodus 30:34.

[34] importance of eating: *Rosh Hashanah* 9a–b.

[35] "I will sin": *Fathers According to Rabbi Nathan*, 40.

[37] crimson thread: Mishnah *Shabbat* 9:3.

[37] Temple thread discontinued: *Rosh Hashanah* 31b.

[39] God's miracle: Rashbam on Leviticus 23:43.

[39] seven clouds: *Mekhilta*, Beshallah, 1.

[39] huts farmers built: H. L. Ginsberg cited in *The JPS Torah Commentary: Leviticus* (Philadelphia: Jewish Publication Society, 1989), 265.

[40] forbidden fruit: Nahmanides on Leviticus 23:40.

[40] four species as parts of body: *Leviticus Rabbah* 30:14.

[40] as heroes or matriarchs of Bible: Ibid., 30:10.

[41] all corners of the earth: *Sukkah* 37b.

[41] "certain person": Mishnah *Sukkah* 4:9.

[41] Josephus on Alexander Yannai: Josephus, *Antiquities of the Jews*, 13:13, no. 5.

[43] Simhat Beit HaSho'evah: Mishnah *Sukkah* 5:1–4.

[43] judgment for rain: Mishnah *Rosh Hashanah* 1:2.

[43] "Anyone who has not seen": Mishnah *Sukkah* 5:1.

[44] ushpizin: *Zohar*, 5:103b.

[46] Jesus' entry: John 12:12–15.

[46] Ani va'ho: Mishnah *Sukkah* 4:5, and Rashi.

[47] whoever does not see his shadow: Joshua Trachtenberg, *Jewish Magic and Superstition* (New York: Meridian Books, 1961), 215.

[47] skin of Leviathan: *Baba Batra* 75a.

[47] parable: Rashi on Leviticus 23:36.

[48] Temple on earth: *Zohar*, 3:140b.

[48] shamir: *Sotah* 48b.

[49] cleaned sewers: *Exodus Rabbah* 6:1.

[49] Temple windows: retold in H. N. Bialik and Y. H. Ravnitzky, *The Book of Legends* (New York: Schocken Books, 1992), 125.

Heshvan: October – November

[53] torrential rains: *Tanhuma*, Noah, 11.

[54] scorpions abound: *Pesikta Rabbati*, piska 53.

[54] not one person harmed: *Ethics of the Fathers* 5:7.

[55] Rachel colludes in substitution: *Megillah* 13b.

[55] she won God's promise: *Lamentations Rabbah*, proem 24.

[55] prohibition against marrying two sisters: Leviticus 18:18.

[56] dies because of curse: Rashi on Genesis 31:32.

[56] exiles would pass burial place: *Genesis Rabbah* 82:10.

[59] "My ancestors were greater": Mishnah *Sanhedrin* 4:5.

[59] sexually dissipated: *Sanhedrin* 108a.

[59] why animals destroyed: *Genesis Rabbah* 28:8; *Sanhedrin* 108a.

[59] Noah and *Gilgamesh*: Nahum M. Sarna, in *JPS Torah Commentary: Genesis*, 48–49.

[60] invented the plow: *Tanhuma*, Genesis, 11.

[60] feeding the animals: *Sanhedrin* 108b.

[60] neighbors laughed: Ibid., 108a.

[60] entered in daylight: *Genesis Rabbah* 32:8.

[60] olive leaf: Ibid., 33:6.

Kislev: November – December

[63] Adam's fright: *Avodah Zarah* 8a.

[67] Shammai and Hillel: *Shabbat* 21b.

[68] "Who . . . commanded us": Ibid., 23a.

Tevet: December – January

[71] young goats: *Pesikta Rabbati*, piska 53.

[72] "Women are obligated": *Shabbat* 23a.

[72] daughter of Mattathias: *Mimekor Yisrael: Classical Jewish Folktales*, collected by Micha Joseph Bin Gorion (Philadelphia: Jewish Publication Society, 1976), 1:268.

[73] "Say to Father Abraham": *Lamentations Rabbah* 1:16, 50–51.

[74] Septuagint legend: *Megillah* 9a.

[75] Septuagint and golden calf: Bialik-Ravnitzky, 450.

[76] "If Moses had not preceded him": *Sanhedrin* 21b.

[76] kept Torah from being forgotten: *Sukkah* 20a.

[77] identified with Malachi: *Megillah* 15a.

[77] Yemenite legend: Ginzberg, *Legends*, 6:431.

[77] "worthy disciple of Ezra": *Song of Songs Rabbah* 8:9.

[78] "exile of King Jehoiachin": Ezekiel 1:2.

[79] Zedekiah's cave: *Erubin* 61b.

[79] Israel compared to moon: *Exodus Rabbah* 15:26.

[79] "Men better": Jacob S. Minkin, *The World of Moses Maimonides* (New York: Thomas Yoseloff, 1957), 98.

[81] "I was agitated": quoted in *A Maimonides Reader*, ed. Isadore Twersky (New York: Behrman House, 1972), 3.

[81] "What can console me?": letter to Japhet ben Eliahu, 1176, in *A Treasury of Jewish Letters*, ed. Franz Kobler (Philadelphia: Jewish Publication Society, 1953), 1:192.

[81] "when night falls": letter to Samuel Ibn Tibbon, September 30, 1199, ibid., 212.

Shevat: January – February

[83] Moses began reviewing: Deuteronomy 1:3.

[83] zodiac sign: *Pesikta Rabbati*, piska 20.

[84] date of plagues: Ginzberg, *Legends*, 5:427.

[85] maidservants rejoiced: Rashi on Exodus 11:5.

[85] animal gods: Ibid.

[85] Aaron effected first two plagues: Rashi on Exodus 7:19.

[86] hardening Pharaoh's heart: Maimonides, *Introduction to Ethics of the Fathers*, ch. 8.

[86] only a single frog: *Sanhedrin* 67b.

[86] "work of My hands": *Sanhedrin* 39b.

[87] angels must wait for humans: *Exodus Rabbah* 23:7.

[87] women servants saw more: *Mekhilta*, Shirata, 3.

[87] timbrels: Ibid., 10.

[88] Miriam's song first: S. D. Goitein, "Women as Creators of Biblical Genres," *Prooftexts* 8 (1988): 7.

[88] "a half brick": *Megillah* 16b.

[88] lowly bramble: *Exodus Rabbah* 2:5.

[89] four New Year days: Mishnah *Rosh Hashanah* 1:1.

[90] plant a sapling: *Fathers According to Rabbi Nathan*, version B, ch. 31.

[91] God's fingers: *Pirkei de-Rabbi Eliezer*, 48.

Adar: February – March

[93] zodiac sign: *Pesikta Rabbati*, piska 20.

[93] fish connected with Israel: *Genesis Rabbah* 97:3.

[93] "When Adar comes . . .": *Ta'anit* 29a.

[94] Haman settled on Adar: *Esther Rabbah* 7:2.

[94] miracle of the flame: II Maccabees 1:19–2:12.

[95] old men crying: Ezra 3:12.

[95] foundation stone: Mishnah *Yoma* 5:2.

[96] world created from that stone: *Yoma* 54b.

[96] traditional answer: Rashi on Numbers 20:12.

[96] Maimonides' view: *Eight Chapters*, ch. 4.

[97] growing haughtiness: Nahmanides on Numbers 20:1.

[97] Rabbinic interpretation: *Numbers Rabbah* 19:13.

[97] "This subject . . .": quoted in Nahmanides on Numbers 20:1.

[98] legend of Moses' death: *Deuteronomy Rabbah* 11:10.

[99] calculations of birth and death date: *Sotah* 12b.

[102] Martin Buber: cited in *The Torah: A Modern Commentary* (New York: Union of American Hebrew Congregations, 1981), 512.

[102] Saul's self-justification: *Yoma* 22b.

[102] "strap of chastisement": *Numbers Rabbah* 19:20.

[102] "cried a loud and bitter cry": *Genesis Rabbah* 67:4.

[104] three-day fast: *Esther Rabbah* 8:6.

[104] arouse the king's jealousy: *Megillah* 15b.

[106] sages argued: Ibid., 7a.

[106] thorn tree for Haman: *Esther Rabbah* 9:2.

[107] "Cursed be Haman": *Megillah* 7b.

[107] definition of walled cities: Mishnah *Megillah* 1:1.

[109] When Messiah comes: Midrash on Proverbs 9:2.

[110] "purify the defiled": *Yoma* 14a.

[110] compared to "sin offering": Jacob Milgrom, in *JPS Torah Commentary: Numbers*, 438–39.

[110] female, not male: *Pesikta Rabbati*, piska 14:14.

[110] seven mentions of seven things: *Numbers Rabbah* 19:2.

[110] Solomon didn't understand: Ibid., 19:3.

[110] Moses didn't understand: *Ecclesiastes Rabbah* 8:1, no. 5.

[111] "When the moon becomes new": Rashi on Exodus 12:1–2.

[111] God like a king: *Exodus Rabbah* 15:30.

Nisan: March–April

[113] every month reminds of first: Nahmanides on Exodus 12:2.

[114] could not destroy Temple: *Pesikta Rabbati*, piska 27/28.

[114] Tabernacle rose: *Exodus Rabbah* 52:4; *Tanhuma*, KiTissa, 35.

[114] first to jump into sea: *Numbers Rabbah* 12:21.

[116] house of holiness: Rashi on Exodus 25:8.

[116] only as token of affection: Ginzberg, *Legends*, 3:148–49.

[116] cave by the sea: *Numbers Rabbah* 12:4.

[116] wood from paradise: Ginzberg, *Legends*, 6:66.

[116] tabernacle corresponds to Creation: *Numbers Rabbah* 12:13.

[116] throne of God: Psalm 80:2.

[119] Amram followed Miriam's advice: *Sotah* 12a.

[119] a son who would redeem Israel: *Megillah* 14a.

[119] Miriam and Aaron danced: *Sotah* 12a.

[120] women's prophecy: Goitein, "Women as Creators . . . ," 13–14.

[120] blackness and beauty: Amos 9:7.

[120] concern about Moses' abstinence: Devora Steinmetz, "A Portrait of Miriam in Rabbinic Midrash," *Prooftexts* 8 (1988): 34–65.

[120] because Miriam waited: *Sotah* 11a.

[121] a wondrous well: *Ethics of the Fathers* 5:8.

[121] well accompanied Israelites: *Ta'anit* 9a.

[121] Moses struck Miriam's well: Rashi on *Ta'anit* 9a.

[121] Ismar Schorsch: from a written teaching on Parashat Hukkat, June 19, 1994.

[121] with kiss of God: *Baba Batra* 17a.

[121] Egyptians worshipped the lamb: *Exodus Rabbah*, 16:3.

[124] yeast in dough and evil impulse: *Berakhot* 17a.

[124] Philo of Alexandria: in *The Passover Haggadah*, ed. Nahum M. Glatzer (New York: Schocken Books, 1989), x.

[125] lesser-known translation: Nahum Sarna, in *JPS Torah Commentary: Exodus*, 56.

[126] "even a poor person": Mishnah *Pesahim* 10:1.

[127] "Your question has exempted us": *Pesahim* 115b.

[127] according to ability: Mishnah *Pesahim* 10:4.

[128] "shameful tale": Ibid.

[128] Isaac's birth: *Rosh Hashanah* 11a.

[128] sun shone: *Pesikta Rabbati*, piska 42.

[129] Sarah's death: Rashi on Genesis 23:2.

[129] Isaac's blindness: *Genesis Rabbah* 65:10.

[131] the fours: *Israel Haggadah*, ed. Menachem M. Kasher (New York: American Biblical Encyclopedia Society, 1950), 82.

[131] Isaac's children: *Pesikta Rabbati*, piska 40:6.

[132] "If You want to have a world": *Genesis Rabbah* 39:6.

[132] deeds of Sodomites: recounted in *Sanhedrin* 109a–b.

[133] "Sodom type": *Ethics of the Fathers* 5:13.

[133] sun and moon visible: *Genesis Rabbah* 50:12.

[133] motherly concern: *Pirkei de-Rabbi Eliezer*, 25.

[133] Lot's daughters: *Genesis Rabbah* 51:8.

[135] midwives save children: *Exodus Rabbah* 1:15.

[135] animal-like women: Ibid., 1:16.

[135] Pharaoh's daughter: Ibid., 1:26.

[136] "on account of the righteous women": Ibid., 1:12.

[136] Song of Songs holiest: Mishnah *Yadayim* 3:5.

[136] Why the Song of Songs: Gerson D. Cohen, "The Song of Songs and the Jewish Religious Mentality," in *Studies in the Variety of Rabbinic Cultures* (Philadelphia: Jewish Publication Society, 1991), 3–17.

[137] Egyptians in darkness: *Mekhilta*, Beshallah, 5.

[137] father protecting his son: Ibid.

[138] all the waters in the universe: Ibid.

[138] mothers held children's hands: *Exodus Rabbah* 21:10.

[138] Egyptian bodies: *Mekhilta*, Beshallah, 7.

[138] Egyptians buried: Ibid., 9.

[139] sea defied Moses: Ibid., 5.

[141] How that specific anniversary: the history of this day is discussed in detail in Irving Greenberg, *The Jewish Way* (New York: Simon & Schuster, 1988), 326–39.

Iyar: April–May

[143] zodiac sign: *Pesikta Rabbati*, piska 20:2.

[147] Rabbi Akiva's students: *Yevamot* 62b.

[147] legend of Rabbi Simeon: *Shabbat* 33b.

[148] conditions for martyrdom: *Sanhedrin* 74a.

[149] "Behold we journey": "The Crusade Chronicle of Solomon bar Simson," in *The Literature of Destruction: Jewish Responses to Catastrophe*, ed. David G. Roskies (Philadelphia: Jewish Publication Society, 1988), 74.

[149] "notable and pious woman": Ibid., 75.

[149] "They stretched forth their necks": Ibid.

[149] father slew son: "The Sacrifice of Isaac ben Meshullam," in *Mimekor Yisrael*, 1:430.

[150] question about martyrdom: Maimonides, *Code*: "Basic Principles of the Torah," 5:1–4.

[151] "joy of the whole earth": *Lamentations Rabbah* 2:15; *Fathers According to Rabbi Nathan*, 28.

[151] "opposite the Heavenly Sanctuary": Nahmanides on Genesis 14:18.

[151] "a port city": Yehuda Amichai, "Jerusalem 1967," in *Poems of Jerusalem and Love Poems* (New York: Sheep Meadow Press, 1994), 61.

[152] "My heart is in the East": Judah Halevi, in *The Penguin Book of Hebrew Verse*, ed. T. Carmi (New York: The Viking Press, 1981), 335.

[153] "The Holy One . . . weeps": *Lamentations Rabbah* 1:2, para. 23.

[153] "ten measures": *Fathers According to Rabbi Nathan*, version B, 48.

Sivan: May–June

[155] every Jew present: *Tanhuma*, Yitro, 11.

[156] the twins: *Pesikta Rabbati*, piska 20.

[157] procession of first fruits: Mishnah *Bikkurim* 3:2–4.

[158] shofar from Isaac's ram: Rashi on Exodus 19:13.

[158] Isaac's fear: Nahmanides on Exodus 19:13.

[159] Torah offered to many nations: *Pesikta Rabbati*, piska 21.

[159] Sinai turned upside down: *Shabbat* 88a.

[159] nature is still: *Exodus Rabbah* 29:9.

[159] voice with no echo: Ibid.

[159] seventy languages: Ibid., 28:6.

[159] according to own strength: Ibid., 5:9.

[160] words of creation: *Pesikta Rabbati*, piska 21:19.

[160] hear all commandments: *Mekhilta*, Bahodesh, 9.

[160] hear only two commandments: *Makkot* 24a.

[161] Moses had to fight angels: *Shabbat* 88b.

[161] "all that a mature disciple": J *Pe'ah* 17:1.

[163] "I am determined to be converted": *Ruth Rabbah* 2:22.

[166] "the John the Baptist": Gershom Scholem, *Sabbatai Sevi: The Mystical Messiah 1626–1656* (Princeton: Princeton University Press, 1973), 207.

[167] "What price messianism?": Ibid., xii.

[167] historical memory: Yosef Hayim Yerushalmi, *Zakhor: Jewish History and Jewish Memory* (Seattle: University of Washington Press, 1982).

[168] "greater than the Fast of Gedaliah": quoted in ibid., 49.

[169] "the Oppressor Chmiel": Nathan Nata Hanover, "The Massacres of the Holy Community of Nemirow," in Roskies, ed., *Literature of Destruction*, 111.

[169] "Men, women, and children": Israel ben Benjamin of Belzyce, "Sermon on Balaq," in Saperstein, ed., *Jewish Preaching*, 289 and 300.

[170] no share in world to come: *Ethics of the Fathers* 5:21.

[171] waters rest on Sabbath: *Genesis Rabbah* 11:5.

[171] *Sambatyon* comes from *Sabbath*: Nahmanides on Deuteronomy 32:26.

Tammuz: June–July

[174] humans scratch: *Pesikta Rabbati*, piska 20.

[174] crab represents Moses: Ibid., piska 27/28.

[175] "And even if you punish *us*": quoted in Jeremy Cohen, *The Friars and the Jews* (Ithaca: Cornell University Press, 1982), 70.

[177] Satan initiating anxiety: *Shabbat* 89a.

[177] miscalculation of forty days: Rashi on Exodus 32:1.

[177] reprimanding God: *Exodus Rabbah* 43:7.

[178] people might kill Aaron: *Leviticus Rabbah* 10:3.

[178] Aaron stalling for time: Rashi on Exodus 32:5.

[178] Aaron man of peace: *Ethics of the Fathers* 1:12.

[178] five events: Mishnah *Ta'anit* 4:6.

[179] every misfortune: *Sanhedrin* 102a.

[179] broken tablets: *Baba Batra* 14a–b.

[179] Ark was hidden: *Yoma* 53b–54a.

[179] idolatry and "hatred without cause": *Yoma* 9b.

[180] Zechariah recorded question: Zechariah 7:2–3; 8:19.

[181] fasts will be abolished: Maimonides, *Code*, "Fast Days," 5:19.

[181] "The daughters of Israel": comment on Exodus 38:8.

[182] at least one daughter: H. Graetz, *History of the Jews*, vol. 3 (Philadelphia, Jewish Publication Society, 1894), 289.

[183] "I . . . am concerned": comment on Genesis 3:8.

[183] legends about Rashi: sources include *Ma'aseh Book*, tr. Moses Gaster, facsimile of 1934 edition (Philadelphia, Jewish Publication Society, 1981), *Mimekor Yisrael*, 1 & 2, and Encyclopedia Judaica, "Rashi."

Av: July–August

[185] lion symbol: *Pesikta Rabbati*, piska 27/28.

[185] "When Adar comes": *Ta'anit* 29a.

[186] "Menahem" another name for Messiah: *Sanhedrin* 98b.

[188] satisfied Jewish needs: Gershom Scholem, "The Messianic Idea in Kabbalah," in *The Messianic Idea in Judaism* (New York: Schocken Books, 1971), 45.

[188] "Oh, hear and see": Solomon Ibn Verga, *Shevet Yehudah*, in Roskies, ed., *Literature of Destruction*, 98.

[189] "enemies on one side": Abraham Zacuto, *Sefer Yuhasin*, quoted in Yerushalmi, *Zakhor*, 60.

[191] anti-Jewish racism: Benzion Netanyahu, *The Origins of the Inquisition* (New York, Random House, 1995).

[191] "Master of the Universe!": Solomon Ibn Verga, *Shevet Yehudah*, in Roskies, ed., *Literature of Destruction*, 98.

[194] "These people have cried": *Ta'anit* 29a.

[195] Rabban Gamaliel: *Makkot* 24a–b.

[195] story of Rabban Johanan: *Gittin* 56a–b.

[197] acts of loving-kindness: *Fathers According to Rabbi Nathan*, 4.

[197] excessive mourning: *Baba Batra* 60b.

[199] dancing in the vineyards: Mishnah *Ta'anit* 4:8.

[199] most beautiful maidens: *Ta'anit* 31a.

[200] story of Benjaminites: Judges 20–21.

[201] reasons for festival: *Ta'anit* 30b–31a.

Elul: August–September

[204] Moses had shofar blown: *Pirkei de-Rabbi Eliezer*, 46.

[204] confuse Satan: *Rosh Hashanah* 16a.

[204] Ba'al Shem Tov letter: in Yitzchak Ginsburgh, *The Alef Beit: Jewish Thought Revealed Through the Hebrew Letters* (New Jersey: Jason Aronson, 1991), 2.

[205] father's piety: *Mimekor Yisrael*, 2:927.

[206] Israel revealed himself: *Ibid.*, 933–34.

[206] "It is the aim": *The Hasidic Anthology*, ed. Louis I. Newman (New York: Schocken Books, 1963), 18.

[207] Besht's death: *Mimekor Yisrael*, 2:968–69.

[209] "The Lord, the Lord" counted twice: *Rosh Hashanah* 17b.

[209] *El* denotes compassion: Rashi on Exodus 34:6.

[210] "Whenever Israel sins": *Rosh Hashanah* 17b.

[210] "Who answered": Mishnah *Ta'anit* 2:4.

[210] letter *bet*: *Genesis Rabbah* 1:10.

[211] not the sequential order: Rashi on Genesis 1:1.

[211] more philosophic vein: Nahmanides on Genesis 1:1.

[211] *be reshit*: *Zohar*, 1:3a–b.

[211] Torah as a blueprint: *Genesis Rabbah* 1:1.

[212] "Before the world was created": *Pirkei de-Rabbi Eliezer*, 10.

[212] no angels: *Genesis Rabbah* 1:3.

[212] Ten utterances: *Ethics of the Fathers* 5:1.

[212] justice and mercy combined: *Genesis Rabbah* 12:15.

[213] "Do not corrupt": *Ecclesiastes Rabbah* 7:13.

Epilogue: The End of Days

[218] contradictory speculations: An overview in Judah Goldin, "Of Midrash and the Messianic Theme," in *Studies in Midrash and Related Literature* (Philadelphia: Jewish Publication Society, 1988), 359–79.

[218] riding on a donkey: Zechariah 9:9.

[218] flying on a cloud: Daniel 7:13.

[218] bandaging sores: *Sanhedrin* 98a.

[218] after one or two Sabbaths: *Shabbat* 118b.

[218] Messiah, son of Joseph: *Sukkah* 52a.

[218] Elijah: Malachi 3:23.

[218] messianic birth pangs: Mishnah *Sotah* 9:15.

[218] "let me not see him!": *Sanhedrin* 98b.

[218] fertility of earth: *Shabbat* 30b.

[218] grapes: *Ketubot* 111b.

[218] In that new age: *Exodus Rabbah* 15:21.

[218] messianic banquet: *Leviticus Rabbah* 22:10; *Baba Batra* 75a.

[218] no more death: *Exodus Rabbah* 15:21.

[219] dressed in clothes they wore: *Ketubot* 111b.

[219] "Blast those": *Sanhedrin* 97b.

[219] "Akiva, grass will grow": *Lamentations Rabbah* 2:4.

[219] universal deliverance: Moshe Greenberg, "Mankind, Israel, and the Nations in the Hebraic Heritage," in *Studies in the Bible and Jewish Thought* (Philadelphia: Jewish Publication Society, 1995), 369–93.

[219] one preoccupation: Maimonides, *Code*, "Kings and Wars," 12:5.

INDEX